THE DEAD SEA SCROLLS TODAY

The
Dead Sea Scrolls
Today

SECOND EDITION

James C. VanderKam

WILLIAM B. EERDMANS PUBLISHING COMPANY
GRAND RAPIDS, MICHIGAN / CAMBRIDGE, U.K.

First edition 1994
Second edition 2010

Published by
Wm. B. Eerdmans Publishing Co.
2140 Oak Industrial Drive N.E., Grand Rapids, Michigan 49505 /
P.O. Box 163, Cambridge CB3 9PU U.K.

Printed in the United States of America

15 14 13 12 11 10   7 6 5 4 3 2 1

Library of Congress Cataloging-in-Publication Data

VanderKam, James C.
The Dead Sea scrolls today / James C. VanderKam. — 2nd ed.
p.   cm.
Includes bibliographical references and index.
ISBN 978-0-8028-6435-2 (pbk. : alk. paper)
1. Dead Sea scrolls. 2. Bible. O.T. — Criticism, Textual.
3. Qumran community. 4. Essenes. 5. Dead Sea scrolls — Relation to the New Testament.
6. Bible. N.T. — Criticism, interpretation, etc.
I. Title.
BM487.V26 2010
296.1′55 — dc22
                                          2009048973

www.eerdmans.com

Contents

Preface to the Second Edition

More than fifteen years have passed since *The Dead Sea Scrolls Today* first appeared, rendering its title increasingly more inappropriate. The early 1990s were exciting and confusing times in research on the Scrolls: publication of fragmentary texts had resumed in earnest after too long a hiatus, articles and books appeared all the time, and conspiracy theories were rife but beginning to be debunked. Now, in 2010, more than sixty years after the first scrolls came to light and when all them have been published, it is possible to view from a larger perspective what has happened and to sketch the current stage in Scrolls research.

The second edition of *The Dead Sea Scrolls Today* retains the format, style, and aims of the first edition, and the same wider audience is envisaged. There seemed no reason to make changes in those respects because the reception the first edition received shows that the book served a useful purpose. It sold far more copies than anticipated and was translated into six languages (Danish, German, Italian, Japanese, Polish, Portuguese). The major kinds of changes in the second edition are these:

First, the information is updated to take into account the full publication of the texts from the caves and the post-1994 debates about the Qumran site, including the later dating of the sectarian occupation of it and the implications following from the revised chronology.

Second, the bibliographies at the end of the chapters have been enlarged.

Third, there is an additional section regarding information the Scrolls provide about Second Temple Judaism and the groups prominent at the time.

Fourth, the phrasing has been changed in many places.

Finally, quotations of the Scrolls are from the fifth edition of Geza Vermes's translation, *The Complete Dead Sea Scrolls in English* (New York/London: Penguin, 1997). The page numbers in that volume follow the citations from it.

It is a pleasant duty to thank those who have helped in the process of preparing the second edition. First, I am grateful to those many good people who, at lectures, Scrolls exhibits, and other venues have offered kind words and helpful suggestions about the book. Second and more specifically, several individuals have read the text and made detailed suggestions for improvements: my wife, Mary VanderKam, who has an aversion to passive verbs and flagged others of my stylistic peculiarities; Molly Zahn, Ardea Russo, and Kevin Haley (all former or present doctoral students at Notre Dame), who compiled lists of changes and suggestions, and Monica Brady, who prepared the manuscript, advised about many matters, including the illustrations and photographs, and read the proofs. A word of thanks is also due to Catherine (Kitty) Murphy for permission to use some of the wonderful photos she has shot of Qumran and its vicinity.

Several friends have also been kind enough to answer questions: Brian Schultz on the War Rule, Eileen Schuller on the Hymn Scroll from Cave 1, Eugene Ulrich regarding the biblical manuscripts, Sue Sheridan on the cemetery, and Marty Abegg and Emanuel Tov regarding some electronic publications. And finally, I am once again grateful to the skillful people at Eerdmans for producing such an attractive book.

Preface to the First Edition

A much better writer once said: "I too decided, after investigating everything carefully from the very first, to write an orderly account for you, most excellent Theophilus, so that you may know the truth concerning the things about which you have been instructed" (Luke 1:3-4). Many have recently written about the Dead Sea Scrolls and aspects of the controversies that have engulfed them. The result has been confusion about what has actually happened. The media tend to publicize the sensational and to give more space to idiosyncratic theories than to the ones more widely held. If anyone claims to have discovered a new messianic reference in a scroll fragment and maintains that it somehow has extraordinary consequences for Christianity, the newspapers will spread the word abroad. But when more considered opinions are reached, they gain little attention. In the light of this situation, it seemed worthwhile to write an orderly account about the Scrolls themselves and what has happened with them since the mid-1980s.

In January 1990 J. T. Milik, one of the first and best editors of the Scrolls, gave to me the right to publish twelve manuscripts that had been assigned to him. After receiving his photographs and notes, I studied the originals in the Rockefeller Museum in Jerusalem, examined the materials Milik had given to me, and with Milik have been publishing those texts. In March 1990 I got a rapid introduction to how controversial the Scrolls had become. When asked by a newspaper reporter whether I would be willing to show the photographs to others, I said yes. That one short answer soon had others on the telephone, and my comment was published and reported in several places. Willingness to show others the photographs was a departure from official policy, so it seems. It was even termed a major breakthrough! I still cannot understand why anyone should deny others the right to examine the pictures of scroll fragments, but the experience illustrated the tensions and strong feelings then surrounding the whole issue of access to the Scrolls. As I have learned more about what had happened in the nearly forty years of scholarship on the Cave 4 manuscripts, I began to understand more about the genesis of people's feelings on both sides of the issue.

The present introduction and update on the Scrolls is intended for a wide audience. I have attempted to cover the major areas of Scrolls research and to bring the latest information to bear on them. Only recently have complete lists of the Qumran texts become available. Now for the first time it is possible to look at the entire extraordinary library that had been hidden away in the eleven caves. The book was written at the suggestion of Jon Pott of Wm. B. Eerdmans Publishing Company. I am grateful to him for the suggestion and for his supervision of the process that has so quickly put the manuscript in print.

Writing the book has provided opportunity to revise and update some essays that I had written previously and to investigate a number of areas on which I had not written before. The only case in which a chapter follows closely the structure and content of an earlier publication is chapter 6: "The Scrolls and the New Testament." It is a version of a two-part article that appeared in the *Bible Review* as "The Dead Sea Scrolls and Early Christianity: How Are They Related?" (*Bible Review* 7/6 [1991] 14-21, 46-47; and "The Dead Sea Scrolls and Early Christianity: What They Share" (*Bible Review* 8/1 [1992] 16-23, 40-41). The two parts were later reprinted as "The Dead Sea Scrolls and Christianity," in *Understanding the Dead Sea Scrolls,* ed. Hershel Shanks (New York: Random House, 1992) 181-202. I have altered the essay in numerous details and made additions to update it. Chapter 7 is a personal account of what has happened especially since 1989.

All quotations from the Dead Sea Scrolls, unless otherwise indicated, are from Geza Vermes, *The Dead Sea Scrolls in English* (3rd ed.; Sheffield: Sheffield Academic Press, 1987). To his translations I have added the reference in the scroll and the page number(s) in his book. My additions to Vermes's translations are indicated by double brackets. Scriptural citations come from the New Revised Standard Version. Rather than burden the text with footnotes, acknowledgments of sources are found in bibliographical notes at the end of each chapter.

The abbreviations for biblical, apocryphal, and pseudepigraphical books are those used by the Society of Biblical Literature and the Catholic Biblical Association, although I do not follow their practice of italicizing the titles of pseudepigraphal and other extrabiblical texts. For the scrolls, I have generally given column (col.) and line numbers in arabic numerals, separated by a period. A text is occasionally called something like 4Q175. The designation means: the text numbered 175 from Qumran Cave 4. At times a more complicated notation, such as 4Q 12-13 i 8 will be used. The numbers *12-13* refer to fragments that belong together, *i* is column 1, and *8* is the line number. As often as possible, I have avoided such designations and used the commonly employed English titles of works.

I owe thanks to several individuals. My colleague Eugene Ulrich, who has been involved in editing the Scrolls since 1980 and is today one of the three general editors of the project, has supplied numerous pieces of useful information from his files and memory. I am also grateful to Emanuel Tov for his corrections and suggestions. I want to offer a special word of gratitude to Ina Vondiziano for all the effort she expended in securing photographs to make this a more attractive book. Thanks also to Bruce and Kenneth Zuckerman, who very graciously provided a number of the photographs. My wife, Mary VanderKam, and my parents-in-law, Agnes and Herman Vander Molen, took the trouble to read through the manuscript and proposed a number of corrections and improvements. To all of these individuals I express hearty thanks for helping to create a more accurate book.

CHAPTER 1

Discoveries

A. INTRODUCTION

The territory of the modern state of Israel has not proved to be congenial for finding written remains from antiquity. Unlike Egypt and Iraq, where excavations have brought innumerable texts to light, Palestine had produced virtually nothing of the kind until 1947. There were reports that centuries ago manuscripts had been found in the region of Jericho, near the Dead Sea. Origen, the Christian scholar who lived from A.D. 185 to 254, was an acute student of the exact wording of the biblical texts. As an aid to text-critical labors, he compiled an enormous work that included in parallel columns six versions of the entire Old Testament (in Hebrew and in Greek). It is called the Hexapla, or sixfold book. He mentioned that the sixth Greek version of the Psalms that he presented in his Hexapla had been found in a jar around Jericho. In describing the same text, the church historian Eusebius, who lived from about 260 to 340, added in his *Ecclesiastical History* (6.16.1) that a Greek version of the Psalms and other Greek and Hebrew manuscripts had been found in a jar at Jericho during the reign of the Roman emperor Caracalla (Antoninus; reigned 211-17). Later, in approximately the year 800, the Nestorian patriarch of Seleucia, Timotheus I (727-819), wrote a letter to Sergius (who died about 805), the metropolitan (a position like that of an archbishop) of Elam. In it he noted:

> We have learnt from trustworthy Jews who were then being instructed as catechumens in the Christian religion that some books

1

were found ten years ago in a rock-dwelling near Jericho. The story was that the dog of an Arab out hunting, while in pursuit of game, went into a cave and did not come out again; its owner went in after it and found a chamber, in which there were many books, in the rock. The hunter went off to Jerusalem and told his story to the Jews, who came out in great numbers and found books of the Old Testament and others in the Hebrew script.

The patriarch goes on to tell how he asked an expert whether passages that in the New Testament are considered quotations from the Old Testament but cannot be found in existing copies of Israel's scriptures were present in these manuscripts. He was assured that they were indeed there, but his attempt to obtain more information on this point failed. The Jewish expert also told him: "We have found more than two hundred Psalms of David among our books." We have no way of checking whether the cave of manuscripts located just before A.D. 800 is one of those in which the Dead Sea Scrolls would be found almost 1,150 years later, but the parallel is at least intriguing, and the description of the scrolls in some ways matches those from Qumran, the site where the Dead Sea Scrolls were discovered. Some Jewish and Arabic sources also refer to a medieval Jewish group that went under the name "the cave people" (*magariyah* in Arabic) because their teachings arose from books found in a cave.

B. THE QUMRAN DISCOVERIES

No other finds of this kind are attested until 1947. In that year some Arab shepherds stumbled upon a cave, and their find led to what was soon hailed as the greatest archeological discovery of the twentieth century. The ways in which the caves were found and the texts in them came to the attention of scholars are a dramatic story in themselves.

1. THE FIRST CAVE

a. The Seven Original Scrolls

John Trever (1915-2006), one of the first scholars to lay eyes on any of the scrolls and the first to photograph those brought to him in 1948, wrote a

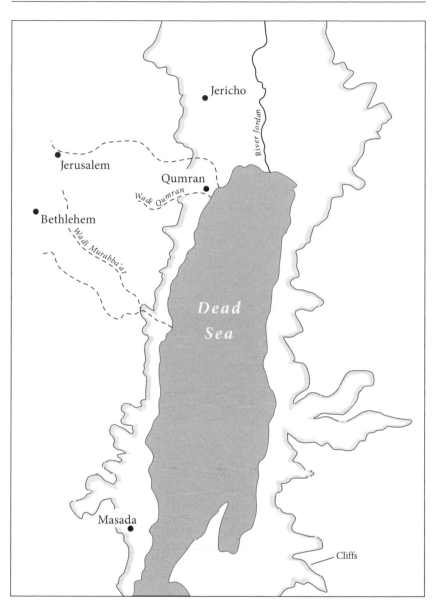

Qumran and the Dead Sea

thoroughly researched and documented history of the initial Qumran finds. Much of his report came from his own experience and notes. According to his account, three Bedouin shepherds were in an area called *Qumran* on the northwest side of the Dead Sea in the winter or spring of 1947 (possibly in late 1946, as the Bedouin claimed). At that time the territory was under the rule of the British Mandate in Palestine. The shepherds, who were cousins and members of the Taʿamireh tribe, were apparently tending their flocks when one of them, named Jumʿa Muhammad Khalil, who enjoyed searching for caves, amused himself by tossing rocks at a cave opening in the cliffs to the west of the plateau at Qumran. One of the rocks went into the mouth of the cave and shattered something inside. The three did not enter the cave at that time to check what had broken, but two days later one of the shepherds, Muhammad ed-Dhib (his real name is Muhammad Ahmed el-Hamed), rose early in the morning before his companions had awakened, located the cave, and squeezed into it. There he found ten jars, each about two feet high. To his dismay, all but two of them were empty. One of these two had dirt in it; the other contained three scrolls, two of which were wrapped in linen. The scrolls were later identified as a copy of the biblical book of Isaiah, the Manual of Discipline (setting forth rules for a community, subsequently called the Rule of the Community), and a commentary on the prophecy of Habakkuk. Later, the Bedouin found four additional scrolls: a collection of psalms or hymns (known as the Thanksgiving Hymns or Hymn Scroll, in Hebrew *Hodayot*), another partial copy of Isaiah, the War Scroll or War Rule (an eschatological text describing the final war between the "sons of light" and the "sons of darkness"), and the Genesis Apocryphon (stories based on some narratives in Genesis).

The scrolls were brought to an antiquities dealer named Kando (Khalil Iskandar Shahin; ca. 1910-1993) in March 1947. Kando, who was a member of the Syrian Orthodox Church, contacted another church member, George Isaiah, who spoke with Athanasius Yeshua Samuel (1907-1995), a metropolitan (archbishop) associated with St. Mark's Monastery in Jerusalem. One must remember that at this time no one knew what the recently discovered scrolls contained, what language they were written in, or how much money they were worth. Members of the Syrian Church were contacted because it was thought the scrolls might be written in the Syriac language. A deal was apparently struck in which the Bedouin would receive two-thirds of whatever amount of money Kando and George Isaiah could get for the scrolls. In the summer of 1947

Muhammed edh-Dhib, the Taʿamireh Bedouin who discovered Cave 1 and the first of the Dead Sea Scrolls in 1947 (John C. Trever)

a meeting between Metropolitan Samuel and the Bedouin was arranged. An oft-repeated story recounts how a monk, who was unaware of the planned meeting and who happened to answer the Bedouin's knock when they arrived at St. Mark's, turned away the poorly dressed tribesmen and thus nearly botched the chance to gain a great treasure. The misunderstanding was eventually rectified, and the metropolitan pur-

A general view of the openings to Cave 1 located in the steep limestone cliffs along the shore of the Dead Sea
(Catherine M. Murphy)

chased four of the scrolls from Kando for £24 (= about $100 at the time). The scrolls bought by the metropolitan were the larger Isaiah scroll, the Manual of Discipline (the Rule of the Community), the commentary on Habakkuk, and the Genesis Apocryphon.

The metropolitan attempted to get information from various experts about his newly purchased scrolls. One of those consulted on his behalf was Professor Eleazar Sukenik (1889-1953), an archeologist from the Hebrew University of Jerusalem. At the time Palestine was a dangerous place indeed, as the British Mandate was staggering toward its end amid an orgy of violence and the United Nations was debating the partition of Palestine. These conditions naturally made travel extremely difficult and perilous. Nevertheless, when Sukenik learned that an antiquities dealer in Bethlehem was offering what appeared to be ancient scrolls for

Cylindrical jar (restored) with bowl-shaped lid from Qumran. At lower right is a Hellenistic-style oil lamp characteristic of Qumran Phase I.
(Israel Antiquities Authority)

sale, he made a secret visit to that city on November 29, 1947, the very date on which the United Nations passed the resolution to partition Palestine and thus to create the state of Israel. The coincidence was not lost on Sukenik. He saw the three scrolls that the metropolitan had not purchased and bought them, after becoming convinced of their antiquity: two on November 29 (the Hymn Scroll and the War Scroll) and the third in December (the second Isaiah scroll). In January an acquaintance, Anton Kiraz, showed him the four scrolls that the metropolitan had, and he was even permitted to keep them for a short time. He was not aware that they had come from the same source as the three he had just obtained. Naturally, he wanted to buy them as well. The Metropolitan Samuel decided, however, that he did not wish to sell them at that time. Thus, the seven scrolls from the first cave were separated into two groups and would be published by different individuals.

By this time several parties had identified the great Isaiah scroll, which the Metropolitan Samuel possessed, but Sukenik seems to have been the first to recognize the antiquity of the parchments. Moreover, he thought that they might have been associated with the *Essenes*, a Jewish group attested in ancient sources. His reason was that the Roman geographer Pliny (A.D. 23-79) had written about a band of Essenes living near the shores of the Dead Sea not far from En-gedi — that is, where the cave of the scrolls seemed to have been located (I examine the passage from Pliny in chap. 3).

By the time the first anniversary of Muhammad ed-Dhib's find had come and gone, few people knew of the Scrolls, and those who did know of them understood little about them. Nor did any but the Bedouin and their immediate contacts know the location of the cave where they had discovered the scrolls. In February 1948 (that is, after his dealings with Sukenik) the metropolitan initiated contacts with the American School in Jerusalem, where two recent recipients of the Ph.D. degree were on duty — William Brownlee (1917-1983) and John Trever. Both had been awarded annual fellowships from the American Schools of Oriental Research. Trever was a photographer, as well as a scholar, and he arranged to have the scrolls brought to the American School. There, under terrible conditions (such as poor film and a very unreliable electrical supply), he took the first photographs of the metropolitan's documents (the larger Isaiah scroll, the Manual of Discipline [Rule of the Community], and the commentary on Habakkuk). The photographs turned out astonishingly well and are still today a priceless record of what could be seen in February 1948 on the now-deteriorating parchments. The scholars at the American School, with the director Professor Millar Burrows (1889-1980) of Yale University, who had been away in Baghdad when the scrolls first arrived, spent hours studying the texts Trever had photographed. One of them reminded Burrows of a Methodist "Discipline"; in this way it received its first modern name "the Manual of Discipline." In February Trever wrote to Professor William Foxwell Albright (1891-1971) of Johns Hopkins University in Baltimore, the leading expert on the ancient Jewish scripts. Albright immediately recognized the antiquity of the script in the sample sent to him and replied: "My heartiest congratulations on the greatest MS [= manuscript] discovery of modern times!"

Dangerous conditions and political problems still precluded any attempt to search for the scrolls cave. The scholars at the American School apparently wanted to encourage such an exploratory effort. To do so,

Millar Burrows (center right) and students in the library of the American School of Oriental Research in Jerusalem, 1948. At left are John Trevor and William Brownlee (John C. Trever)

they finally divulged to the Syrians associated with St. Mark's, who had been giving them misleading information about the source of the scrolls, how old they thought the texts were. They also arranged for a news release. On April 11, 1948, the American Schools of Oriental Research office in New Haven, CT, released a statement. It carried a New York dateline and read (as given in *The Times* of London on April 12, 1948):

> Yale University announced yesterday the discovery in Palestine of the earliest known manuscript of the Book of Isaiah. It was found in the Syrian monastery of St Mark in Jerusalem, where it had been preserved in a scroll of parchment dating to about the first century BC. Recently it was identified by scholars of the American School of Oriental Research at Jerusalem.
>
> There were also examined at the school three other ancient Hebrew scrolls. One was part of a commentary on the Book of

Habakkuk; another seemed to be a manual of discipline of some comparatively little-known sect or monastic order, possibly the Essenes. The third scroll has not been identified.

The press release is interesting for several reasons. First, it says nothing about the cave and its possible whereabouts. Readers were misled into thinking that the scrolls had been discovered at St. Mark's. Second, the dating of the Isaiah scroll was considered reliable enough to announce (based on the paleographical or script analyses of Trever and Albright). Third, the one document already had the name "Manual of Discipline." Fourth, the American scholars introduced the notion that the "Manual" was associated with a "sect or monastic order." Contrary to the impression later given, the idea did not derive from one of the priests (such as R. de Vaux) who later played such an important role in Scrolls research. Fifth, the Essene connection is already there. Finally, the last scroll, now known as the Genesis Apocryphon, was in such poor condition that it could not even be opened, much less identified.

On April 26 Sukenik announced the news about the scrolls he had bought. He later remarked that, after seeing how inaccurate the American press release was, he felt it was fitting to issue a statement to the newspapers in order to set the record straight. That he, too, had scrolls from the cave was news not only to the world at large but also to the scholars of the American School, so poor was communication in Jerusalem at that time. It so happens that Millar Burrows, who had written the original press release, did not formulate it the way it was printed. As he wrote later,

Unfortunately a mistake had somehow been introduced into the version given to the press. I had written, "The scrolls were acquired by the Syrian Orthodox Monastery of St. Mark." As released to the press in America the statement said that the scrolls had been "preserved for many centuries in the library of the Syrian Orthodox Monastery of St. Mark in Jerusalem." Who inserted this I do not know.

His quotation from the American press release does not agree with the wording of the one in *The Times*. Even though Sukenik's press release was dated April 26, the *New York Times* carried a story in the April 25 issue (p. 6), written specially for the *Times* by J. L. Meltzer. It reported that ten ancient Hebrew scrolls had been found "some time ago in a hillside

**Butrus Sowmi (with 1QpHab), Metropolitan Samuel, and John Trever (with 1QIs^a)
at the ASOR on February 21, 1948** (John C. Trever)

cave near En-Geddi, halfway down the western shore of the Dead Sea." The *Times's* correspondent knew about the texts of the American School and those of the Hebrew University (including fragments of Daniel that Sukenik had subsequently acquired) and was aware that Bedouin had discovered the scrolls. The article included the claim that the leather scrolls were "sealed with pitch." Later it was learned that what appeared to be pitch was actually decomposed leather. In the same month — April 1948 — Albright, who by that time knew of the four texts of the American School and the ones held by Sukenik (he thought there were at least eight manuscripts), announced the finds in the *Bulletin of the American Schools of Oriental Research* (110 [April 1948] 3). To the news he added a prophetic comment: "It is easy to surmise that the new discovery will revolutionize intertestamental studies, and that it will soon antiquate all present handbooks on the background of the New Testament and on the textual criticism and interpretation of the Old Testament."

While the story of these seven scrolls and their fate took many twists and turns, all of them were published at a very early date. The American Schools of Oriental Research published photographs and transcriptions of the Isaiah scroll, the commentary on Habakkuk, and the Manual of Discipline (Rule of the Community) in 1950 and 1951, while Sukenik's texts appeared in a posthumous volume dated 1954 (English translation in 1955). He and the Americans had, however, begun issuing photographs and transcriptions in preliminary form already in 1948. The last of the seven scrolls to appear, the Genesis Apocryphon, was a particular problem because of the advanced state of decay it had attained. But after it was opened what could be read on it at the time was published in 1956.

In 1948 Metropolitan Samuel had, at the urging of the Americans, removed his four scrolls from Jerusalem to Lebanon for safekeeping. His actions raised questions about the legality of transporting antiquities from the country where they were discovered. He eventually brought them to the United States and attempted to sell them. His efforts produced no results for some time. People were apparently reluctant to invest considerable sums of money in scrolls whose ownership was in dispute. For one, Anton Kiraz, a member of Metropolitan Samuel's church and a good friend, claimed that he had loaned money to him because of his financial problems at the time he purchased the scrolls. Kiraz said they had agreed to split any proceeds from the sale of them. While in the

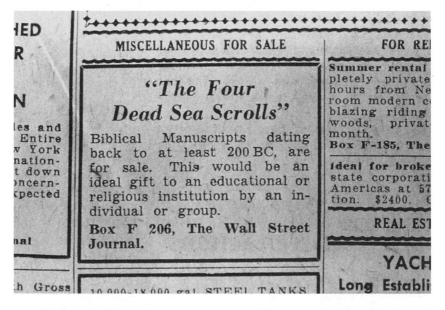

The ad placed in the *Wall Street Journal* by Metropolitan Samuel dated June 1, 1954, under the category "Miscellaneous for Sale" (Werner Braun)

United States Metropolitan Samuel placed a now-famous ad in the *Wall Street Journal* of June 1, 1954 (p. 14), which was brought to the attention of Yigael Yadin, Sukenik's son, who happened to be in the United States at the time. "'THE FOUR DEAD SEA SCROLLS' Biblical Manuscripts dating back to at least 200 BC are for sale. This would be an ideal gift to an educational or religious institution by an individual or group. Box F 206." Through middlemen Yadin arranged to purchase for $250,000 the scrolls advertised by Metropolitan Samuel. The four scrolls were then presented to the State of Israel, where they were reunited with Sukenik's three. A special structure called the Shrine of the Book (shaped like the top of the vase in which some of the scrolls were discovered) was constructed to house them at the Israel Museum. There the seven remain today. Contributions from Samuel Gottesman (1885-1956) and later from his family were instrumental in the purchase of these scrolls and in financing the Shrine of the Book.

b. The Cave Itself

Interviews conducted later revealed that the Bedouin and others, including the Syrians, visited the cave several times after the initial discovery and before officials knew where it was. During these visits, the last of which occurred in August and November 1948 (by George Isaiah and Kando), more written material was removed from the cave. The scholars who first dealt with the scrolls were understandably eager to find the cave, and plans to visit the area were discussed. Some intrigue and the danger of travel in much of 1948 frustrated any hopes of reaching it. With the creation of the State of Israel in May 1948, the British Mandate had ended, and the area where the scrolls had been found became part of the Kingdom of Jordan.

Not until January 1949 did someone with official connections succeed in finding the cave — about two years after the initial discovery. A Belgian soldier, Captain Philippe Lippens, who was an observer in the area for the United Nations, became interested in locating the cave. He gathered all the information he could from those people who had had any connections with the scrolls and received help from military and archeological authorities. With the assistance of the data gathered and the plans made by Lippens, Captain Akkash el-Zebn succeeded in finding the cave on January 28, 1949. It was located eight or nine miles south of

Original entrance to Cave 4, first discovered by the Bedouin in 1954 (Corel)

Jericho, in a cliff situated more than one-half mile from the northwest shore of the Dead Sea. G. Lankester Harding (1901-1979), the chief inspector of antiquities in Jordan, and Father Roland de Vaux (1903-1971), director of the Ecole Biblique et Archéologique Française in Jerusalem, then came to the site and began studying it.

The first archeological excavation of the cave took place from February 15 to March 5, 1949. Jars, bowls, pieces of cloth, and other artifacts were removed at this time. More importantly, fragments of perhaps seventy additional manuscripts were uncovered, some of which were pieces broken from the manuscripts that the Bedouin had found in the cave. The fragments confirmed that this was indeed the cave in which the original works had been discovered. The archeologists who were working at the cave noticed building ruins about a half-mile to the south. They examined them for a short time and also dug up some tombs near the ruins. At the time, based on the limited evidence available to them, they concluded that the ruins had no connection with the scrolls cave. Rather, they thought they had come upon the remains of a Roman fort from the first century A.D. In their conclusion they agreed with what another visitor to the site had determined. Gustav Dalman, a distinguished German scholar, had inferred in 1914 that the structures were from a Roman fort.

Cave 3 where the Copper Scroll was discovered in 1952 (Zev Radovan)

Others had identified the site differently. In 1861 Félicien de Saulcy thought he had found the Gomorrah of biblical Sodom and Gomorrah fame; he made his decision on the basis of the way in which local Arabs pronounced the modern name of the place — Qumran as Gumran. The French archeologist C. Clermont-Ganneau had visited the area in 1873 but had drawn no conclusions about it. F. M. Abel later concluded that the tombs were part of a cemetery of an early Muslim sect. Since none of these visitors, including the archeologists who were there in early 1949, had much data on which to base their deductions, they carry little weight.

As scholarly debates about the scrolls and the ruins grew more intense in the early 1950s, archeologists decided to conduct a full-scale excavation at the Qumran site. It took place from November 24 to December 12, 1951. The excavators, Harding and de Vaux, found evidence that led them to change their minds regarding the relation between the cave and the buildings. In particular, in the buildings they found pottery resembling that from the cave and a jar of the same kind as the scrolls jars. Thus, although only one manuscript cave had been located at that time, scholars now had reason to believe that it was in some way connected with the structures whose ruins jutted above an extension of the plateau to the east of the cliffs. Subsequent excavations at the site have confirmed their conclusion many times over.

2. THE OTHER CAVES

Not until 1952 were a series of other caves in the vicinity of the buildings discovered. The one labeled Cave 2 was found by Bedouin, who had been busily exploring as many caves as they could find in the area, now that they knew scrolls could bring a decent price. In October 1951 they had found manuscript fragments in remote caves in the Wadi Murabbaʿat region, a few miles from Qumran. There, among others, some documents from the Second Jewish Revolt against Rome (A.D. 132-35) were unearthed. Included in the Murabbaʿat documents were letters signed by Simon Bar Koseba, the Jewish leader of that doomed struggle. While the Murabbaʿat caves were being excavated in January-February 1952, the same Taʿamireh Bedouin continued their explorations, and in February 1952, one and one-half months after the archeologists had left, they found the second Qumran cave, not far from the first. Although what was discovered in it (fragments of 33 manuscripts) was not nearly as exciting as the contents of the first cave, the presence of another cave with ancient written materials in the same area impelled archeologists to conduct a systematic survey of the entire region. Between March 10 and 29, a group from the American School explored some 225 caves or cavities (including Cave 2). Their efforts led to the discovery of Cave 3 on March 14, 1952 — the first Qumran cave to be found by archeologists. From it they recovered fourteen manuscripts and the intriguing Copper Scroll (which lists treasure sites; for more on the Copper Scroll, see chap. 2).

The discoveries of that extraordinary year were not yet completed. Once again the Taʿamireh Bedouin (who in July and August had chanced upon two other nearby sites — Khirbet Mird and Nahal Hever — containing written materials) were responsible for an incredible find. In August 1952 they entered Cave 4, which is just a few hundred feet from the building remains at Khirbet (= the ruin of) Qumran. A visitor to the area might justifiably wonder why it took so long to find this cave when one can nearly see it from the buildings. The archeologists had apparently assumed that caves would be present only in the cliffs, not in the marl terrace near the buildings.

The Taʿamireh Bedouin later told a story about the discovery of Cave

4. An elderly member of the tribe recalled that when he was young he had been hunting and had pursued a partridge into a hole in the area of Qumran. The hole led down to a cave in which he found several items, including a lamp and pottery. Younger members of the tribe followed the elderly gentleman's directions and quickly spotted the cave described in his story. In it they dug up countless fragmentary manuscripts. They attempted to sell about fifteen thousand of them in Jerusalem and, to conceal the source of their new income, gave false information about the cave's whereabouts. The facts were soon discovered, however, and the cave was excavated by Harding and Fathers de Vaux and J. T. Milik (1922-2006) from September 22 to 29, 1952. The cave turned out to be two caves (called Cave 4a and 4b), but the Bedouin had mixed the fragments from the two so that they are always identified as coming from Cave 4, without specifying which chamber. The archeologists were able to recover fragments of about one hundred manuscripts from the cave. The pieces held by the Bedouin were eventually purchased by the Jordanian government and by various foreign institutions. While the archeologists were at work on Cave 4, they found a fifth one next to it. It proved to have few written remains — fragments of perhaps twenty-five manuscripts. Nearby the Bedouin then found a sixth cave that contained fragments of some thirty-one scrolls.

With this flurry of discoveries, it was only natural that the site of the building remains would undergo further investigation. A second season of excavation took place from February 9 to April 4, 1953, that is, after Caves 2-6 had been discovered. A third campaign followed from February 15 to April 15, 1954, and a fourth from February 2 to April 6, 1955. During this fourth season of excavation archeologists found Caves 7-10, all in the marl terrace. None of these partially eroded caves produced much written evidence: Cave 7, about nineteen very fragmentary manuscripts, all in Greek; Cave 8, five broken texts; Cave 9, one unidentified papyrus fragment; and Cave 10, one piece of pottery with writing on it. Finally, the Ta'amireh struck again in January 1956 when they located the eleventh cave. They waited until February to divulge the news about the latest cave, which proved to be a rich find in that, while only twenty-one manuscripts were removed from it, some of them were nearly as complete as the original seven from Cave 1. That discovery was followed almost immediately by a fifth archeological expedition to the site (February 18–March 28, 1956). While it was taking place, preliminary investigations were also made at Ain Feshka, which is south of Qumran. A sixth and final season,

Cave 11, discovered by the Bedouin in 1956, contained the Temple Scroll, the longest scroll found
(David Harris)

which involved excavations only at Ain Feshka, occurred in 1958 (January 25–March 21).

The result was that from 1947 to 1956 eleven caves containing written material or remains of one kind or another were found within a rather small area in the vicinity of a set of building ruins. Similar artifacts connected the ruins with the caves. The Bedouin proved to be the big winners in the race to find manuscripts. They succeeded in locating the three richest caves (1, 4, 11) and two others (2 and 6), while the professional archeologists found Caves 3, 5, and 7-10, none of which contained impressive manuscript remains.

Efforts to find additional caves in the hope of uncovering more written deposits have failed, even with advanced techniques (such as sonar

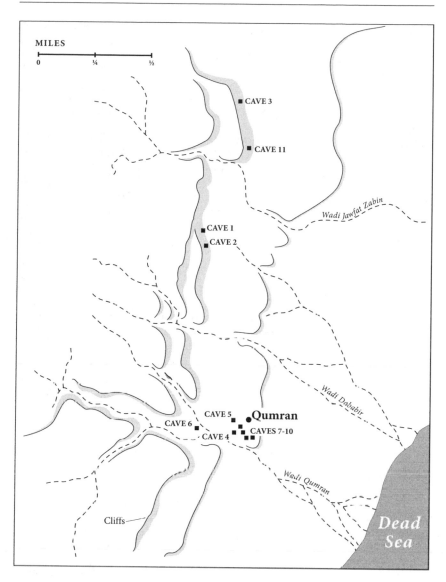

The Caves in the area of Qumran

John Strugnell sorting some of the 15,000 fragments found in Qumran Cave 4
(Estate of John Allegro)

resonancing) for spotting holes in the ground whose openings are now closed. The total of the fragmentary manuscripts uncovered is around 930 — an incredible treasure from an area that was thought to be an unlikely repository of ancient texts. But finding and purchasing the manuscripts and fragments, though a long and difficult process, was one thing; preparing and interpreting them, and understanding the evidence from the buildings, proved to be even more complicated.

3. The Ruins of Qumran

For five seasons archeologists investigated the building ruins occupying a plateau in the vicinity of the caves. The leader of these digs was Father Roland de Vaux of the Ecole Biblique, a French Dominican school in Jerusalem. De Vaux had distinguished himself as a biblical scholar and archeologist and by 1949 had been appointed director of the Ecole. The Ecole had been one of the institutions contacted by Metropolitan Samuel when he was trying to identify the scrolls that he had purchased. In fact, a scholar visiting there, J. van der Ploeg of the University of Nijmegen in the Netherlands, seems to have been the first expert to recognize that one of the scrolls contained the book of Isaiah.

a. The de Vaux Excavations and Interpretations

(1) *The Buildings*

On the basis of the evidence uncovered during the seasons of excavation, de Vaux wrote a series of articles in the journal *Revue Biblique* and later a book in which he articulated a hypothesis about the site that, though it always had its critics, long dominated historical reconstructions of its history. De Vaux identified two principal periods of occupation. (1) In the eighth-seventh centuries B.C. a small city stood on the site. It may be the one named Secacah in Josh 15:61, where it is listed with various others including "the City of Salt" and En-gedi, a place just south of Qumran. The remains of a rectangular building were traced to this phase. (2) After a gap of several centuries one finds evidence for the sectarian period, that is, the time when the people associated with the scrolls occupied the area. De Vaux divided the two centuries that he thought were involved in this second period into two phases, the first of which he further subdivided. A brief third phase seems to have followed. The next paragraphs summarize his understanding of this period.

Phase Ia Few remains survive from this early reoccupation because later construction and destruction removed most of them. On the basis of coins and other artifacts from the *next* phase, de Vaux concluded that phase Ia began not far from 140 B.C. and that it did not last very long. That is, it is possible to date phase Ia only relative to the next phase in the sense that the former had to precede the latter.

Phase Ib De Vaux argued that phase Ib began probably during the reign of the Hasmonean ruler and high priest John Hyrcanus (134-104 B.C.). The people then using the site added upper storeys to the older structures and expanded the buildings to the west and south. They extended the impressive water system of Qumran at this time and constructed the aqueduct that brought water from the hills into the building complex. They then coated the entire system with plaster. The remains from phase Ib indicate that the population associated with the complex had grown

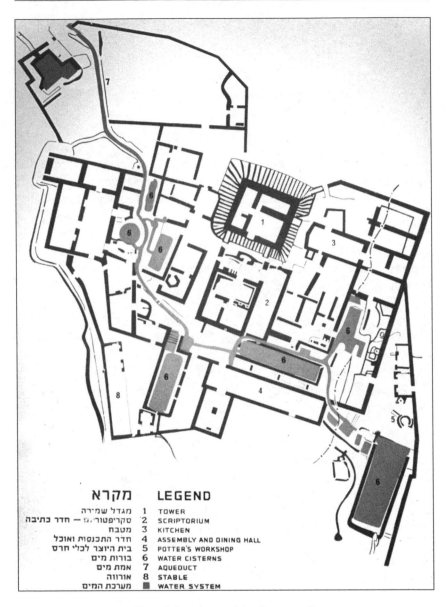

מקרא   LEGEND

מגדל שמירה	1	TOWER
סקריפטורי.ם – חדר כתיבה	2	SCRIPTORIUM
מטבח	3	KITCHEN
חדר התכנסות ואוכל	4	ASSEMBLY AND DINING HALL
בית היוצר לכלי חרס	5	POTTER'S WORKSHOP
בורות מים	6	WATER CISTERNS
אמת מים	7	AQUEDUCT
אורווה	8	STABLE
מערכת המים	■	WATER SYSTEM

Plan of the layout of the Qumran site

(Joel and Neal Bierling)

22

Overview of the Qumran site and the surrounding area. Four of the caves where Dead Sea Scrolls were found can be seen. (Werner Braun)

dramatically from the much smaller number accommodated in phase I*a*. There is evidence that a fire and an earthquake contributed to the end of the phase. Especially in the north and northwest a layer of ash lies beneath the remains of phase II (see below). It is not certain that the two disasters were connected, but the Jewish historian Josephus (A.D. 37-about 100) does record that an earthquake struck the area in 31 B.C. — the date at which de Vaux put the end of phase I*b*.

Phase II De Vaux believed that the people who used the site abandoned it after the earthquake and that it remained unoccupied until the death of King Herod in 4 B.C. He pointed to some meager evidence in the writ-

ings of Josephus that Herod and at least a few Essenes enjoyed good relations, perhaps implying that they were more comfortable living with
other Jews during his reign. Around the time of Herod's death, the site
was rebuilt. Phase II lasted until A.D. 68 when, de Vaux thought, Roman
troops who were quelling the Jewish revolt in the area (the revolt lasted
from 66 to 70) attacked and destroyed the structures. There is again
widespread evidence of a fire. The date of 68 is consistent with the fact
that eighty-three bronze coins of the second year of the revolt were
found at Qumran but only five from the third year. A decisive event must
have occurred to account for the difference. Some iron arrowheads characteristic of a Roman type of the first century A.D. were also uncovered.

Phase III Roman soldiers who were stationed at Qumran after the end
of phase II apparently constructed a few barracks, primarily in the south-
western corner of the central building. The series of coins belonging to
this phase continues until about A.D. 90, although the few identified
from the Bar Kokhba period (A.D. 132-35) suggest that rebels of this later
uprising also used Qumran.

De Vaux concluded that the structures at Qumran in phases I and II
were not intended as residential quarters. Rather, the buildings and ruins
had the appearance of a communal center with a sizable meeting place
and dining area. The people associated with the site probably lived in
makeshift shelters in the area or even in the caves. They assembled in the
buildings only for communal purposes. He identified the fallen remains
of one second-storey room (in archeological terminology, locus 30) as
coming from a scriptorium, a place where scribes copied scrolls. The
pieces of furniture and the two inkwells found in the room entailed for
him that it was indeed the place in the settlement where the scrolls from
the caves were written.

No manuscripts were unearthed in the building ruins. The excavations did, however, turn up some jars and ostraca with writing on them.
The many coins recovered (over 700) are also inscribed.

De Vaux himself wrote a number of technical articles that kept
scholars abreast of the finds, but no final and exhaustive publication of
the data was ever made. The most comprehensive statement about the
evidence and de Vaux's interpretations is in the printed version of his
Schweich Lectures, which he delivered in 1959. The revised English edition, entitled *Archaeology and the Dead Sea Scrolls*, was published in 1973,
two years after his death.

(2) The Cemeteries

As one would expect for a site that was used by a group for many decades, Qumran had several cemeteries. The large main cemetery, which lies to the east of the buildings, is about fifty meters away from them. It holds approximately eleven hundred individual tombs, arranged in neat rows and divided into three sections by alleys between them. All the graves are aligned on a north-south axis, with the head of the skeletons at the southern end. De Vaux excavated only twenty-eight of these tombs, selected from different parts of the main cemetery. All the skeletons identifiable by gender and found in the neat, ordered parts of the cemetery were male. One unusual grave, set apart from the others, contained a female skeleton. In the extensions of the cemetery farther to the east,

The large main cemetery at Qumran. More than 1,100 graves have been counted.
(Catherine M. Murphy)

however, the nine tombs investigated yielded four female skeletons and one of a child. De Vaux also studied what he called two secondary cemeteries, one north of the site and the other south of Wadi Qumran. In the northerly one just two tombs were opened; they held a male and a female skeleton. In the southern cemetery, the four graves that were investigated provided the final resting place for one woman and three children. (In chap. 3, I discuss the implications of these finds in connection with the problem of celibacy at Qumran.)

b. Subsequent Studies and Interpretations

(1) The Buildings

De Vaux's theory was the dominant one for decades, although there were dissenters from his conclusions. So, for example, not all were convinced about his period Ia for which he cited so little evidence, and his interpretation of the gap in occupation from 31-4 B.C. was also not universally accepted. Everyone has agreed that the failure of de Vaux (and his successors) to publish all of the evidence is unfortunate. The materials from his excavations have been appearing slowly but are still not fully available for study.

In the post–de Vaux debate about the Qumran site, there have been experts who largely accept his interpretation while adjusting the chronological limits for the phases of occupation that he hypothesized; others have read the evidence in a much different way.

The most widely cited revision of de Vaux's overall theory is the one articulated by Jodi Magness in her 2002 monograph *The Archaeology of Qumran and the Dead Sea Scrolls.* Magness rightly observes that any conclusions regarding the archeology of the site must be tentative as long as the full body of relevant evidence from it remains incompletely published. But, working with the data available, she defends the following points regarding the phases distinguished by de Vaux:

1. There was no period corresponding to de Vaux's Ia.

2. De Vaux's dating of the beginning of Ib is unconvincing: he argued on the basis of the high number of coins minted by Alexander Jannaeus and found at Qumran that the phase began no later than the reign of this king/high priest (103-76 B.C.). Magness concludes that the site was first reoccupied (after the Israelite settlement centuries before) at some point in the first half of the first century B.C. (between 100 and 50) and, as

items such as the ritual baths indicate, the site was sectarian from the beginning (she also thinks the sectarians were Essenes). Her dating for the beginning of sectarian occupation of the site had earlier been defended by Ernest-Marie Laperrousaz, a scholar associated with the Ecole and also director of studies at l'Ecole Pratique des Hautes-Etudes who had participated in the de Vaux expeditions from 1954 onwards, although his overall interpretation of the chronology differs from that of de Vaux and Magness at several points.

3. The gap in occupation between I and II was not the lengthy time suggested by de Vaux (31-4 B.C.). Magness's argument involves the proper interpretation of a collection of Tyrian silver coins (561 of them) that de Vaux reported were found in three pots buried beneath Period II ruins and above those of his Period I*b*. Since the latest among them dated to 9/8 B.C., he reasoned that phase II must have begun after that time. Magness assigns the coins to phase I and understands them as evidence that it extended into the last decade B.C. That is, the earthquake of 31 B.C. did not lead to an extended abandonment of the site. Rather, a fire decades later caused people using the site to leave it for a shorter time — from one winter to perhaps a couple of years — before returning to rebuild it. Damage to the water system shows that there was a period of disuse. Early in the reign of Herod's son Archelaus (4 B.C.–6 A.D.) the same group returned to the site and rebuilt it nearly as it was before the fire. Magen Broshi, professional archeologist and former curator of the Shrine of the Book at the Israel Museum, had earlier objected to de Vaux's reading of the evidence and did not think it required the lengthy gap in time he suggested.

The building ruins have elicited other interpretations, several of which should be surveyed here.

The Ruins of a Fortress I have already mentioned that some visitors to Qumran had identified the ruins as those of a fortress. Included among them was de Vaux himself, although after he excavated the site more thoroughly he came to a much different conclusion. The fortress thesis has had its defenders over the years, with Norman Golb of the University of Chicago advocating it in a series of publications. His understanding of the site is part of a larger theory, which I analyze in chap. 3. Here it suffices to say that, according to Golb, the scrolls in the caves have no integral connection with the buildings at Khirbet Qumran. The scrolls were brought from Jerusalem by people of various persuasions and hidden in the caves for safekeeping at the time of the revolt against Rome (A.D. 66-

70). The fortress had been standing at the site for some time before this event. Golb notes, among other arguments, the thick walls of the tower and the likelihood that the structures were destroyed as a result of a military attack.

Golb has not found much of a following. In general, we can say that if Qumran was a fortress it assumed a unique form. The layout of the site is unparalleled in other fortresses of the time, and, apart from the tower area, the thickness of the outer walls is not adequate for military needs. True, the many cisterns would have provided space for enough water to last for months, but the water supply could easily have been cut off by an enemy since the aqueduct is exposed for long stretches outside the enclosure. Would a fortress have been planned so carelessly? The buildings also seem to be located at a poor place for military security. If Qumran was destroyed by Roman troops, as de Vaux maintained, it would not follow that it was a military installation, unless we knew that the Romans attacked only fortresses, not civilian targets. Finally, ancient literature makes no reference to a fortress in the Qumran area. Since the ruins show no clear evidence of being a military establishment and parts of them would be unexpected in one, Golb's theory has rightly been rejected as implausible.

A Villa with a Dining Room As already mentioned, no complete excavation report on Qumran was ever made, although de Vaux and others have written extensively on the material remains and their interpretation. A group of archeologists was assigned to complete the publication project. Among them was the wife-husband team of Pauline Donceel-Voûte and Robert Donceel. They apparently think that the ceramic evidence and other data suggest that Qumran was the villa of a well-to-do owner. Donceel-Voûte wrote an essay in which she argued against de Vaux's notion that locus 30 contained a scriptorium on the upper level. Donceel-Voûte claimed that the data favor identifying it as a dining room in which the banqueters ate reclining (a *triclinium*) and from which they had an unobstructed view toward the south and southeast. This identification would be consistent with the theory that the site was a villa. She has reexamined in detail the fragments of furniture that were found on the ground, their relation with one another, and parallels to them from elsewhere in the Hellenistic and Roman worlds.

In the light of her arguments, it is interesting to read de Vaux's words about those broken pieces of furniture and what they might have been.

In this way it was found possible to reconstruct a table from them
... a little more than 5 m. in length, 40 cm. in breadth, and only 50
cm. in height. There were also further fragments from two smaller
tables. These tables had certainly fallen from the upper floor
where the long table had been set up parallel to the eastern wall;
they had been used there in association with a low bench fixed to
this wall. This might have suggested the furniture of a dining-
room except for the fact that we had already identified this in another part of the buildings which did not contain a table. (*Archaeology and the Dead Sea Scrolls*, 29)

He also mentions the two inkwells found in this area. The pieces of furniture were set up in the Palestine Archaeological Museum in Jerusalem
(now called the Rockefeller Museum) in the form of a table with a bench.
The theory was that scribes sat on the bench and copied scrolls on the table. De Vaux was aware that pictures of ancient scribes at work usually
did not show them in such posture; rather, they would sit on the ground
or on a bench with a tablet in their lap and write in this way. He was,
however, able to list a number of cases in which they are pictured as writing at tables or desks.

A few comments about Donceel-Voûte's theory are in order. First, it
seems unlikely that a wealthy person would build a villa at Qumran when
a lush place like Jericho lies close by. Donceel-Voûte may have misread the
value of the ceramics at Qumran as a result of misunderstanding the nature of wealth and private property in the Qumran community (for a
fuller study of this issue, see chap. 3). Second, regarding the scriptorium
or dining room, Donceel-Voûte did admit that the exact form of what she
considered couches in a dining room are not attested elsewhere. She was
correct in saying that the inkwells could be associated with tasks other
than copying scrolls; but the obvious fact is that they are especially consistent with the scribal function de Vaux assigned to locus 30.

More recently, two archeologists have incorporated aspects of the
fortress or villa theory into their reading of the evidence.

Yitzhar Hirschfeld (1950-2006; he was a professor of archeology at the
Hebrew University of Jerusalem), in his 2004 volume *Qumran in Context:
Reassessing the Archaeological Evidence*, maintained that Qumran served
different functions at different times: during the Hasmonean period (that
is, before 37 B.C.) it was a field fort and road station; in the Herodian age it
was a manor house. In other words, it was never a sectarian site, and the

buildings at Qumran had nothing to do with the scrolls in the caves. The scrolls came from the Jerusalem temple and were deposited there just before the Roman destruction of Jerusalem. Hirschfeld commendably attempts to place the Qumran site within the larger context of the region and the agricultural and economic life in it.

J.-B. Humbert, an archeologist at the Ecole Biblique in Jerusalem, has proposed an interpretation that also involves different stages. The site first was a Hasmonean villa serving an agricultural purpose. It began during de Vaux's period I*a* and was destroyed in 57 or 31 B.C. Essenes took over the site in 31 B.C. and turned it into a cultic center with an altar on the north side facing Jerusalem. There they carried out a sacrificial system. There was no gap in the Essene occupation of the site although parts of it underwent some changes over time. For example, at a later point they abandoned the northern cultic area and built another on the southern side (in locus 77, de Vaux's dining hall). He thought only a small number of "guardians" lived permanently in the buildings; others who worked there came from elsewhere. The site was destroyed in A.D. 68.

Other experts have been unable to find parallels to the sorts of manor houses or villas posited by Hirschfeld and Humbert. In the case of Hirschfeld, the large cemetery at the site is a problem as are indications that the structures served a sectarian community (e.g., the unusually high number and large size of the ritual baths). Furthermore, he completely divorced the scrolls in the nearby caves from the buildings and fell victim to the more common assumption that the presence of fine ware or other signs of wealth implies the site could not have served an Essene community. The sources indicate the Essenes were not driven to seek wealth, but they do not say they were poor. As for Humbert's theory, other archeologists have found no evidence for the practice of a sacrificial system in the buildings at Qumran.

Magness's modification of de Vaux's theory has the strongest standing today as the best interpretation of all the evidence — the evidence of the scrolls as well as the building ruins. Any visitor to the site realizes how difficult it is to separate the scrolls found in, say, Cave 4 (housing some 600 of them) from the buildings, because the cave and the site are so close together. Moreover, the full configuration of the archeological data from Qumran remains unique despite the growing number of sites excavated in ancient Judea and surrounding areas. All readings of the artifacts are hypotheses, but Magness's thesis appears to enjoy the fullest explanatory power.

(2) The Cemeteries

The cemeteries at Khirbet Qumran have always been a focal point of debate, but the discussion took on a new form beginning in the late 1990s. There are two aspects of the renewed conversation: the likelihood that not all the burials at Qumran date from the Second Temple period, and the availability of new data regarding the excavated bones.

As for the first, in 2000 Joseph Zias, former Curator of Archaeology and Anthropology for the Israel Antiquities Authority, reported that the presence of beads and other grave goods in some of the tombs in the Qumran cemeteries made him doubt that they were Second Temple period Jewish burials. After noting five traits of Bedouin burials, he concluded that the Qumran tombs oriented E-W are Muslim, graves of Bedouin who were interred in them in much more recent times than when the buildings were in use (after A.D. 1450). That the skeletons of women and children which are usually less well preserved were the best preserved at Qumran also suggested they were more recent. He added: "The absence here of extended family tombs comprising several generations, as seen in other nearby Jewish sites such as Ein Gedi and Jericho, along with the absence of females and children, strengthens in my opinion the belief that we are dealing here in fact with a celibate community of males" (p. 242). Questions have been raised about aspects of Zias's work, but the possibility of intrusive burials, i.e., reuse of the cemeteries in later times, has opened a new perspective in the analysis of the tombs at Qumran.

The second aspect of the renewed discussion is the publication of data resulting from rigorous scientific analyses of the bones available for research. De Vaux had given some bones taken from various tombs to anthropologists for analysis: Gottfried Kurth of Gottingen, who had visited Qumran during the excavations and seen some of the tombs firsthand, and Henri Victor Vallois, director of the Musée de l'Homme in Paris. The bones in the possession of these experts seem to have disappeared from sight for decades before they were "rediscovered" more recently. The Kurth Collection of material retrieved from fourteen graves (containing bones from sixteen individuals) in the main cemetery and from four tombs (with bones of five individuals) in the southern cemetery has been examined by a team of experts organized by Olav Rohrer-Ertl, Kurth's former assistant and now at the University of Munich; they have issued publications detailing the results of their work. The French

Collection, consisting of the bones that Vallois had in Paris supplemented with ones later found at the Ecole Biblique in Jerusalem, was entrusted to Susan Sheridan, professor of anthropology at the University of Notre Dame, who has also worked with a team who have published the results of their studies. Included in this lot are remains from seventeen graves with parts of seventeen individuals.

There are various complications in working with the limited amount of poorly preserved material, but the reported results regarding sex identification of the skeletons are as follows. The Kurth Collection consists of 9 males, 7 females, and an approximately seven-year-old girl (all from the main cemetery) and one female, three boys, and a child of undetermined sex (from the southern cemetery). Regarding the French Collection, all were over thirty years of age when they died, other than a boy buried in tomb 15, and all were likely male except a woman in tomb 15 and possibly a second woman in tomb 5.

In 2006, Brian Schultz, now of Fresno Pacific University, surveyed all of the available data and also compared the Qumran evidence with Muslim burial practices as known from published results of excavated cemeteries. He concluded that direction of orientation was not a reliable pointer to Muslim burials. In fact, of the fourteen intrusive burials that he identifies at Qumran, six are oriented N-S. In the 32 excavated tombs that, in his view, can be confidently dated to Second Temple times, there were skeletons of five women, each one of which is problematic or debatable in some way. The only primary burial (as distinct from a reburial) of a female about which there is no debate is the one from Tomb A which is located in a separate cemetery (although exactly where is debated). He concludes:

> . . . the cemetery unequivocally points to a special treatment of women in an otherwise male-oriented community. The unusual character of the community which used this cemetery in the Second Temple period is further confirmed by a total absence of any children. These results, when combined with the fact that the Qumran cemetery exemplifies greater uniformity with respect to burial orientation than any other Second Temple period cemetery of its kind, point to its total uniqueness, and fit best with the majority opinion that Qumran was a community center for a predominantly male, Jewish sectarian group in the first century BCE and CE. (219-20)

Of the individuals sampled, then, most are male, which may corrob-
orate other evidence that a male sectarian group used the site of Qumran
in the Second Temple period. But several points should be underscored:
Only a small percentage of the graves have been excavated so that the
sample size is questionable. There was a lack of rigor in the sampling
procedure when the excavations occurred so that we do not have a random sampling representative of the cemeteries. The preservation is poor,
the conservation has been deficient, and only skulls and pelvises were removed by the archeologists when excavating, resulting in limits on the
kinds of anthropological tests that can be applied to them today.

4. METHODS FOR DATING THE DISCOVERIES

At this point, it will be useful to sketch the kinds of evidence that have
been used for dating the scrolls and the other archeological remains from
Qumran. One may distinguish several kinds for the two types of artifacts.

a. Methods for Dating the Texts

Well before the Qumran ruins had been explored in a systematic way,
scholars were already proposing dates for the writings from the first cave.
These and later conclusions arose from application of several techniques
for determining when a text or copy might have been written.

(1) Paleography

Paleography is the study of ancient scripts or the ways in which scribes
shaped the letters of the texts they were writing or copying. Styles of letter
formation change over time. By observing the changes, the paleographer
can determine roughly where on the line of development a particular
manuscript belongs. In order to translate the relative position on the line
into a chronological date, the expert must have some fixed points — especially texts that contain their own dates — from which to extrapolate for
those works whose dates are under investigation. Fortunately a growing
number of ancient Hebrew and Aramaic texts date themselves to a particular year (there are more Greek documents of this kind). For example,

1QIsaᵃ column VI with small fragment that added six letters to the second line from the end, where Isa 7:14 appears (John C. Trever) some of the Elephantine papyri, Aramaic texts from a Jewish military colony in Egypt, contain dates in the regnal year of Darius II (423-404 B.C.) of Persia. Others, from Wadi ed-Daliyeh north of Jericho, date themselves to the reign of Artaxerxes III (358-338). Others exist for later times. Good examples are the documents from Masada, which cannot be later than A.D. 73 or 74 (when Masada was taken by the Romans), and those from Murabba'at and Nahal Hever that bear dates during the Second Jewish Revolt (A.D. 132-35). By examining the handwriting in dated texts and noting the developments that have affected the script, the paleographer can situate an undated text at some point between them, relatively closer to the one whose script it more generally resembles. Paleographers have some advantages in working with ancient rather than modern writing samples. Since they were usually written by professional scribes, the penmanship tended to follow conventions, with only gradual modification. Paleographically assigned dates tend to become more precise as the number of dated texts increases. Nevertheless, one should remember that dates assigned to texts on the basis of their script alone are relative, not exact.

Frank Moore Cross, then of McCormick Theological Seminary and later of Harvard University, published the standard study of the Qumran and related scripts in 1961. He distinguished three paleographical periods in the scrolls: archaic (250-150 B.C.), Hasmonean (150-30 B.C.), and Herodian (30 B.C.–A.D. 68/70). Within these limits he made further subdivisions and also distinguished different kinds of writing styles: formal, semiformal, cursive, and semicursive. He found that a few manuscripts date to the archaic period (such as 4QSamuel^b); these were presumably brought to Qumran from outside, since they are earlier than the sectarian use of the site. Many more come from the Hasmonean period (the Manual of Discipline [Rule of the Community] and the larger Isaiah scroll from Cave 1 are good examples), but most were copied in the Herodian age (for example, the commentaries). Cross believes that paleographical analysis of these texts has reached such a level of precision that a trained paleographer can date a manuscript to within twenty-five or fifty years of when it was copied.

(2) Accelerator Mass Spectrometry

Assigning rather precise dates on the basis of paleographical evidence alone has long been a controversial matter. Some scholars, who tend not

Fragment from 11Q10 Targum of Job, column XXXVII

(Photograph by Bruce and Kenneth Zuckerman, West Semitic Research. Courtesy Shrine of the Book.)

to be paleographers, believe that more caution is in order. In their opinion, external controls must supplement the data of script analysis. One such external control is now available — accelerator mass spectrometry (AMS), a more refined form of carbon-14 dating. The carbon-14 method of dating was discovered in 1947, the year when the first scrolls were found. No scroll was subjected to carbon-14 dating in the early years, however, because the amount of material that had to be destroyed in the process would have required the loss of too much of a manuscript — 1-3 grams, more than some of the fragmentary texts weighed. Some linen in which scrolls had been wrapped was tested in 1950-51 (see below). More recently, the new AMS method has been refined. Testing by means of it can be done with only a fraction of the organic material needed for the older carbon-14 method (0.5-1.0 mg.).

Both carbon-14 and AMS testing supply ranges of dates for the age of the material on which the texts are written. Unfortunately, we lack information about whether materials were prepared and then not used for long stretches of time, but perhaps it is not rash to suppose that normally when one prepared a hide to serve as a writing surface it was soon put to use. If so, the age of the hide would roughly correspond with the time at which someone wrote on it.

There have been tests of two groups of manuscripts from the Qumran caves along with some others for comparative purposes. One test took place at the Institut für Mittelenergiephysik in Zurich, Switzerland, in 1991; the results were published in 1991 and 1992. A second batch underwent testing in 1994 at the NSF Accelerator Mass Spectrometry Facility at the University of Arizona in Tucson, with the results published in 1995 and 1996. The outcomes of AMS testing are expressed as two ranges of dates: +/-1, a narrower range, means the laboratory reports with 68% confidence that the actual date lies within the years specified, while +/-2σ, a wider range, indicates a 95% level of confidence. Only the Tucson lab expressed the 2σ data.

The laboratories also tested several samples from ancient manuscripts that contained their own dates as a check on the method. The results appear in Table 1.

TABLE 1

Text	Internal Date	1σ	2σ
1. WDSP 2	352/51 B.C.	399-357 or 287-234	408-203 B.C.
2. 5/6 Hev 19	A.D. 128	131-240	A.D. 84-322
3. 5/6 Hev 21	A.D. 130	132-324	A.D. 80-389
4. XHev/Se 11	A.D. 130/131	32-129	A.D. 2-220?
5. Mur 30	A.D. 134/135	77-132	A.D. 32-224?
6. XHev/Se 8a	A.D. 134/135	237-340	A.D. 140-390
7. Mird	A.D. 744	676-775	A.D. 660-803

In each instance, the actual date of the text (the internal date) falls within the limits of the 2σ range, except the sixth for which the earlier date (A.D. 140) is 6/5 years later than the actual date. As for the 1σ dates, the internal dates fall just before the earlier AMS date (examples 2, 3), just after the later one (examples 4, 5 and the first set of dates for #1), within them (#7), or rather noticeably outside them (the second range for ##1, 6). The correspondence between the dates of the texts and of the materials on which they are written is quite close, with no really wide deviations.

The samples from the Qumran caves were 19 in number, with one tested twice (4Q258); none of the Qumran texts has an internal date (see Table 2).

TABLE 2

Text	Paleographic Date	1σ	2σ
1. 4Q542 (Qahat)	125-100 B.C.	385-349 or 317-208 B.C.	395-181 B.C.
2. 4Q365 frg. 3	40-10 B.C.	339-327 or 202-112 B.C.	351-296 or 230-53 B.C.
3. 1QIsaiah[a]	125-100 B.C.	201-93 B.C.	351-296 or 230-48 B.C.
4. 4Q213 (Levi)	50-25 B.C.	197-105 B.C.	344-324 or 203-53 B.C.
5. 4Q53 (Sam[c])	150-30 B.C.	196-47 B.C.	349-318 or 228 B.C.–A.D. 18
6. 11Q19 (Temple)	30 B.C.–A.D. 30	53 B.C.–A.D. 21	166 B.C.–A.D. 67
7. 1QGenesisApoc	30 B.C.–A.D. 30	47 B.C.–A.D. 48	89 B.C.–A.D. 69
8. 1QH[a]	30-1 B.C.	37 B.C.–A.D. 68	47 B.C.–A.D. 118
9. 4Q266 (DamDoc)	100-50 B.C.	A.D. 4-82	44 B.C.–A.D. 129
10. 1QpHab	A.D. 1-50	88-2 B.C.	160-148 or 111 B.C.–A.D. 2
11. 1QS	100-50 B.C.	164-144 or 116 B.C.–A.D. 50	344-323 or 203 B.C.–A.D. 122
12. 4Q258	30-1 B.C.	A.D. 133-237	129-255 or A.D. 303-318
13. 4Q258	30-1 B.C.	36 B.C.–A.D. 81	50 B.C.–A.D. 130
14. 4Q171 (pPs[a])	A.D. 1-70	A.D. 29-81	A.D. 3-126
15. 4Q521 (MessAp)	125-75 B.C.	39 B.C.–A.D. 66	49 B.C.–A.D. 116
16. 4Q267	30-1 B.C.	168-51 B.C.	198-3 B.C.
17. 4Q249	190-150 B.C.	196-47 B.C.	349-304 or 228 B.C.–A.D. 18
18. 4Q317		166-48 B.C.	196-1 B.C.
19. 4Q208	225-175 B.C.	167-53 B.C.	172-48 B.C.
20. 4Q22 (palEx)	100-25 B.C.	164-144 or 116 B.C.–A.D. 48	342-324 or 203 B.C.–A.D. 83 or A.D. 105-115

Three other texts were tested (4Q342, 344, 345), but there is some debate about whether they are from Qumran and hence they have been omitted from the list. For two of them, the 1σ and 2σ ranges overlap with the paleographical date (342, 344); for 4Q345, the 2σ range does. Summarizing the results for the 2σ column, of 19 examples, 7 of the paleographic dates fall outside the date range; of these 7, four come within a few years of being included. For the 1σ figures, 9 fall outside the range, with two coming within a few years. In the majority of cases, then, the AMS and paleographical dates overlap. In that sense, the AMS results confirm that experts have been correct to see the origins of the manuscripts in the last centuries B.C. and the first century A.D.

The interesting cases are the ones in which the two types of dates — paleographical and AMS — differ markedly. We should recall that in such cases either of the kinds of testing could have produced erroneous results. In the case of 4Q258 it appears that the initial testing done in Switzerland was performed on a piece of parchment that was covered with a contaminant. Once it was properly removed, the resulting year range overlapped with the paleographically determined date. It is not known why the results diverge more significantly for 4Q542 (at least 56 years) and 4Q521 (at least 26 years). For 4Q542, one could argue that the scribe used an older piece of parchment, but that argument would not work for 4Q521 since the handwriting is supposed to be older than the material on which it is written.

While these data do not prove that the paleographical dates are exact, they do show, as nearly as AMS testing can, that they are accurate and even that they tend to be conservative. Thus, although we may not know the exact date of a manuscript, we can be confident that the paleographers have placed them in the correct periods. Such information makes it highly likely that the Scrolls come from the last centuries B.C. and the first century A.D., not from the medieval period, for example, as some (such as Solomon Zeitlin of Dropsie College) maintained in the late 1940s and early 1950s.

(3) Internal Allusions

A third means for obtaining a general idea of when the scrolls were written is provided by references in them to known individuals (like Nabonidus in the Prayer of Nabonidus) or peoples. If a text names a recognizable individual, then it could not have been written before that person's lifetime. These references, like coins (see below, 4.b.3), define a point after which a text was composed, although they do not indicate how long after. If, however, the manuscripts from the caves were written before A.D. 68, then a scroll that names a person would have been written between the time of that individual and 68.

The Nahum Commentary mentions a few people by name, and several other texts do as well. The commentary, in its interpretation of Nah 2:11b, refers to "[Deme]trius king of Greece who sought, on the counsel of those who seek smooth things, to enter Jerusalem. [But God did not permit the city to be delivered] into the hands of the kings of Greece, from the time of Antiochus until the coming of the rulers of the Kittim. But then she shall be trampled under their feet" (1.2-3). Demetrius is almost certainly Demetrius III Eucerus. In approximately 88 B.C. some Pharisees invited him to help them in their opposition to the Jewish king Alexander Jannaeus (reigned 103-76 B.C.; see Josephus, *Antiquities* 13.375-76; *Jewish War* 1.90-92). Antiochus may be Antiochus IV, who sacked Jerusalem in 168 B.C. Since several Seleucid (Greek) monarchs assumed the names Demetrius and Antiochus, some uncertainty remains about the references, but these two are the most likely. At any rate, the two kings could be no later than about 65-64 B.C., when the Seleucid monarchy came to an end. If the incident involving Demetrius and the Pharisees is the one the commentator describes (the subsequent reference in 1.6-8 to crucifixion makes this identification likely), the passage would be another clear indication that the "seekers of smooth things" are Pharisees, eight hundred of whom Jannaeus hanged at one time. Most would agree also that the Kittim in this and many other passages are the Romans, specifically Pompey and his army, who did in fact trample Jerusalem under their feet in 63 B.C. (for more on this passage, see chaps. 3 and 4).

A few other individuals are named elsewhere: Shelamsion (= Alexandra Salome), who was queen in Judea in the years 76-67 B.C. (4Q331 1 2.7; 4Q332 2.4 says, in a broken context, "Shelamsion came"); Hyrcanus, either John Hyrcanus or Hyrcanus II (he ruled with his mother [76-67] and held a sort of control in the years 63-40 [4Q332 2.6: "Hyrcanus the King"; the title would be accurate only for Hyrcanus II; 4Q341 1.7]); and Aemilius, who seems to be Marcus Aemilius Scaurus, the Roman governor in Syria (65-62; 4Q333 1.4, 8: in both places the text says "Aemilius killed"). Another text that has garnered much attention — 4Q448 — mentions "Jonathan the king." His name appears once for sure and possibly a second time. The only "Jonathan the king" in Jewish history was Alexander Jannaeus, whose Hebrew name, stamped on his coins, is Jonathan. In 4Q468e line 3 the name Peitholaus probably appears. He was involved with the Romans after Pompey's conquest. Apparently no individual who lived in the first century A.D. is named in the Scrolls.

b. Methods for Dating the Other Archeological Remains

(1) Carbon 14

As noted above, some of the linen from Cave 1, supplied by G. Lankester Harding, the excavator of the cave, was subjected to carbon-14 testing. On November 14, 1950, the material was given to W. F. Libby, the University of Chicago scientist who had discovered the carbon-14 technique for dating. He reported on January 9, 1951, that the linen had been dated by the carbon-14 test to A.D. 33, plus or minus 200 years. Although the result was not very precise, it at least made a likely case that the linen, and hence presumably the scroll wrapped in it, were ancient. The central date — A.D. 33 — was comfortably within the range established by other methods. One could raise questions about the linen and the relationship between its age and any scroll that might have been safeguarded in it (was an old piece of linen used to encase a more recent scroll or vice versa?), but the carbon-14 data were a welcome addition to the growing body of evidence that the Scrolls came from around the turn of the eras.

(2) Pottery

The innumerable pieces of pottery found in the ruins and in the caves belong to types from the late Hellenistic and early Roman periods, that is, the last centuries B.C. and the first centuries A.D. Although de Vaux was not able to assign any pottery confidently to his phase Ia at Qumran, the examples are numerous for the last century B.C. and the first century A.D. That the same sorts of jars were found both in the caves and in the buildings had originally suggested a connection between the two.

(3) Coins

Hundred of coins were found in the ruins of the settlement, but apparently none was found in the caves. In antiquity as today, coins regularly had dates stamped on them, normally the regnal year of the king who was entitled to mint them. At times they bore the dates of particular eras. Since they often date themselves, coins found at a site can point to the approximate time when it was occupied. Their presence does not, of course, specify a particular date, since dates on coins indicate only the year(s) during and after which they were used. If King X minted a coin in his third year, then that coin could not come from a time before that year, only from that year and it could have been in use for some time after it. An important limitation on the use of numismatic (coin) evidence for determining dates is that we do not know precisely how long coins stayed in circulation. Nevertheless, they do furnish a rough guide to when a site was occupied.

De Vaux reported that the various coins which could be associated with specific rulers or events were distributed in this way:

1. Seleucid coins
   a. Silver: three dated to the reign of Antiochus VII (138-129 B.C.) and two others not dated but probably from his time. Another may be from the reign of Demetrius II (145-139 B.C.).
   b. Bronze: five dated from Antiochus III (223-187 B.C.), IV (175-164 B.C.), and VII (139/138-129 B.C.), and an undated one, probably from Antiochus IV.
2. Jewish coins (which begin late in John Hyrcanus's reign [134-104 B.C.])
   a. one from John Hyrcanus
   b. one from Aristobulus (104-103 B.C.)
   c. 143 from Alexander Jannaeus (103-76 B.C.)
   d. one from the joint reign of Alexandra Salome and Hyrcanus II (76-67 B.C.)
   e. five from Hyrcanus II (63-40 B.C.)
   f. four from Antigonus Mattathias (40-37 B.C.)
3. Herodian coins
   a. ten from Herod (37-4 B.C.)
   b. sixteen from Herod Archelaus (4 B.C.–A.D. 6)
4. Procuratorial coins — 91 (33 from Nero's reign [A.D. 54-68])
5. Agrippa I (A.D. 41-44) — 78
6. The First Revolt (A.D. 66-70)
   a. zero from Year 1
   b. 83 from Year 2

c. five from Year 3
d. zero from Year 4

Many other coins were found, including a hoard of 561 Tyrian coins dating between 126 and 9/8 B.C. There were also a few from the Period III level of the ruins (they were left there after the revolt when a Roman garrison was stationed at Qumran): thirteen coins minted in Nero's reign and still in use; and one that may be from A.D. 87. Finally, a few coins date from the Second Jewish Revolt against Rome (A.D. 132-35) when the site was reused, apparently only briefly.

De Vaux used the numismatic evidence to argue a number of points. Among them were that one could not push the origin of the buildings associated with the sectarian phases very far before John Hyrcanus's reign and that the site was destroyed in A.D. 68, as suggested by the vast difference in the number of coins before and after this date. Whether or not one accepts all of de Vaux's conclusions, the coins from the different times again point toward the last century B.C. and the first century A.D. as the likeliest period when Qumran was occupied.

BIBLIOGRAPHICAL NOTES

The translation of the letter from Timotheus to Sergius is quoted from G. R. Driver, *The Hebrew Scrolls from the Neighbourhood of Jericho and the Dead Sea* (London: Oxford University Press, 1951) 25-26.

The section on the discoveries in the first cave is indebted to John C. Trever, *The Untold Story of Qumran* (Westwood, N.J.: Fleming H. Revell Co., 1965), who supplied much more detail and documentary evidence than is given here.

For Eleazar Sukenik, the information comes from his Hebrew-language book, published posthumously, entitled *The Collection of the Hidden Scrolls in the Possession of the Hebrew University* (ed. Nahman Avigad; Jerusalem: Bialik Institute, 1954) 14 (for his explanation of his press release) and 26 (for his suggestion that the authors of the scrolls were Essenes). His entire account of how he learned about the scrolls and eventually acquired several of them is fascinating.

For Anton Kiraz's claims about ownership of the scrolls, see G. A. Kiraz, ed., *Anton Kiraz's Dead Sea Scrolls Archive* (Piscataway, NJ: Gorgias, 2005).

The dating of key events in the history of Scrolls discoveries and study is aided by the list prepared by Stephen J. Pfann and published in *The Dead Sea Scrolls on Microfiche: Companion Volume* (ed. Emanuel Tov, with the collaboration of S. J. Pfann; Leiden/New York/Cologne: E. J. Brill, 1993) 97-108. Pfann has also compiled in the same volume the section entitled "Sites in the Judean Desert Where Texts Have Been Found," 109-19.

The quotation of Millar Burrows is taken from his *The Dead Sea Scrolls* (New York: Viking Press, 1955) 17.

The standard older work on the archeology of Qumran and a book that I quote in the chapter is Roland de Vaux, *Archaeology and the Dead Sea Scrolls* (Schweich Lectures 1959; rev. ed.; London: Oxford University Press, 1973). Also useful is Philip R. Davies, *Qumran* (Cities of the Biblical World; Grand Rapids: Wm. B. Eerdmans, 1983). On p. 30 he mentions the pre-1947 visitors to the site. On this matter, see also Pfann in *The Dead Sea Scrolls on Microfiche,* 110. For the fullest statement of her reading of the evidence, see J. Magness, *The Archaeology of Qumran and the Dead Sea Scrolls* (Studies in the Dead Sea Scrolls and Related Literature; Grand Rapids: Wm. B. Eerdmans, 2002).

For Magen Broshi's view on de Vaux's gap in occupation from 31-4 B.C. and related issues, see his essay, "The Archeology of Qumran — A Reconsideration," in *The Dead Sea Scrolls: Forty Years of Research* (ed. Devorah Dimant; Studies on the Texts of the Desert of Judah 10; Leiden: Brill, 1992) 103-15.

For Norman Golb's views, see for example his essays: "The Problem of Origin and Identification of the Dead Sea Scrolls," *Proceedings of the American Philosophical Society* 124 (1980) 1-24; "The Dead Sea Scrolls: A New Perspective," *The American Scholar* 58 (1989) 177-207; and *Who Wrote the Dead Sea Scrolls?: The Search for the Secret of Qumran* (New York: Scribner, 1995).

Pauline Donceel-Voûte's article is "'Coenaculum' — La salle a l'étage du locus 30 a Khirbet Qumrân sur la mer morte," *Banquets d'Orient* (Res Orientales 4; 1993) 61-84.

For Y. Hirschfeld, see his *Qumran in Context: Reassessing the Archaeological Evidence* (Peabody, MA: Hendrickson, 2004).

For J.-B. Humbert's understanding of the Qumran site, see "L'espace sacre a Qumran: Propositions pour l'archéologie," *Revue Biblique* 101 (1994) 161-214; and "Some Remarks on the Archaeology of Qumran," in *Qumran: The Site of the Dead Sea Scrolls: Archaeological Interpretations and Debates.*

For Joseph Zias's essay, see "The Cemeteries of Qumran and Celibacy: Confusion Laid to Rest?" *Dead Sea Discoveries* 7 (2000) 220-53.

For one place to read reports about the studies on the bones from the Qumran graves, see *Qumran: The Site of the Dead Sea Scrolls: Archaeological Interpretations and Debates: Proceedings of a Conference Held at Brown University, November 17-19, 2002* (ed. K. Galor, J.-B. Humbert, and J. Zangenberg; Studies on the Texts of the Desert of Judah 57; Leiden: Brill, 2006). O. Rohrer-Ertl's essay, "Facts and Results Based on Skeletal Remains from Qumran Found in the Collectio Kurth — a Study in Methodology," is on pp. 181-93; the essay by S. Sheridan and J. Ullinger, "A Reconsideration of the Human Remains in the French Collection from Qumran," follows on pp. 195-212. Brian Schultz's article is "The Qumran Cemetery: 150 Years of Research," *Dead Sea Discoveries* 13 (2006) 194-228.

The project for publishing completely the results of de Vaux's excavations has produced the following works: J.-B. Humbert and A. Chambon, *Fouilles de Khirbet Qumran et de Ain Feshkha I Album de photographies, Reportoire du fonds photographique, Synthese des notes de chantier du Pere Roland de Vaux OP* (Novum Testamentum et Orbis Antiquus Series Archaeologica 1; Fribourg: Editions Universitaires/ Göttingen: Vandenhoeck & Ruprecht, 1994); J.-B. Humbert and A. Chambon, *The Excavations of Khirbet Qumran and Ain Feshka IB: Synthesis of Roland de Vaux's Field Notes* (translated and revised by S. Pfann; Novum Testamentum et Orbis Antiquus Series Archaeologica 1B; Fribourg: Editions Universitaires/Göttingen: Vandenhoeck & Ruprecht, 2003; the volume is an English translation of the previous one with some new material); J.-B. Humbert and J. Gunneweg, *Fouilles de Khirbet Qumran et de Ain Feshka II: Etudes d'anthropologie, de physique et de chimie* (Novum Testamentum et Orbis Antiquus Series Archaeologica 3; Gottingen: Vandenhoeck & Ruprecht, 2003).

Frank Moore Cross's essay on the Qumran scripts is "The Development of the Jewish Scripts," in *The Bible and the Ancient Near East: Essays in Honor of William Foxwell Albright* (ed. G. E. Wright; Garden City, N.Y.: Doubleday, 1961) 133-202.

The information about the AMS testing is taken from G. Bonani, S. Ivy, W. Wölfli, M. Broshi, I. Carmi, and J. Strugnell, "Radio Carbon Dating of Fourteen Dead Sea Scrolls," *Radiocarbon* 34 (1992) 843-49 (for the Zurich tests). For the Tucson tests, see A. J. T. Lull, D. J. Donahue, M. Broshi, and E. Tov, "Radiocarbon Dating of Scrolls and Linen Fragments from the Judean Desert," *'Atiqot* 28 (1996) 85-91. The numbers from both tests were then presented according to the 1997 calibration data by D. Doudna, "Dating the Scrolls on the Basis of Radiocarbon Analysis," *The Dead Sea Scrolls After Fifty Years: A Comprehensive Assessment* (2 vols.; ed. P. Flint and J. VanderKam; Leiden: Brill, 1998, 1999) 1.430-71. His figures are cited above.

Weston W. Fields, *The Dead Sea Scrolls: A Short History* (Leiden: Brill, 2006), is a short version of the two-volume work he has prepared regarding the early years of Scrolls discoveries and scholarship. He has allowed me to read a pre-publication copy of the larger work that includes extensive quotations from correspondence and other documents. The larger work will be a most valuable resource for those who wish to follow events and to read what the individuals involved, including the members of the original Scrolls publication team, wrote about the Scrolls, one another, and their work.

CHAPTER 2

Survey of the Manuscripts

The eleven caves at Qumran have yielded the remains of over 900 manuscripts. It seems likely that many of them were copied or written at Qumran, but certainly not all of them were. A few of them can be dated on paleographical grounds to the third or early second century B.C., well before the site was occupied. They must have been brought to it from elsewhere. The same may be true for many others; unfortunately, it is difficult to tell which ones they might be.

Some of the scrolls I mentioned already in chap. 1; the following is an overview of the works found and of the contents of a few texts that are particularly interesting and important. The survey includes most but by no means all of them.

A. BIBLICAL TEXTS

Using the word *biblical* for the time frame with which we are dealing is anachronistic because, insofar as we are able to tell, there was no final, fixed, and authoritative understanding of which works were scriptural and which ones were not in the last centuries B.C. and the first century A.D. A final agreement about which books constituted the Hebrew Bible (= the Protestant Old Testament) probably did not come about until later, although we do not know when that might have been. It is fair to say that many did agree about the authoritative status of a considerable number of books that eventually were regarded as part of the Bible: the five books constituting the Law of Moses (Genesis through Deuteronomy = the Torah), the historical and prophetic works, and the Psalms. Questions remained about a few others, especially books like Esther, Song of Solomon (also called Song of Songs or Canticles), and Sirach (also called the Wisdom of Jesus ben Sira or Ecclesiasticus). In the remainder of this book, I use the word *biblical* simply for the sake of convenience to refer to those works that later constituted the Hebrew Bible. Use of the term does not, however, imply that everyone in the period in question had the same list of authoritative scrolls/books. In chap. 5, I devote a section to the textual significance of the Qumran biblical scrolls and another to the issue of which books were considered supremely authoritative by the people who wrote and copied the Dead Sea Scrolls.

1. BIBLICAL SCROLLS

The latest published lists of the manuscripts indicate that the biblical books are represented in the following numbers of copies in Hebrew/Aramaic (using a common order for the books in Hebrew Bibles; the numbers in parentheses include manuscripts whose identity is uncertain):

Genesis	20	(21)	Psalms	34	(36)
Exodus	16		Proverbs	4	
Leviticus	12	(13)	Job	4	
Numbers	6	(7)	Song of Solomon	4	
Deuteronomy	30	(32)	Ruth	4	
Joshua	3		Lamentations	4	
Judges	4		Ecclesiastes	2	
1–2 Samuel	4		Esther	0	
1–2 Kings	3		Daniel	8	
Isaiah	21		Ezra	1	
Jeremiah	6		Nehemiah	1	
Ezekiel	6		1–2 Chronicles	1	
Twelve Prophets	8			206	(213)

These biblical manuscripts were distributed among the caves in this way:

Cave 1	16 (17)		Cave 7	0
Cave 2	16 (17)		Cave 8	2
Cave 3	3		Cave 9	0
Cave 4	148 (149)		Cave 10	0
Cave 5	7		Cave 11	8 (9)
Cave 6	6 (9)			206 (213)

These numbers include some scrolls that contain more than one book (for example, Exodus and Leviticus). To the overall numbers we could add the Greek copies (Exodus — 1, Leviticus — 2, Numbers — 1, and Deuteronomy — 1). Identification of some of the fragments is debated, because they are so small that it is impossible to tell, for example, whether we have a copy of a biblical book or have just stumbled on a fragment of another work that happens to quote a scriptural book in the preserved section.

If one works with the numbers listed above, the total for the biblical manuscripts is 211 (218) copies, or a little less than one-quarter of 930 manuscripts found at Qumran. (Perhaps as many as 25 more copies were unearthed at other sites in the Judean desert.) The total documents the fact that the people who lived in the Qumran area considered the scriptural writings important. Moreover, we know from the Qumran literature that scriptural study was part of daily life for the members of the group(s). The raw totals probably also indicate which books were used frequently. The book of Psalms is present in the largest number of copies (34 or 36), with the next two being Deuteronomy (30 or 32) and Isaiah (21). Of the others, only Genesis (20 or 21), Exodus (16), and Leviticus (12 or 13) break into double figures. At the other extreme, not a single recognizable scrap from a manuscript of Esther has been located, and not a single fragment from a copy of Nehemiah was identified until 2008. Before the Nehemiah fragment came to light, some had assumed that at Qumran Ezra and Nehemiah were already considered a single book, as they are in the Hebrew Bible. In this fashion they were able to regard the one copy of Ezra as representing both works. There is no proof the two were considered a single entity at the time, but the appearance of a copy of Nehemiah in Cave 4 entails that Esther is the only book of the later official Hebrew Bible not attested in the Qumran caves. (As explained below in B.2.a-b, some other books that did not make their way into the official Hebrew Bible are present in more copies at Qumran than almost any work of the Hebrew Bible.)

The numbers alone give a fairly reliable impression of where the

Qumran group(s) placed its (their) emphases. The Psalms could be used for a variety of reasons: for worship, meditation, and prooftexting. The legal books (Exodus, Leviticus, Numbers, and Deuteronomy) served as the authoritative basis for the way of life developed by the group(s). They, with Genesis, also supplied historical examples from the biblical period. That in some manuscripts the books of Moses (and Job, which may have been associated with Moses) are copied in paleo-Hebrew script (a script ancient already at that time) may be a way of expressing the esteem in which they were held. The prophecies of Isaiah proved to be a rich mine of predictions about the group(s) and the messianic leaders who would soon appear. Perhaps it is not strange that the three books that appear on the largest number of copies at Qumran are also the three that are quoted most frequently in the New Testament. The relatively low number of copies for the historical books (Joshua, Judges, 1–2 Samuel, 1–2 Kings, Ezra, Nehemiah, and 1–2 Chronicles) implies that they played only a modest role at Qumran. Esther, which provides the explanation for the festival of Purim — a holiday that is never mentioned in the Qumran texts, though all other biblical festivals are — was apparently not used, unless its absence is a result of sheer chance.

2. TARGUMS

When gradually in the last centuries B.C. Hebrew ceased being the spoken language of most Jewish people, understanding the Hebrew scriptures as they were read in worship became a problem. The modern Roman Catholic Church dropped Latin in the services because few parishioners understood it, and replaced it with vernacular languages. In ancient Judaism the difficulty was solved somewhat differently for synagogue services: after the scriptural passage was read in Hebrew, it was immediately translated orally into Aramaic, the language that most Jewish people in Israel spoke. These translations into Aramaic were eventually written down, and a number of them have survived. They provide yet another witness to the Hebrew text of the Bible and also to how it was understood in the first centuries A.D. A much-debated question has been when these translations or *targums* (*targum* is the Hebrew word for "translation") first came into being. Some scholars maintained that they were pre-Christian, but others concluded from the relatively late (medieval or later) dates of the surviving targumic manuscripts that it was unsafe to posit an early date for such works. Now the debate has taken a new turn with the discovery at Qumran of the remains from targums for two biblical books — Leviticus and Job. The fragments of the targum to Leviticus come from Cave 4 and are very small: they translate only Lev 16:12-15 and 16:18-21 (4Q156). The small pieces have been dated to the second century B.C. Two targums to Job have also been found. Fragments from Cave 4 (4Q157), copied in the first century A.D., preserve an Aramaic rendering of Job 3:5-9 and 4:16–5:4. Cave 11 has, however, produced the major targumic find. The targum of Job found in it is one of the best-preserved manuscripts from any of the Qumran caves and dates from the last half of the first century B.C. It contains Aramaic translations of most verses, in whole or in part, from Job 17:14 to 42:11. The number of the targums discovered in the Qumran caves is not large, but they indicate that targums were being written down in the pre-Christian era.

3. Tefillin and Mezuzot

Although they are not copies (in a technical sense) of biblical books, tefillin (or phylacteries) and mezuzot are small parchments containing passages from Exodus and Deuteronomy (including Exod 12:43–13:16; Deut 5:1–6:9; 10:12–11:21; and at times verses from Deuteronomy 32). The tefillin were and still are placed in small boxes tied to the head or left arm, while mezuzot are attached to the doorpost of a house. They were made to fulfill the scriptural requirement about the words God had commanded Israel: "Bind them as a sign on your hand, fix them as an emblem [or: frontlet] on your forehead, and write them on the doorposts of your house and on your gates" (Deut 6:8-9). A large number of these were found at Qumran and other sites in the Judean wilderness. From Cave 4 a total of twenty-one tefillin were recovered (4Q128-48), one from Cave 1, one from Cave 5, and one from Cave 8. Four others came from another cave but no one knows which one. Mezuzot are fewer: seven from Cave 4 (4Q149-55) and one from Cave 8. The scriptural passages in them can vary from the wording in the traditional (Masoretic) Hebrew text, and at times these variants agree with readings in other ancient versions of the Bible.

B. APOCRYPHAL AND PSEUDEPIGRAPHAL TEXTS

It is difficult to find an adequate word or phrase for the books that fall into this category. These books are neither biblical (in the sense that they did not become part of the Hebrew Bible) nor specifically sectarian (that is, books written for the purposes of the separated group(s) that lived around Qumran). In this section I first survey copies of works that belong in the traditional categories of Apocrypha and Pseudepigrapha and then indicate how the Qumran collection has augmented the number of works that we can categorize in this way.

1. APOCRYPHA

Apocrypha is an anachronistic but useful term. Its meaning depends on the one who is speaking. Here I use it in the Protestant sense to refer to those books that are in the Catholic but not in the Protestant Old Testament (= the Hebrew Bible). The extra books found in the Catholic Bible derive ultimately from the Septuagint (the Greek translation of the Old Testament). At the time of the Reformations their authority was rejected by Protestants but reaffirmed by Catholics. The Catholic biblical books that fall into this category today are: Tobit, Judith, 1–2 Maccabees, Wisdom (of Solomon), Sirach (= the Wisdom of Jesus ben Sira, or Ecclesiasticus), Baruch (of which chap. 6 is called the Letter of Jeremiah), and eight additional sections in Esther and three in Daniel (Susanna, the Prayer of Azariah and the Song of the Three Young Men, and Bel and the Dragon). If we use the word *Apocrypha* in a broader sense to mean all those books present in the Greek Bible (the Septuagint) but not in the Hebrew, we could add Psalm 151 (and a few others) to the list.

Of these apocryphal works, four have been identified among the Dead Sea Scrolls.

a. Tobit

The book contains a dramatic story about Tobit, a Jewish exile from the northern kingdom of Israel. He rose to prominence in the Assyrian bureaucracy only to lose his position. In his reduced condition, he continued to perform acts of charity but eventually became poor and was later accidentally blinded. He sent his son Tobias to get the family treasure, which had been deposited with a relative for safekeeping. Although Tobit and Tobias did not know it, Tobias's hired traveling companion was the angel Raphael. After sundry adventures, Tobias married a relative named Sarah and found a remarkable remedy for his father's blindness. All ends well. The entertaining tale may have been written in the third century B.C. Before the Qumran discoveries, the earliest surviving version of Tobit was in Greek, though scholars thought it had been translated from a Semitic base. Among the Qumran manscripts experts have identified four copies of the book in Aramaic and one in Hebrew (4Q196-200). So, we have an early instance of a book that was translated or perhaps an example of a work that circulated in two languages. The Aramaic copies have been important for textual criticism of the book: they often agree with the longer Greek text of the book and thus make it likely that it is the more original form. Parts of all fourteen chapters are represented in the Qumran copies of Tobit.

b. Sirach (Ecclesiasticus or the Wisdom of Jesus ben Sira)

Jesus ben Sira was a Jewish teacher who wrote a book of wise sayings and instructions in about 190-180 B.C. The work was composed in Hebrew and later translated into Greek by the author's grandson, who also added a preface to his rendering. The Hebrew text must have survived for some centuries because rabbinic writings cite and discuss it; but it passed out of use in most Jewish communities and was not recopied. In modern times several discoveries have brought to light portions of the lost Hebrew original. In the late nineteenth century a large amount of the text was recovered on several medieval manuscripts found in the geniza (a synagogal storage place for discarded manuscripts) in the Ezra synagogue in Cairo. At Masada, the famous fortress where more than nine hundred Jewish rebels committed suicide in A.D. 73 or 74, a fragmentary copy containing 39:27–43:30 in Hebrew was discovered (it dates from the first century B.C.). Qumran has made some smaller additions to these finds. Cave 2 (2Q18) contained some small pieces on which one could recognize parts of a few verses from the book. Cave 11 yielded another section of the book but in a surprising place: a manuscript of the book of Psalms (11QPs^a) includes the poem that is now found in Sirach 51. That the poem is attested in two literary compositions shows that it was a floating piece. Where it may have belonged originally is an open question.

c. Letter of Jeremiah (= Baruch 6)

This single-chapter work is largely an attack on idolatry. Nothing from the first five chapters of Baruch has been found at Qumran, but the Letter of Jeremiah appears on one copy from Cave 7 (7Q2) that is written in Greek, which was apparently the original language of the book. Cave 7 is, incidentally, one of the few places where Greek manuscript fragments were found at Qumran. In fact, all legible fragments from Cave 7 have Greek texts.

d. Psalm 151

This extra psalm, also found in the Septuagint, is a strongly Davidic piece and forms a fitting conclusion to the Psalter, which is so closely associated with the poetic, musical king. The psalm is another of the compositions in the first Psalms scroll from Cave 11 (11QPs^a) that is not part of the Psalter in the traditional Hebrew Bible. As in the Septuagint, in the Psalms scroll from Cave 11 it is the concluding poem.

2. PSEUDEPIGRAPHA

This word is a cover term for Jewish religious books, written in the last centuries B.C. and the first century or two A.D., that did not become part of the Hebrew Bible or the Septuagint. The term itself derives from the practice found in some of these books by which the author hides his identity beneath the name of some ancient worthy from biblical times (for example, Adam, Abraham, Moses, Elijah). One could characterize the procedure as a reverse form of plagiarism: the author does not publish the work of another under his own name; he publishes his work under the name of someone else. Scholars debate whether the practice is found in the Old and New Testaments, but that it was used frequently in antiquity is indisputable and it may not have been considered disreputable. Since the definition of this category of books is vague, there is some disagreement about what belongs in it. *The Old Testament Pseudepigrapha,* the most recent English translation (2 volumes edited by James H. Charlesworth), includes more than fifty texts that meet the editor's requirements for the category *Pseudepigrapha.*

Of the previously known Pseudepigrapha only three have surfaced at Qumran. All three examples teach us something about the text in question, but each one does so in a distinctive manner.

a. Enoch or 1 Enoch

The text as known before 1947 consisted of five units or booklets, each of which contained revelations supposedly given to Enoch, the seventh in the genealogy of Adam (Gen 5:21-24). The full text of the 108 chapters is preserved only in an Ethiopic translation of a Greek rendering of the Semitic original (written in Aramaic or Hebrew). One of the main themes in most of the booklets is a story about the angels who descended from heaven, married women, and became the fathers of gigantic offspring. These giants became the cause of the great evil and violence that resulted in God's sending the flood to punish them. The story is based on Gen 6:1-4 — the tale about the sons of God who married the daughters of men. The phrase "sons of God" was interpreted to mean "angels," a sense it carries elsewhere in the Bible (see, for example, Job 38:7, which uses almost the same Hebrew expression), while "the daughters of men" was understood in a literal sense. These verses in Genesis come just before the flood story and so were believed to be related to it. In the Enoch literature the angel story, far more so than the story of Adam, Eve, and the serpent, served as the fundamental way of explaining how human sin exploded to such an extent that God was compelled to send the annihilating flood. In the Enoch booklets, the combination of great evil and divine response in judgment also serves as a warning of the judgment to come. In fact, the flood is referred to as the first end (93:4). It serves as an example of the way in which God responds to rampant evil. In his exhortations Enoch frequently cites this example, as do some New Testament writers (the authors of 2 Peter, Jude). The Enoch booklets have many other important traits: several of them offer what appear to be the earliest Jewish examples of apocalypses that survey human history from start to finish; and one of them is devoted to astronomical information — the earliest Jewish text of this kind (perhaps written in the third century B.C.).

55

Among the many fragments found in Cave 4, a relatively large number of manuscripts of Enoch have appeared. All of them are written in the Aramaic language. Seven of the manuscripts include parts of three of the booklets: the Book of Watchers (chaps. 1–36); the Book of Dreams (83–90); and the Epistle of Enoch (91–107). The other four manuscripts give parts of another booklet — the Astronomical Book (chaps. 72–82). What has been intriguing to scholars is that none of the eleven manuscripts contains a word from the Similitudes or Parables of Enoch (chaps. 37–71). These chapters have always been of special interest to scholars of the New Testament because in them a character named "the son of man" plays a central role. In the end he is identified as Enoch. Scholars have long debated whether this concept of a superhuman son of man who will be involved in the final judgment may have been a source from which the writers of the New Testament Gospels drew in elaborating their pictures of Jesus as the son of man. That debate has now taken a new turn. Some, including J. T. Milik, who edited the fragments of Enoch, have concluded that since the Similitudes of Enoch are not present at Qumran and all the other parts of 1 Enoch are, the Similitudes must be a later composition. If so, they were probably written after the Gospels and thus could not have served as a source for the evangelists. Others think that the Similitudes may have come from a different strand of Judaism, not the Qumran kind, and that the text is pre-Christian in date. Whatever may be the answer to these historical problems, it is quite likely that the Similitudes, unlike all the other parts of 1 Enoch, were never part of the manuscript collection at Qumran.

It is also possible, even likely, that some of the Enoch manuscripts make a further intriguing point: in place of the Similitudes, the version of 1 Enoch known at Qumran had a different composition altogether, one that has been named the Book of Giants. There are nine, perhaps ten, Qumran copies of it, and two of the Enoch manuscripts mentioned above may include it as well. The Book of Giants tells about the enormous sons of the angels. In itself, this fact might not be very interesting, but this Book of Giants was to have a remarkable history. Some centuries later it was rewritten by Mani, a religious leader (from Babylonia) who synthesized various elements of Zoroastrianism, Judaism, and Christianity. His reworked Book of Giants became a canonical or biblical work for Mani and his followers. If the Book of Giants was the third composition in the Qumran version of 1 Enoch, then it was later replaced by the very different Similitudes of Enoch.

The four manuscripts of the Astronomical Book have an interest of their own. The first of them dates from shortly after 200 B.C., thus indicating that the booklet itself was probably written sometime before this copy was made. Hence, the Astronomical Book of Enoch is probably one of the rare surviving pieces of Jewish literature from the third century B.C. This first copy and the other three also reveal a major textual variation between the Aramaic and the Ethiopic versions. The Astronomical Book is full of long lists of information, such as the position of the sun and moon on the various days of the months and years and of the amount of the lunar surface that is illuminated by the sun during all the nights of a month. At some point a translator or copyist apparently grew weary of all this and abbreviated it. That truncated version now stands in the Ethiopic manuscripts, while the Aramaic shows something of the full, numbing scope of the original. The booklet describes a solar calendar that had 364 days in it and also a lunar calendar with 354 days.

b. Jubilees

The author of the book presents his work as a revelation from God, through an angel of the presence (that is, one who serves in God's presence). He in turn tells it to Moses, who writes it down. The book is largely a retelling of the biblical stories from creation (Genesis 1) until the Israelites arrive at Mount Sinai and Moses ascends the mountain to receive God's words (Exodus 19 and 24). It was written around 160-150 B.C., before the Qumran community was formed. The writer uses the biblical text as the medium through which he communicates his own views about theological and legal matters. Jubilees has received its name from the fact that it divides the history it covers into fifty units of forty-nine years each. That is, the author took the word *jubilee* to mean not the fiftieth year (as in Leviticus 25) but the forty-nine-year period that was marked off by the fiftieth year. One of the legal points on which he insists is that the true annual calendar is a solar one of 364 days, the same system as the one found in Enoch's Astronomical Book and, as we shall see, in the writings of the Qumran community. Before the scroll discoveries, it was widely believed that the book had been composed in Hebrew and later translated into Greek. Those versions had disappeared, however, and only translations made from the Greek had survived: a complete Ethiopic translation, and about two-fifths of a Latin rendering.

Soon after archeologists had explored Cave 1, they announced that fragments from two Hebrew copies of Jubilees had been found in it. The same proved true for Cave 2, while Cave 3 produced yet another. A sixth turned up in Cave 11, but, as usual, Cave 4 proved to be the richest depository: it contained fragments from eight or possibly nine manuscripts of Jubilees. The total of fourteen or fifteen copies of the book is most impressive. If we compare it with the number of copies for the biblical books listed above, only Psalms, Deuteronomy, Isaiah, Genesis and Exodus were represented by as many as or more copies than Jubilees. I explore the implications of the high number in the section about the canon of scripture at Qumran (see chap. 5).

In contrast to what we find for parts of 1 Enoch, the Qumran copies of Jubilees reveal a text that is close to the wording in the Ethiopic and Latin versions. In many cases entire passages agree word for word, while the deviations that exist tend to be minor. No evidence suggests that the later versions lack whole sections of the original or have augmented it to any significant degree. For whatever reasons, the text of the book was reproduced with great care. Jubilees served as an authority at Qumran and is cited as such in one of the central legal documents of the community, the Damascus Document. 4Q225-27 are called Pseudo-Jubilees in that they resemble material in Jubilees but are not copies of it. 4Q228 may cite the book by its Hebrew title.

c. Testaments of the Twelve Patriarchs

The twelve patriarchs of the title are the twelve sons of Jacob. In this pseudepigraph, each of the twelve, as their father Jacob did in Genesis 49, summons his children to his deathbed and offers them the benefit of the wisdom he had acquired in his lifetime. Testaments of this kind seem to have been popular in antiquity. The deathbed scene proved to be an effective setting for moral instruction. Scholars have had a long, lively discussion about whether the Testaments of the Twelve Patriarchs is a Jewish or Christian work. The various testaments have some unmistakable Christian passages. Are they additions to a Jewish base text, or were the Testaments written by a Christian using Jewish sources? On either view, it is clear that the Testaments are filled with Jewish material and that the Christian contributions are minor. Scholars often suggest a date in the late second century B.C. for the Testaments, if they are a Jewish composition.

The Qumran caves have yielded no copies of any of the Testaments of the Twelve Patriarchs. The work is included in this section, however, because sources for some of the individual testaments have turned up at Qumran. One very fragmentary text is about Naphtali (4Q215); another two or three, represented only by tiny pieces, have been named a Testament of Judah (3Q7; 4Q484, 538); and one other has received the title Testament of Joseph (4Q539). The most interesting of these sources is the one that scholars still often call the Testament of Levi but that should be termed the Aramaic Levi. This work appears in what may be six copies from Cave 4 (4Q213-14; the editors have subdivided each into three copies) and on a fragment or two from Cave 1 (1Q21). Levi was the third son of Jacob and ancestor of the Levitical tribe, which included all the priests. With such credentials, one might expect him to be praised highly or to act heroically in the Bible, but the opposite is the case. He is criticized in the only story in which he plays a part. With his brother Simeon he avenged the rape of their sister Dinah by massacring the men of Shechem while they were recovering from the effects of circumcision. In the aftermath, their father Jacob blamed them for leaving him with a bad reputation among the peoples of the area (Genesis 34), and he repeated his sentiments when he cursed the two brothers in his last words to them (Gen 49:5-7). Their reputations improved, however, in later texts. In Jubilees, for instance, Levi and Simeon are lauded for what they did in Shechem. Also in Jubilees and in the Testament of Levi the Shechem incident becomes one of the reasons why Levi himself became a priest (compare Mal 2:4-7) and received the promise of an eternal priesthood for his family.

These ideas, which were important for the Qumran group, are also part of the Aramaic Levi. The Shechem episode forms an early section of the text, one that leads to Levi's ordination as a priest. Careful comparison of the Aramaic text with the Testament of Levi (the earliest version of it is in Greek) shows that, while the two are similar, they also differ considerably. Since the Aramaic work may have been written already in the third century B.C., it is almost certain that it served, directly or indirectly, as one of the sources used by the author of the Testament of Levi, which is one part of the Testaments of the Twelve Patriarchs (cf. also 4Q540-41).

These three texts — 1 Enoch, Jubilees, and the Testaments of the Twelve Patriarchs — have, then, surfaced in one form or another at Qumran. The Hebrew text of Jubilees and the later translations of the book are very similar to one another; the Aramaic originals of 1 Enoch are less close to the later translations and may have a different composition — the Book of Giants — as the third part of the text; and the Testaments of the Twelve Patriarchs themselves do not appear, only sources from which their authors seem to have drawn.

d. New Pseudepigrapha

Although the net result for the Pseudepigrapha known before 1947 is slim — three texts (represented on about 40 copies) from a corpus numbering more than fifty documents — the caves have furnished students of ancient Jewish pseudepigrapha with a wide variety of previously unknown texts that may also fit in the category. A quick summary shows how many texts of this kind we have. One should keep in mind that correct identifications are often difficult because of the poor state in which most of these texts have survived. The following is a sampling meant to illustrate the diversity and size of the category — it is not intended to be exhaustive.

1. Genesis Apocryphon. The Aramaic work, one of the first seven scrolls to be found, retells and adapts the stories of Genesis. The extant parts of the text tell of the angelic marriage story that is connected with the birth of Noah: he was such a wondrous child that his father suspected his mother had been consorting with one of the fallen angels. The text continues with Noah and the flood, the division of the earth among Noah's descendants, and the Abra(ha)m stories as far as the covenant of Genesis 15. The scroll once contained much more, but it has come to us in the worst condition of the first seven. In the 1990s more letters and words were deciphered through use of the advanced photographic techniques. It remains the case, though, that much of the composition is irretrievable. What has survived often resembles Jubilees.
2. Noah texts: 1Q19; 4Q246(?), 534-36?
3. Jacob text: 4Q537
4. Joseph texts: 4Q474, 539
5. Qahat (also spelled Kohath; grandfather of Moses, Exod 6:18) text: 4Q542
6. Amram (Moses' father, Exod 6:20) texts: 4Q543-48, 549 (?)

7. Moses texts: 1Q22, 29; 2Q21; 4Q368, 4Q374?, 375-76?, 377, 408?
8. Joshua texts: 4Q378-79, 522
9. Samuel texts: 4Q160; 6Q9
10. David text: 2Q22 (see also the first Psalms scroll from Cave 11); cf. 4Q479
11. Elisha text: 4Q481a
12. Jeremiah texts: 4Q383-84(?) (see 4Q385b, 4Q387b)
13. Ezekiel texts: 4Q384(?)-90, 391
14. Zedekiah text: 4Q470
15. Daniel texts: 4Q242 (Prayer of Nabonidus), 4Q243-45, 4Q551(?)
16. Esther text: 4Q550, 550a-e

Some of these may be misidentified, and in no case is anything close to the complete text extant. But the bits and pieces that have turned up in the caves, especially Cave 4, demonstrate that at least for the Qumran group(s) the category of books ascribed to the pens of biblical heroes was large, with many entries not known before. In a sense, all of them could also be classified as examples of biblical interpretation in that they amplify something in the scriptural text or use it as a springboard for development in independent directions.

C. OTHER TEXTS

Under this pleasantly vague rubric I include all those texts in which the distinctive views of the separated group that inhabited the Qumran area come to expression. Also treated here are some works whose connection with the Qumran community is disputed. Again, the precise boundaries of this literature are uncertain because we know so little about the Qumran group(s) and the others living at the same time in Judea. Yet most of the caves have produced texts that seem to have been written for the purposes of the community (which I understand to have been Essene; see 3.A. below), either the part of it that resided in the wilderness at Qumran or the wider association of Essenes living throughout the country and in closer daily contact with others. The list here is only a sampling of the remaining texts, almost all of which were unknown to scholars before 1947.

1. COMMENTARIES ON BIBLICAL MATERIAL

We know that the residents of Qumran spent a portion of each day in scriptural study and that the ancient revelations were central to the life and teachings of the community. As the Rule of the Community says: "And where the ten are, there shall never lack a man among them who shall study the Law continually, day and night, concerning the right conduct of a man with his companion. And the Congregation shall watch in community for a third of every night of the year, to read the Book and to study the Law and to bless together" (6.6-8; p. 105). The centrality of the scriptures comes to light in a number of ways, the most obvious of which is the quantity of biblical manuscripts found in the caves. Another way in which it finds expression is in the commentaries on biblical books found there. A term that recurs in these texts is the Hebrew word *pesher* (plural *pesharim*), which means "interpretation." It is the cover term that scholars have given to the sort of interpretation found especially in the first type of commentary treated below.

a. Continuous Commentaries

The Qumran caves have disclosed a type of scriptural exposition that is the earliest-known antecedent of the modern running commentary. Like the modern commentator, the Qumran expositor would begin with the first words of a biblical book or section, cite them, and attach his understanding of the passage to them. He would then turn to the next verse or verses, quote it (them), and offer an explanation. He would proceed in this fashion throughout the entire composition on which he was commenting, or at least as far as his interests dictated. He separated his interpretation from the scriptural text with a word or phrase such as "its interpretation concerns." Because the commentator quoted from the scriptural text, the commentaries are another source of information for the wording of the biblical text.

Very early in the study of the Scrolls, it became evident that at least two fundamental assumptions underlay Qumran exegesis in these commentaries. The first is that the *biblical writer* referred in his prophecy to the latter days, not to his own time; the second was that the *commentator* assumed he was living during the latter days and that therefore the ancient prophecies were directed to his own days. His duty, then, was to unlock the secrets of the prophets' mysterious words and thus to find the divine message that addressed the commentator's circumstances. Since the interpreters often mention people and events who, in their opinion, were the referents of the prophecy, the commentaries are one of the few sorts of texts that give historical clues about the group and the period when it lived (see chap. 1 B.4.a.3).

The Qumran exegetes were assisted in their special kind of interpretation by an additional assumption. In their view, God had revealed the mysteries of his servants the prophets to the Teacher of Righteousness, who was an early leader of their movement. This belief finds expression in the commentary on Habakkuk, specifically in the explanation of Hab 2:1-2:

> *I will take my stand to watch and will station myself upon my fortress. I will watch to see what He will say to me and how [He will answer] my complaint. And the Lord answered [and said to me, "Write down the vision and make it plain] upon the tablets, that [he who reads] may read it speedily* [= Hab 2:1-2]."
>
> . . . and God told Habakkuk to write down that which would happen to the final generation, but He did not make known to him when time would come to an end. And as for that which He said, *That he who reads may read it speedily:* interpreted this concerns the Teacher of Righteousness, to whom God made known all the mysteries of His servants the Prophets. (1QpHab 6.12–7.5; p. 481)

With both an inspired text — the scriptures — and an inspired interpreter — the Teacher — the Qumran group was confident it enjoyed a great advantage over any other readers of the sacred prophecies. They convinced themselves that for them alone the vagaries of the prophets had become clear through the inspiration of their leader.

A few of the continuous commentaries are fairly well preserved, but most of them are rather fragmentary. Seventeen or eighteen (one may be a *pesher,* but the text on which it comments has not been identified) works belong in this category. Their distribution is interesting in itself: six on Isaiah; three on various psalms; two each on Hosea, Micah, and Zephaniah; and one each on Nahum and Habakkuk. Here, too, as with the biblical scrolls, the book of Isaiah and the Psalms are prominent. It may be surprising that there should be continuous commentaries on the

Psalms, since all the others are on prophetic books. It is likely, however, that the Qumran group regarded the Psalms as prophetic in some sense. Note what the first Psalms scroll from Cave 11 says about David:

> YHWH [Yahweh] gave him an intelligent and brilliant spirit, and he wrote 3,600 psalms and 364 songs to sing before the altar for the daily perpetual sacrifice, for all the days of the year; and 52 songs for the Sabbath offerings; and 30 songs for the New Moons, for Feast-days and for the Day of Atonement.
>
> In all, the songs which he uttered were 446, and 4 songs to make music on behalf of those stricken (by evil spirits).
>
> In all, they were 4,050.
>
> All these he uttered through prophecy which was given him from before the Most High. (11QPs^a 27.4-11; p. 307)

The New Testament, too, speaks of David as a prophet and interprets his poetry as pointing to events in the life of Jesus and in the early church (Acts 2:29-31; see also 1:15-26; Matt 13:34-35).

The relation between the biblical text and the commentary varies from passage to passage. Sometimes the explanation follows the scriptural words rather closely, at other times it seizes on a word or two in scripture (perhaps interpreting them as symbols), and on still other occasions the connection is less obvious. The best-preserved continuous commentaries are the Habakkuk *pesher* (one of the seven original scrolls), the Nahum commentary, and the exposition whose surviving parts center on Psalm 37. The commentaries on Isaiah are a major source of information about messianic beliefs at Qumran.

(1) The Habakkuk Commentary (1QpHab)

The scroll contains the text and accompanying commentary on Habakkuk 1-2. The poem in Habakkuk 3 is not explained. At the end of the manuscript is space for more material (about two-thirds of the last written column is empty, as is the next column), but the *pesher* ends without filling it. This space suggests that the interpreter wrote as much as he intended; the poem in chapter 3 did not serve his purposes. Habakkuk himself was active at some point in the period from about 650 to 600 B.C. He prophesied that the Lord was rousing the Chaldeans (the

Column VIII of the Habakkuk Commentary (John C. Trever)

Babylonians) to punish wayward Judah. As he describes the power and violence of these invaders, he offers a complaint to the Lord, who responds by speaking of the future punishment of the Chaldeans. The Qumran commentator interpreted the Chaldeans as the *Kittim*, a name by which he apparently meant the Romans. The prophet was told to write the vision he saw: "For there is still a vision for the appointed time; it speaks of the end and does not lie. If it seems to tarry, wait for it; it will surely come, it will not delay" (2:3). Thus, the Lord himself told Habakkuk that the vision pertained to the end, and the commentator knew that history had not ended in Habakkuk's day. Here he had a clue to the time that the prophet was addressing. Habakkuk also devoted a few verses to the contrast between the righteous and the wicked (1:13;

2:4). These, too, were ciphers for the expositor who saw such contrasts as exemplified in his own day.

A few passages should be quoted to illustrate how the commentator works. First, Hab 1:5 talks of the nations' marveling at what happens in Judah: "for I accomplish a deed in your days, but you will not believe it when told." The commentator finds in these words a prediction of what happened in the history of his group:

> [Interpreted, this concerns] those who were unfaithful together with the Liar, in that they [did] not [listen to the word received by] the Teacher of Righteousness from the mouth of God. And it concerns the unfaithful of the New [Covenant] in that they have not believed in the Covenant of God [and have profaned] His holy Name. And likewise, this saying is to be interpreted [as concerning those who] will be unfaithful at the end of days. They, the men of violence and the breakers of the Covenant, will not believe when they hear all that [is to happen to] the final generation from the Priest [[= the Teacher]] [in whose heart] God set [understanding] that he might interpret all the words of His servants the Prophets, through whom he foretold all that would happen to His people and [His land]. (1.17–2.10; p. 479)

The Liar seems to have been a member of the community who refused to accept what the Teacher of Righteousness claimed. The same point is made in the commentary on Hab 1:13b: "*O traitors, why do you stare and stay silent when the wicked swallows up one more righteous than he?* Interpreted, this concerns the House of Absalom and the members of its council who were silent at the time of the chastisement of the Teacher of Righteousness and gave him no help against the Liar who flouted the Law in the midst of their whole [congregation]" (5.8-12; p. 481). Others proved unfaithful to what the Teacher's group considered a new covenant, and some will prove unfaithful at the end. The real issue here is the authority of the Teacher and the claims he made. That some did not accept them was foretold in the prophetic scriptures. Here we encounter interpretation that is hardly concerned in the first place with the historical setting of the prophecy; it is transparently driven by other concerns.

A second example illustrates how the commentator, with his assumption that the biblical text spoke of his time, provides some historically useful pieces of information. The interpreter understood the Chaldeans of Habakkuk to be the Kittim, a term that referred to people who came from the sea to the west of Judea (see Gen 10:4). But in some places the expositor elicited more specific details from the text of Habakkuk:

> *The wind then sweeps on and passes; and they make of their strength their god* (Hab 1:11).
>
> Interpreted, [this concerns] the commanders of the Kittim who, on the counsel of [the] House of Guilt, pass one in front of the other; one after another [their] commanders come to lay waste the earth. (4.9-13; p. 480)

The Kittim are the Romans, whose leaders (the consuls) changed yearly and were under the control of the Senate (= the House of Guilt). Later (Hab 1:16) the prophet says that the enemy sacrifices to his net. "And as for that which He said, *Therefore they sacrifice to their net and burn incense to their seine:* interpreted, this means that they sacrifice to their standards and worship their weapons of war" (6.2-5; p. 481). Worship of standards is a clear reference to a Roman practice.

One other passage may be cited because it is one of the best known in the Qumran literature.

> *Woe to him who causes his neighbours to drink; who pours out his venom to make them drunk that he may gaze on their feasts!* (2:15).
>
> Interpreted, this concerns the Wicked Priest who pursued the Teacher of Righteousness to the house of his exile that he might confuse him with his venomous fury. And at the time appointed for rest, for the Day of Atonement, he appeared before them to confuse them, and to cause them to stumble on the Day of Fasting, their Sabbath of repose. (11.2-8; p. 484)

The Wicked Priest may have been a high priest. In chap. 4 I discuss the significance of this passage, in which the two archenemies — the Teacher and the Wicked Priest — appear together.

(2) The Nahum Commentary (4Q169)

The prophecies of Nahum also come from the late 600s B.C. but at a time when Assyria still survived (therefore before 612 or 609). The prophet looks to a rapidly approaching moment when the Lord will come for judgment against Nineveh, the capital city of Assyria. He compares the city to a lion's den and says that its young lions will be killed so they can take no more prey. He also compares Nineveh to a prostitute who will be shamed before all for her debaucheries. The prophecy of Nahum is a poem of judgment against Nineveh, a song celebrating its destruction: "There is no assuaging your hurt, your wound is mortal. All who hear the news about you clap their hands over you. For who has ever escaped your endless cruelty?" (3:19).

The Nahum commentary is not as well preserved as the Habakkuk *pesher,* but it, too, offers some important historical clues about the time when the Qumran group(s) existed. The surviving parts cover sections of chapters 1–2 and as far as verse 12 or perhaps verse 14 in chapter 3 (the last chapter in the book). Like the Habakkuk commentary, it mentions the Kittim. Unlike the Habakkuk commentary, the exposition of Nahum also calls individuals by their names.

> *Whither the lion goes, there is the lion's cub, [with none to disturb it]* (Nah 2:11b).
>
> [Interpreted, this concerns Deme]trius king of Greece who sought, on the counsel of those who seek smooth things, to enter Jerusalem. [But God did not permit the city to be delivered] into the hands of the kings of Greece, from the time of Antiochus until the coming of the rulers of the Kittim. But then she shall be trampled under their feet. . . . (1.1-3; p. 474)

The Demetrius in question appears to be Demetrius III Eucerus (95-88 B.C.), who did attack Jerusalem. The epithet "seekers after smooth things" is probably a punning allusion to the Pharisees (the word translated "smooth things" is a play on the Pharisaic word for "laws"); they are criticized several other times in the commentary. The Antiochus mentioned later may well be Antiochus IV Epiphanes (175-164 B.C.), who temporarily banned the practice of Judaism in the 160s.

The following passage also supplies a valuable historical clue.

> *[And chokes prey for its lionesses; and it fills] its caves [with prey] and its dens with victims* (Nah 2:12).
>
> Interpreted, this concerns the furious young lion [who executes revenge] on those who seek smooth things and hangs men

alive, . . . formerly in Israel. Because of a man hanged alive on [the] tree, He proclaims, *"Behold I am against [you, says the Lord of Hosts."]* (1.4-8; p. 474)

The reference is to an act of Alexander Jannaeus, a king of Judah (103-76 B.C.) who hanged eight hundred Pharisees on one occasion (note that they are "those who seek smooth things"). The commentary mentions neither the Teacher nor the Wicked Priest and seems to deal with a time subsequent to their careers.

(3) The Commentary on Psalms (4Q171, 173)

While the commentary on Psalms deals with more biblical passages than the one psalm, most of the surviving pieces treat different parts of Psalm 37. As he explicates the psalm, the expositor finds a number of predictions about contemporary events. Psalm 37 speaks of the tribulations suffered by the righteous at the hand of the wicked and of the vindication that the former will enjoy as they wait patiently for the Lord. Since "righteous" and "wicked" were code words for the commentator, he found in them allusions to the Teacher and his opponents. Note in particular these passages:

> *The steps of the man are confirmed by the Lord and He delights in all his ways; though [he stumble, he shall not fall, for the Lord shall support his hand]* [Ps 37:23-24].
>   Interpreted, this concerns the Priest, the Teacher of [Righteousness whom] God chose to stand before Him, for He established him to build for Himself the congregation of . . .

> *The wicked watches out for the righteous and seeks [to slay him. The Lord will not abandon him into his hand or] let him be condemned when he is tried* [Ps 37:32-33].
>   Interpreted, this concerns the Wicked [Priest] who [watched the Teacher of Righteousness] that he might put him to death [because of the ordinance] and the law which he sent to him. But God will not *aban[don him and will not let him be condemned when he is]* tried. And [God] will pay him his reward by delivering him into the hand of the violent of the nations, that they may exe-

cute upon him [judgement]. (fragments 1-10, cols. iii 14-16; iv 7-10; p. 489-90)

The commentary adds to the picture of the strong opposition between the two leaders and also mentions "the law which he [[the Teacher]] sent to him [[the Wicked Priest]]." Their disagreements may have been spelled out in this document, and it is possible that the text has been found among the Scrolls. This matter will be treated below in section 3, on the legal literature.

b. Thematic Commentaries

Many other works found in the Qumran caves base themselves in one way or another on the scriptures, although they do not take the form of continuous or running commentaries. They tend to assemble a number of biblical passages that pertain to a single or a few themes. The passages may be taken from different books or from separate parts of the same biblical book. A few examples follow.

(1) Florilegium (4Q174)

This collection of texts revolves especially around 2 Samuel 7 (the promise of an eternal dynasty for David) and Psalms 1 and 2. Along the way, other passages are adduced for commentary and clarification. 2 Sam 7:10 mentions that God would establish a place for his people where they could live securely. The Qumran commentator understood that place to be the house that the Lord will build for his people in the last days (Exod 15:17-18 is cited in support). "[Its glory shall endure] for ever; it shall appear above it perpetually. And strangers shall lay it waste no more, as they formerly laid waste the Sanctuary of Israel because of its sin. He has commanded that a Sanctuary of men be built for Himself, that they may send up, like the smoke of incense, the works of the Law" (1.5-7; p. 493). This section is speaking about a sanctuary of the last days that God, not humans, will construct; it will be a "Sanctuary of men," that is, it will not be a building; and the sacrifices offered in it will not be animal and grain offerings but "the works of the Law." In other words, the Lord's sanctuary will be like the Qumran community or perhaps equal to it.

The Florilegium has interested scholars not only because of its notion of a spiritual temple but also because it divulges important details about the eschatological characters awaited by the group.

> The Lord declares to you that He will build you a House [2 Sam 7:11]. I will raise up your seed after you [2 Sam 7:12]. I will establish the throne of his kingdom [for ever] [2 Sam 7:13]. I [will be] his father and he shall be my son [2 Sam 7:14]. He is the Branch of David who shall arise with the Interpreter of the Law [to rule] in Zion [at the end] of time. As it is written, I will raise up the tent of David that is fallen [Amos 9:11]. That is to say, the fallen tent of David is he who shall arise to save Israel. (1.10-13; p. 494)

At a later point (chap. 4.B.6) I examine more closely the anticipation that the Interpreter of the Law would accompany a Davidic messiah.

(2) The Testimonia (4Q175)

This short text is divided into four sections, each of which focuses on a biblical text (or two) that is cited: the first quotes two sections from Deuteronomy (5:28-29; 18:18-19); the second cites from the Balaam chapters of Numbers (24:15-17); the third adduces Deut 33:8-11 (Moses' blessing of Levi); and the fourth, which is also in 4Q379 22 ii 7-14, deals with Josh 6:26 (the curse on anyone who rebuilds Jericho). The first three paragraphs are united around the theme of future leaders: the prophet like Moses, a star who rises from Israel (the Davidic messiah apparently), and the priests (one like Levi, but his descendants as well). The fourth paragraph is less obviously related, but it seems to intend the fortification of a city by brothers (the Maccabees?) and the curse that awaits them. The unusual feature of the Testimonia text is that it is almost all quotation; only the fourth section has an interpretation added to it. However, Testimonia is a form of interpretation. For example, by appearing side-by-side with Num 24:15-17, Deut 18:18-19 takes on messianic overtones. Hanan Eshel thinks 4Q175 is directed against John Hyrcanus (134-104 B.C.), who claimed all three offices and built extensively in the Jericho area.

4Q175 Testimonia

(Photograph by Bruce and Kenneth Zuckerman, West Semitic Research, in collaboration
with Princeton Theological Seminary. Courtesy Department of Antiquities, Jordan.)

(3) *The Melchizedek Text (11QMelch)*

A scroll from Cave 11 makes Melchizedek the center of its attention. Melchizedek was the priest-king of Salem who met Abram after he had defeated the kings and rescued Lot (Gen 14:17-20). Abram gave him a tenth of his spoils and Melchizedek blessed him. Psalm 110:4 speaks of Melchizedek's eternal priesthood, a point elaborated in the Letter to the Hebrews, which presents Christ as a priest for all time after the order of Melchizedek. Melchizedek is a puzzling figure who appears suddenly and then as quickly disappears from the pages of the Old Testament.

Despite the fact that the Melchizedek text from Qumran is poorly preserved, enough survives to show that he was an object of speculation on the part of these groups. They thought of him as an angelic creature who would participate in the last judgment. The extant part of the text begins with a citation of Lev 25:13 and Deut 15:2, verses that deal with the year of jubilee and the year of release; to them is added Isa 61:1 ("to proclaim liberty to the captives"), which is understood to address the last days:

> [Its interpretation is that He] will assign them [[= the captives]] to the Sons of Heaven and to the inheritance of Melchizedek; f[or He will cast] their [lot] amid the po[rtions of Melchize]dek, who will return them there and will proclaim to them liberty, forgiving them [the wrongdoings] of all their iniquities.
>
> And this thing will [occur] in the first week of the Jubilee that follows the nine Jubilees. And the Day of Atonement is the e[nd of the] tenth [Ju]bilee, when all the Sons of [Light] and the men of the lot of Mel[chi]zedek will be atoned for. [And] a statute concerns them [to prov]ide them with their rewards. For this is the moment of the Year of Grace for Melchizedek. [And h]e will, by his strength, judge the holy ones of God, executing judgement as it is written concerning him in the Songs of David, who said, ELOHIM *has taken his place in the divine council; in the midst of the gods he holds judgement* [Ps 82:1]. And it was concerning him that he said, (Let the assembly of the peoples) *return to the height above them; EL (god) will judge the peoples* [Ps 7:7-8]. And as for that which he s[aid, *How long will you] judge unjustly and show partiality to the wicked? Selah* [Ps 82:2], its interpretation concerns Belial and the spirits of his lot [who] rebelled by turning away

from the precepts of God to. . . . And Melchizedek will avenge the vengeance of the judgements of God . . . and he will drag [them from the hand of] Belial and from the hand of all the sp[irits of] his [lot]. And all the "gods [of Justice"] will come to his aid [to] attend to the de[struction] of Belial. (2.4-14; p. 501)

The writer seizes on the fact that the word for "God" (*'elohim*) can also be used for angels. When, therefore, he finds the word in a place such as Ps 82:1, he is able to explain the passage as referring not to God himself but to the angel Melchizedek. His judging work is explicitly dated to the end of time because it involves the destruction of Belial. By interweaving sundry biblical texts and interpreting them in his special way, the writer fashions a memorable portrait of Melchizedek. While it does not tie in directly with the picture of him in Hebrews, it shows nevertheless something of the status he enjoyed within one Jewish circle. One should also note that scriptural texts which do not speak of the end of time are explained as if they did in this text and in other commentaries from Qumran.

(4) A Commentary on Genesis (4Q252)

The fragments of the commentary cite and interpret several non-consecutive passages from Genesis. At times the author slows down to present a passage at great length (the flood), and at other times he moves quickly through long stretches (the Abraham, Isaac, and Jacob stories), arriving finally at Jacob's "blessings" on his sons in Genesis 49. The work is unusual among the scrolls closely tied to the biblical text. It does not fit the *pesher* pattern in the sense that it does not reproduce and explain successive parts of a text, yet it may not belong in the category of thematic commentaries either because all the passages are from Genesis and in the scriptural order. If a consistent theme emerges from all the texts selected, it is not obvious from the fragments. Later I present the messianic passage at the end of the work; here it suffices to summarize what the author stresses most in his treatment of the flood story — the chronology.

1. The 120 years of Gen 6:3 are the time between when the warning contained in the verse was issued and the beginning of the flood. This time frame is indicated by putting the warning in Noah's 480th year; the flood came in his 600th year.

2. The flood begins on the same date as in Gen 7:11 — month 2, day 17. The other numbers are the same as well.
3. The flood ends the next year in month 2, but contrary to the traditional text of Gen 8:14, which has day 27, this text puts its conclusion on day 17. Thus the flood lasts exactly one year.
4. That year is explained as lasting precisely 364 days, which was the total for a solar year according to the Qumran group(s). In this respect they agreed with Jubilees and the Astronomical Book in 1 Enoch.

2. Paraphrases

The official list labels only a few manuscripts "paraphrases" of the Bible. The reason for distinguishing them from other close treatments of the scriptural text is that they very nearly resemble the wording but do not reproduce it exactly; or they reproduce it but splice other material into it here and there. The texts so designated are 4Q123 (on Joshua), 127 (on Exodus; it is in Greek), 4Q382 (on Kings), and 4Q422 (on Genesis and Exodus). 4Q158, 364-67 (on the Pentateuch) were also so named, but their latest title is Reworked Pentateuch (see below, chap. 5). It is not always clear why the scholars who have identified these documents call them paraphrases rather than straightforward biblical manuscripts; but, whatever we name them, they provide further illustration of how important the biblical text was at Qumran.

3. Legal Texts

Only since 1977 have the true scope and significance of the legal compositions at Qumran become apparent. From the beginning of Qumran research, scholars knew that the caves held texts which included numerous laws drawn from the scriptures and from biblical interpretation. But several major works that have been published or made available since the late 1970s have transformed law into one of the central areas of Qumran studies. It is a field in which Jewish scholars have led the way in analyzing the new documents and exploring their similarities to and differences from the great compilations of rabbinic law written down long after Qumran was destroyed. Four of the most important are noted here.

a. The Damascus Document

The composition goes under several names: the Zadokite Fragments and, as Damascus is mentioned in it several times, the Damascus Covenant or the Damascus Document. It has had an unusual history among the communal texts discovered at Qumran, because it was known before 1947. Solomon Schechter, a Jewish scholar who worked around the turn of the twentieth century, found two copies of the work in the *geniza* (the storage room where old, discarded manuscripts were kept) of the Ezra Synagogue in Old Cairo in 1896 (hence the name Cairo Damascus = CD). These he published in 1910. One copy, called A, has sixteen columns; text B has two columns (they were labeled 19-20 and overlap considerably with cols. 7-8 in manuscript A). They were copied in the tenth and twelfth centuries A.D. respectively. Although the Damascus Document did become the object of intense study for a short time, interest in it was renewed when fragmentary manuscripts of it were identified in Cave 4 (4Q266-73), 5 (5Q12), and 6 (6Q15). The Qumran copies demonstrate that the work, which had previously been known only from medieval manuscripts, was indeed ancient; the oldest of the cave 4 copies (4Q266) dates from about 75-50 B.C.

The Damascus Document has two principal parts: an exhortation, which covers much of columns 1-8 and 19-20; and a legal section, which includes columns 15-16 and 9-14 (the numbers are from the medieval copies). The fifth copy from Cave 4 shows that columns 15-16 belong between columns 8 and 9 in text A. The evidence from Qumran indicates that the version used there not only ordered the material somewhat differently but also had a longer text than the copies from the *geniza* (e.g., some material preceding col. 1). The laws in the Damascus Document cover, among other topics, the purity of priests and sacrifices, diseases, marriage, agriculture, tithes, relations with non-Jews, entry into the covenant community and the oaths involved, life within the community, sabbath, and communal organization.

In his exhortation the author calls on "all you who know righteousness" (1.1; p. 127), "all you who enter the Covenant" (2.2; p. 128), "my sons" (2.14; p. 128), and encourages them to follow the ways of God as members of the new covenant "in the land of Damascus" (6.19; p. 132). Scholars have disputed the meaning of "Damascus": is the Syrian city meant, or is the name symbolic for a place of exile, as some think it is in Amos 5:27? No one knows the answer, but the appearance of the name in the text (seven times) has so caught the attention of those who have studied it that it has received the name "the Damascus Document/Covenant." The addressees are encouraged not only to live according to the stipulations of the new covenant but also to avoid evils such as the three nets of Belial: fornication, riches, and profanation of the temple (4.14-18). The possibility exists, therefore, that the covenanters could fall away from their earlier resolve. Moreover, "None of those brought into the Covenant shall enter the Temple to light His altar in vain" (6.12; p. 132). This command may mean that the group did not participate in the cult of the temple in Jerusalem. They considered themselves a remnant, and it was for them that God had raised the Teacher of Righteousness to lead them in the proper way (1.10-11). Throughout his exhortation, the writer cites scriptural passages and interprets them for the reader.

The author also makes mention of "camps" (7.6), "the camp" (10.23), "the assembly of the towns of Israel" (12.19), and "the assembly of the camps" (12.23). Such references and the assumption in the text that the group(s) addressed are living among other people have led many scholars to conclude that the Damascus Document was not intended for the group living at Qumran but for others who adopted similar beliefs and practices and yet had not exiled themselves to the wilderness. Instead, they lived with one another in the towns and villages where they came into contact with Jews and non-Jews. Nevertheless, the presence of copies at Qumran suggests that these people too found it valuable, however they read it. A prominent leader mentioned frequently is the *guardian*, who, among other tasks, assesses the qualifications of those who desire to join and teaches the members about the works of God.

The legal sections, now known to be longer than in the medieval copies, deal with a variety of subjects, as indicated above. In many particulars they coincide with legal statements in other Qumran documents; at times they are at variance with them. One of the largest sections is devoted to laws about the sabbath.

b. The Rule of the Community

A copy of the Manual or Rule of the Community was one of the seven original scrolls, and it has served as the core text in the scholarly understanding of the Qumran group(s). Besides the nearly complete copy from Cave 1, there are ten fragmentary manuscripts from Cave 4 (4Q255-

64), one or possibly two from Cave 5 (5Q11, and perhaps 5Q13, unless it just quotes from 3.4-5), and one additional text that seems to combine aspects of the Rule and the Damascus Document (4Q265).

One may fairly call the Rule a constitution for the community. It begins with a statement about what the leader is supposed to teach those who seek admission to the fellowship.

> He shall admit into the Covenant of Grace all those who have freely devoted themselves to the observance of God's precepts, that they may be joined to the counsel of God and may live perfectly before Him in accordance with all that has been revealed concerning their appointed times, and that they may love all the sons of light, each according to his lot in God's design, and hate all the sons of darkness, each according to his guilt in God's vengeance. (1.7-10; pp. 98-99)

These opening words precede a description of the ceremony for entrance into the group(s) and for the annual renewal of the covenant. The sharp division of humanity into two camps — one of light and one of darkness — is elaborated at length in an oft-quoted section of the scroll (3.13–4.26). "From the God of Knowledge comes all that is and shall be. Before ever they existed He established their whole design, and when, as ordained for them, they come into being, it is in accord with His glorious design that they accomplish their task without change. The laws of all things are in His hand and He provides them with all their needs" (3.15-17; p. 101). The fifth, sixth, and seventh columns deal in large part with the life of the community. Included in them are regulations for the process of joining the fellowship and for meetings of the group(s) and also a list of penalties for violations. The Rule continues by speaking of the original members and dealing with the appropriate way of life in the present age. It concludes with a lengthy poem in praise of God. Like the Damascus Document, the Rule sets its legal material within or next to sections that take other literary forms.

The full manuscript from Cave 1 has two additional compositions on it. The Rule of the Congregation (1QSa) is a two-column text that provides regulations for the latter days and for the assembly and messianic banquets to be held then. The Rule of Blessings (1QSb) gives benedictions for the various leaders of the community. None of the other copies of the Rule of the Community includes either of these works, but Ste-

The beginning of 1QS Rule of the Community Scroll. This document contains the rules and regulations for a wilderness community. This scroll is important in the debate as to who actually lived at Qumran (John Trever) phen Pfann has identified 4Q249 a-i as copies of the Rule of the Congregation (they are written in a cryptic script).

c. The Temple Scroll

In some respects the publication of the Temple Scroll in 1977 by the Israeli scholar, soldier, and statesman Yigael Yadin (1917-1984) introduced a new phase of Qumran studies in which for the first time the centrality of law in the life and thought of the community was recognized. The best-preserved of the copies — 11QTª (11Q19) — seems to have had at least sixty-six columns (more than 8 meters) and is thus the longest of the Dead Sea Scrolls. 4Q524 and perhaps 11Q20 and 11Q21 are other copies of the Temple Scroll. 4Q524 dates from about 150-125 B.C.; the implication is that the Temple Scroll was written before the community

11Q19 Temple Scrollª, columns XLIII-XLIV
(Photograph by Bruce and Kenneth Zuckerman, West Semitic Research. Courtesy Shrine of the Book.)

moved to Qumran. Yadin had learned of the scroll's existence through correspondence with a Virginia clergyman. After the Six-Day War in 1967, Yadin obtained the scroll from the antiquities dealer Kando (who was mentioned in chap. 1). Although Kando was paid for it, he was given no choice about delivering it to Yadin.

One of the outstanding characteristics of the composition is that, when it quotes a biblical passage that presents God's words in the third person ("and God said"), it changes it to the first person ("and I said"). The author, then, could hardly make a more straightforward claim for the inspiration of his work: It is spoken by God himself to Moses, not by an angel of the presence as in Jubilees. The Temple Scroll's fragmentary beginning contains some words that recall the second covenant made on Mount Sinai (Exodus 34). It then moves into a long section regarding the temple (cols. 3-13) and the festivals and sacrifices observed there (13-29). The temple depicted matches none of Israel's historical sanctuaries. It was meant as a blueprint for a new temple to be built in the future when the right people were in control. The calendar that underlies the dated festivals is likely the 364-day solar arrangement familiar from Jubilees, 1 Enoch, and other Qumran texts. The next extended section (cols. 30-45) describes the large courts of the temple compound, and a shorter one (cols. 45-47) treats people and items that are to be excluded from the pure temple. The last columns offer a series of laws regarding a variety of subjects; they are generally drawn from the book of Deuteronomy. The Temple Scroll often groups in one passage laws on subjects that are scattered in the Pentateuch. The sections about the festivals and the groups of laws have been studied and compared with other bodies of Jewish law in order to situate the text within the history of Jewish legal reflection. The scroll clearly departs from what became the rabbinic system and shows interesting points of agreement with what is known about the stands of some other ancient Jewish groups such as the Essenes. And, not surprisingly, its legal material corresponds closely with legal texts from Qumran and with Jubilees.

d. Some of the Works of the Torah (4QMMT)

If the Temple Scroll inaugurated a new era in Qumran studies, the document called "Some of the Works of the Torah" (in Hebrew, *Miqṣat Ma'ase ha-Torah,* hence the abbreviation 4QMMT) or the "Halakhic Letter,"

4Q394 MMTª and 4Q395 MMTᵇ fragments from the "Some of the Works of the Torah" document. Controversy has surrounded this text because of sharp disagreement about access to it.

(Courtesy Israel Antiquities Authority)

available in six copies (4Q394-99), has brought legal concerns to the very heart of investigations into the nature and history of the Qumran community. More than any other, this text also stood for a time at the center of controversy because of sharp disagreements about access to it. The editors suggested that it is a letter from the Qumran group, perhaps written by the Teacher of Righteousness and his colleagues, to their opponents in Jerusalem, including the high priest (= the Wicked Priest). The purpose of the letter was to spell out the differences between the two parties and to summon the opponents to amendment of life. All this is done in a surprisingly friendly manner (e.g. "For [we have noticed] that prudence and knowledge of the law are with you" [C27-28; p. 228]). If the suggested scenario should prove correct, an important conclusion would emerge: the differences between the two parties were strictly legal ones, often matters that would seem excessively minor to many people today. 4QMMT begins with a detailed, year-long calendar; once again it is the 364-day solar calendar. In the sequel the writer presents twenty-two points of law on which the correspondents differ. These legal statements have also been compared with other legal texts. They too oppose rabbinic or Pharisaic views and coincide with Essene and, in some cases, Sadducean positions.

4. Writings for Worship

Various sorts of texts from the caves appear to have served the community and its individual members in their worship of God. Naturally, the scriptural books functioned in this way, particularly, one would think, the book of Psalms. Apart from the biblical books, however, many new works may be subsumed under various headings within the broader area of worship or liturgy.

a. The Cycle of Worship

The Bible prescribes that Israel observe the weekly sabbath as a day for rest. It was marked at the temple with a special sacrifice. But the Bible has no requirement that Israelites be present at the temple on that day. The biblical calendars (such as Leviticus 23) also mention Passover (it falls on month 1/day 14) and the three pilgrimage festivals: Unleavened Bread (1/15-21), Weeks (in the third month), and Tabernacles (or

Booths; 7/15-21). During the pilgrimage holidays, the Israelite males were to journey to the sanctuary, there to offer the firstfruits of the harvest for the appropriate season. The Bible also mentions the first of the seventh month as important and describes the Day of Atonement (7/10) and its rites as well as the festival of Purim (or Lots; 12/14 or 15). The Qumranites observed all these holidays except Purim, which is based on the book of Esther, the one biblical book of which no copy has been found in the caves. They also added several other festivals that they might have deduced from biblical givens: firstfruits festivals of wine and oil and a wood festival.

(1) Liturgical Texts

The first Psalms scroll from Cave 11 says that King David composed "52 songs for the Sabbath offerings" (27.7; p. 307). Thus, he wrote one for each sabbath in a solar year. Another document, which has been called "The Angelic Liturgy" or "Songs of the Sabbath Sacrifice" (4QShirShabb), presents thirteen such poems, enough to cover one-fourth of a year. This text exists in eight copies from Cave 4, one from Cave 11, and one from Masada. The sabbaths are dated in each case according to the 364-day calendar, which has been mentioned several times already. For instance, the first sabbath occurs on the fourth day of the first month. This date was selected because, according to Genesis 1, time began to be measured on the fourth day of the week when the sun was created; hence, the first sabbath would occur on 1/4. The Songs of the Sabbath Sacrifice vary between words of adoration for God, summonses to praise him, and descriptions of how the praising takes place. One of their striking features is the correspondence that they posit between the liturgy offered by angels in the heavenly sanctuary and that rendered by humans on earth. The document's picture of the celestial temple borrows from the language of Ezekiel 1, with its image of God enthroned on a chariot.

Among the Scrolls is a set of liturgical texts that include:

Daily Prayers (4Q503)
Festival Prayers (1Q34, 1Q34bis, 4Q505, 507-509)
Words of the Luminaries (4Q504, 506)
Blessings (4Q286-90)
Times for Praising God (4Q409)

Besides these texts that express the heartfelt piety of the community at special occasions are works that have been labeled Prayer Texts (e.g., 4Q291-93, 443), a communal confession (4Q393), Grace after Meals (4Q434a), and Purification Liturgies (4Q414, 512). The liturgical works draw upon scriptural models but also share much with Jewish liturgical texts known from later times. Although the community's festival calendar of 364 days in a year differed from that of many other Jews, they used similar language in their worship on the holidays.

(2) Calendrical Texts

A number of texts state or presuppose the 364-day calendar and align the biblical and extrabiblical festivals with it. That the calendar existed before the Qumran community was established follows from its presence in earlier works such as the Astronomical Book in 1 Enoch and the book of Jubilees. The book of Enoch does not connect the solar calendar with the religious festivals, but Jubilees does. This tendency is enhanced in a series of Qumran texts (4Q317-30 can all be characterized as calendrical in some sense) that not only date the festivals according to the 364-day solar calendar but also coordinate the calendar with the weekly rotation of priestly groups on duty in the temple. 1 Chr 24:7-19 lists twenty-four priestly groups or watches that rotated sanctuary duty so that all the priests could carry out their sacred duties without taking too much time each year from their daily occupations. In a normal year, the turn of a priestly watch would come up only twice, three times at most. The Qumran texts that scholars have labeled *mishmarot* (= watches) use the list in Chronicles and tie it in with the days in the week or dates in the year. At times the lists establish equivalences between three items: the day in a seven-day priestly watch, the date in a solar month, and the date in the corresponding lunar month. Some of the texts indicate that tables were worked out so that one could check which priestly watch would be on duty for any date in any year within a forty-nine-year cycle (a jubilee) or even within seven of these (343 years). In the tables one also learns which priestly shift would be serving during each of the festivals. The Temple Scroll (see above C.3.c) gives detailed prescriptions for the offerings to be made in the sanctuary on each of the festival days. It too dates these festivals according to the 364-day solar calendar.

b. Poetic Compositions

Several scrolls contain poems that resemble to some extent the kinds of compositions found in the book of Psalms.

(1) The Thanksgiving Hymns

One of the seven original scrolls was given the name *Hodayot* (or Thanksgiving Hymns), a noun which is related to the verb that regularly introduces the poems: *'odekah,* "I thank you [Lord]." The large copy from Cave 1 is joined by a second less well-preserved one from the same cave, six others from Cave 4 (4Q427-32; 4Q433 and 433a are called Hodayot-like Text A and B, and 4Q440 and 440a are Hodayot-like Text C and D). The implication is that it was an important work in the Qumran collection. The approximately thirty psalms contained in the text are individual, not communal, in character.

The poems in the text fall into at least two categories. In one group the "I" who is voicing his feelings and beliefs makes powerful claims for his person and divine mission. He also speaks emphatically about ferocious opposition to him and to his personal claims. For example, he complains:

> And they, teachers of lies and seers of falsehood,
>> have schemed against me a devilish scheme,
> to exchange the Law engraved on my heart by You
>> for the smooth things (which they speak) to Your people.
> And they withhold from the thirsty the drink of Knowledge,
>> and assuage their thirst with vinegar,
> that they may gaze on their straying,
>> on their folly concerning their feast-days,
>> on their fall into their snares.
>
> (1QH 12.9-12; p. 263)

The reference to God's "Law engraved" on the poet's heart, the fact that his opponents traffic in "smooth things," and association of their festivals with "folly" are interesting points for understanding the nature of the speaker, his group, and their opponents. Later, the poet sings of how God has hidden his law within him (13.11) and of how the men of the

86

covenant, those who follow God's ways, inquire of him and listen to him (12.23-24; see the paternal imagery in 15.20-22). Nevertheless, the mystery concealed in him led to problems even with his friends (13.22-25). From clues such as these some scholars have concluded, quite understandably, that the speaker is the Teacher of Righteousness himself, who recounts in autobiographical poetry the depths of his convictions and the burden of the struggles he endured because of his calling.

In a second set of poems in the Thanksgiving Hymns the speaker articulates experiences that may have been more characteristic of the regular members of the community. In them we read no extraordinary claims for the poet. Yet, in these, as in the first type, one often encounters a small series of basic themes: (1) God is the creator before whom humans, mere creatures of clay, are painfully lowly and inadequate; (2) the wicked attack the righteous, who suffer intensely, but God saves them from their troubles and judges the evil; (3) he gives wisdom to the righteous, that is, knowledge of himself and his will, and with them he enters into a covenant; (4) the righteous in turn sing his praises. Scriptural quotations and allusions dot the collection. In addition, the Thanksgiving Hymns express the notion that the psalmist is raised to an everlasting height where he enjoys communion with the angels (see, for example, 11.19-29; 14.13).

(2) Other Poems

Besides the copies of the Thanksgiving Hymns, the caves contained many other poetic compositions that praise and thank God. There are two copies of a work called "Psalms of Joshua" (4Q378-79), two manuscripts containing "apocryphal Psalms" (4Q380-81), two that are called "liturgical" works (4Q392-93), five manuscripts of poetic works that begin with the phrase "my soul, bless" (4Q434-38), and a number of other prayer and poetic texts (4Q439-56). Several similar kinds of compositions were found in Cave 11 (11Q11, 14-16). In at least some of the poetic works of Qumran we find, in comparison with biblical psalms, a greater emphasis on creation as a cause for praising God and a stronger tendency to speak of knowledge, wisdom, and teaching.

5. Eschatological Works

The category of Qumran texts that mention or have sections about the last days is very large. A number of works that were written before the community settled near the Dead Sea but became part of the Qumran library contain eschatological passages. This is true for sections of 1 Enoch, such as the Apocalypse of Weeks (in chaps. 93 and 91) or the Animal Apocalypse (chaps. 85–90), both of which culminate in predictions about the final judgment and the afterlife. Jubilees, too, contains passages about the future (see chap. 23), while Daniel is saturated with them. One could also include here the commentaries, which frequently relate scriptural verses to the final days, or the Rule of the Community (cols. 3-4), which speaks of the final divine victory over evil. The Rule of the Congregation (1QSa), sometimes called an appendix to the Rule of the Community, specifies that it is "the Rule for all the congregation of Israel in the last days" (1.1; p. 157). It concludes with an account of a meal at which a messiah and his priestly colleague are present. To these one could add the series of texts that mention a messiah or messiahs (I treat these texts in chap. 4). Even a thoroughly legal work like the Temple Scroll speaks once of the final temple that God himself will construct in the new creation (29.8-10). These are only examples. Yet, though much of what the residents of Qumran wrote and read was concerned with the latter days (in which they thought they were living), some documents focus on the end time more single-mindedly than others.

a. The War Rule

The most famous of the eschatological compositions is probably the War Scroll from Cave 1 (in Hebrew, war = *Milhamah,* hence the abbreviation 1QM) — another of the seven scrolls first taken from the cave in 1947. It is more damaged than some of the others, but parts of nineteen columns have been preserved. Cave 4 yielded fragments from six manuscripts (4Q491-96) whose precise relation to the Cave 1 copy may not all be the same. They are either copies of the War Rule, sources for it, or possibly from similar compositions. There are also some other related works, especially 4Q285 and 11Q14 — called the Book of War. Whatever the correct identification of 4Q491-96 may be, the text of the War Rule may have been edited and reedited as it continued to be copied. The first part of the War Rule summarizes the course of a forty-year war that will be fought between those whom it calls "the sons of light" and "the sons of darkness." The first column makes abundantly clear that the war is to be no ordinary one; rather, it is to be the final conflict.

> This shall be a time of salvation for the people of God, an age of dominion for all the members of His company, and of everlasting destruction for all the company of Belial. . . . The dominion of the Kittim shall come to an end and iniquity shall be vanquished, leaving no remnant; [for the sons] of darkness there shall be no escape. [The sons of righteous]ness shall shine over all the ends of the earth; they shall go on shining until all the seasons of darkness are consumed and, at the season appointed by God, His exalted greatness shall shine eternally to the peace, blessing, glory, joy, and long life of all the sons of light. (1QM 1.5-9; pp. 163-64)

Other passages term the war the "day of vengeance" (7.5; see 15.3) and "the battle of God" (9.5). Several lines also state that the sons of light, far from fighting alone, battle alongside their allies the angels. Unfortunately, the sons of darkness have their angelic companions as well, so that the conflict is a draw until the last battle (see cols. 12 and 17). The first column speaks of three "lots" during which the sons of light prevail against evil and three in which the sons of darkness gain the upper hand. This material apparently means that each side will be victorious in three engagements. After they have battled to a 3-3 tie, "with the seventh lot, the mighty hand of God shall bring down [the army of Belial, and all] the angels of his kingdom, and all the members [of his company in everlasting destruction]" (1QM 1.14-15; p. 164). Thus, the eschatological war will reflect the ongoing struggle between good and evil, light and darkness, throughout human history. Only God is able to tip the balance in favor of righteousness (compare Rule of the Community cols. 3-4).

Not all the clues about the chronological sequence and division of the fighting are clear, but the forty years seem to transpire in this way: (1) The forty years include five sabbatical years, and in them no warfare is permitted. (2) The remaining thirty-five years are divided into two periods: (a) a time during which all the army fights against the Kittim (here apparently the Seleucids) and Israel's neighbors (cols. 1, 15-19); this is the conflict in which the seven lots or battles occur, with God's intervention in the seventh proving utterly decisive; (b) a twenty-nine year-period for the war of the divisions when only a part of the army engages the various nations of the world in a series of battles (cols. 2-9). All of this could be predicted because God had long ago determined the time for annihilating evil.

The author devotes a considerable amount of space to describing the trumpets, banners, formations, and weapons used in the battles. He also deals at length with the physical and age requirements for the combatants and the roles carried out by leading priests (and Levites) in the rituals of the war. Another substantial portion of the text is dominated by poems and declarations of praise to God, who had assisted Israel in its historical battles. They laud him as the only source of victory, call on him to act now as he had in the past, and glorify him for effecting the great victory (cols. 10-14).

b. Texts about the New Jerusalem

Caves 1, 2, 4, 5, and 11 yielded seven copies of an Aramaic composition that describes the New Jerusalem of the future. The fragmentary remains leave many uncertainties of interpretation, but where the text can be followed it lays out a town plan that has some ancient parallels outside Israel and in the sketches of Ezekiel 40–48 and Revelation 21. We can infer that Jerusalem is the city under consideration only from the fact that the temple is mentioned (its gates are named after the twelve tribes). The text takes the form of a speech by a tour guide who shows the visionary the houses, streets, doors, towers, entrances, and staircases in the city. For each item that the guide shows he provides the measurements. The text is modeled on Ezekiel 40–48 to a considerable extent.

Additional texts that might be included here are discussed elsewhere, e.g., in dealing with the community's beliefs about the afterlife (3.A.2.a.2) and the messiahs (4.B.6).

6. Wisdom Texts

The Scrolls include several works that remind one of Proverbs, Job, Ecclesiastes, Sirach, and the Wisdom of Solomon. One should recall that much of the poetry or hymnic material from Qumran contains sapiential language (see above, C.4.b.2), but a number of texts are more properly classified as works of wisdom.

a. 4Q184 Wiles of the Wicked Woman

The text focuses on a lady who is a threat to seduce the righteous from the path they are to follow. She is pictured in terms reminiscent of Proverbs' strange woman or adulteress (see Proverbs 7) who allures the simple with the wiles of a prostitute.

b. 4Q185 Sapiential Work

The author encourages the readers to become wise and to remember the miracles that accompanied the exodus from Egypt. Like the ancient wisdom teachers, he refers to them as his sons. They are told to seek God's wisdom, from which all sorts of blessings flow:

> and He will put to death those who hate His Wisdom.
> Seek it and find it, grasp it and possess it!
> With it is length of days and fatness of bone,
>   the joy of the heart and . . .
> Happy is the man who works it.

(2.11-13; p. 398)

c. Instruction

A long wisdom text that has attracted much attention has been named Instruction. It has survived in very fragmentary form in seven (1Q26; 4Q415-18, 418a, 423) and perhaps eight (4Q418c) copies. In it a sage, in traditional fashion, offers guidance to a younger person who is called an "understanding one." He instructs him in subjects that are familiar from the wisdom tradition — finances, family relations, dealings with the poor, and more — but the advice is framed in a way that differs from older works such as Proverbs. The sage appeals to revelation as the basis for his instruction, and the instruction also has to do with eschatology. A key concept mentioned fairly frequently is "the approaching mystery" or "the mystery that is to be."

> Look at the approaching mystery
> and grasp the sources (or: begetters) of salvation,

and know who is to inherit glory or injustice.

(4Q417 1 i; p. 403)

"The approaching mystery" is what God reveals to those who are open to it, and it seems to involve a proper understanding of the workings of creation and the course of history, including what is to come.

7. THE COPPER SCROLL (3Q15)

In Cave 3 two sections of one text impressed on copper were found (3Q15). It is the only work from the Qumran caves on a material other than parchment or papyrus. When found, the copper had been so thoroughly oxidized that it could not be unrolled. Some four years after it was removed from the cave, an expert at Manchester College in England — Professor H. Wright Baker — separated it into strips with vertical cuts. In 1962 J. T. Milik published the twelve columns of text in the third volume (Les 'petites grottes' de Qumrân) of the official series, Discoveries in the Judaean Desert. Already in 1960, however, John Allegro had edited and translated the text in his Treasure of the Copper Scroll.

This scroll has proved a conundrum in Qumran studies because no one really knows what it is or, rather, what the author meant to convey. Some consider it extemely important for understanding the nature of the manuscript collection found at Qumran, while others are inclined to dismiss it as fanciful, the product of an overheated imagination starved for treasure. Milik dated it to about A.D. 100 (Cross dated the script to A.D. 25-75), well after the Qumran settlement was destroyed. If he is right, it would not have come from that community; someone else would have put it in the third cave at a later time.

The contents are tedious and matter-of-fact. The scroll names sixty (?) places in the land where treasures were supposed to be hidden. The treasures consist of metal (gold and silver) and other valuables, including writings that are said to be hidden near these items. Though hard to calculate in terms of their value, the amounts are staggering — tons of precious metals, for example. One thesis often defended by those who take the text literally is that it enumerates the hiding places where the temple treasures were stashed to keep them from the Romans at the time of the First Jewish Revolt (there are temple-related items in some of the hiding places), or where Bar Koseba and his supporters placed their wealth dur-

John Marco Allegro examining the unopened rolls of the Copper Scroll
(Estate of John Allegro)

ing the Second Revolt. Milik's dating would preclude the latter suggestion. It is likely that, if a writer took the trouble to have his many words stamped into copper, he intended for it to be a lasting record.

Needless to say, attempts have been made to find some of the valuables named in the scroll. For example, in 1962 Allegro led an expedition that excavated some places the scroll seems to mention. As one might expect, the treasure hunters were disappointed. If such caches ever did exist, they were emptied in the past. It is fair to say that uncertainty remains the dominant note in the study of the Copper Scroll, which has been elaborately treated, cleaned, analyzed, copied, and photographed by Electricite de France and is now housed in Amman, Jordan.

8. Documentary Texts

The lists of fragmentary works found at Qumran include a number of items that relate to business dealings. In Cave 4 were found letters (4Q342-43), an acknowledgment of debt (344), documents concerned with the sale of land (345-48, 359), and several accounts (350-58). Perhaps there are more among the still-unidentified pieces. As mentioned below (chap. 3 C.2), these sorts of documents, though they do not provide very interesting reading, have their own significance for determining the type of group(s) that might have been associated with the Scrolls. There has been debate about whether some of these actually came from Qumran Cave 4 (examples are 4Q347, 359), but there is no decisive evidence against their presence in that cave.

The Qumran caves have yielded more fragmentary works, but enough have been noted to give a good impression of what was found in them. The texts surveyed in the major categories above represent the vast majority of the total of over nine hundred Qumran manuscripts. Many of the remaining ones are simply too small or too damaged to identify or do not add much to the information supplied here. Chapter 3 deals with the question of who wrote all these scrolls.

BIBLIOGRAPHICAL NOTES

The complete list of Qumran manuscripts is: E. Tov in Consultation with S. J. Pfann, "List of the Texts from the Judaean Desert," in *The Texts from the Judaean Desert: Indices and An Introduction to the* Discoveries in the Judaean Desert *Series* (ed. E. Tov; DJD 39; Oxford: Clarendon Press, 2002) 27-89.

A rich source of information regarding the texts surveyed in this chapter is: *Encyclopedia of the Dead Sea Scrolls* (ed. Lawrence H. Schiffman and James C. VanderKam; New York: Oxford University Press, 2000).

For the Pseudepigrapha see *The Old Testament Pseudepigrapha* (ed. James H. Charlesworth; 2 vols.; Garden City, N.Y.: Doubleday, 1983-85).

The references to the positions that J. T. Milik has taken on the book of Enoch are found in his *Books of Enoch: Aramaic Fragments of Qumrân Cave 4* (Oxford: Clarendon Press, 1976).

For the War Rule, see Yigael Yadin, *The Scroll of the War of the Sons of Light Against the Sons of Darkness* (Oxford: Oxford University Press, 1962).

For much more on the wisdom texts within the Jewish sapiential tradition, see John J. Collins, *Jewish Wisdom in the Hellenistic Age* (The Old Testament Library; Louisville: Westminster John Knox, 1997).

For an engaging account of the Copper Scroll and study of it, see

Hershel Shanks, *The Copper Scroll and the Search for the Temple Treasure* (Washington, DC: Biblical Archaeology Society, 2007).

There are now several series that offer studies of individual texts or kinds of texts:

One is the Companion to the Qumran Scrolls (Sheffield: Sheffield Academic Press, now by London: T&T Clark; the later volumes are also part of the series Library of Second Temple Studies).

1. Charlotte Hempel, *The Damascus Texts* (2000)
2. Sidnie White Crawford, *The Temple Scroll and Related Texts* (2000)
3. Timothy H. Lim, *Pesharim* (2002)
4. Jonathan G. Campbell, *The Exegetical Texts* (2004)
5. Jean Duhaime, *The War Texts: 1 QM and Related Manuscripts* (2004)
6. Hannah Harrington, *The Purity Texts* (2004)
7. Philip Alexander, *The Mystical Texts: Songs of the Sabbath Sacrifice and Related Manuscripts* (2006)
8. Daniel K. Falk, *The Parabiblical Texts: Strategies for Extending the Scriptures in the Dead Sea Scrolls* (2007)
9. Sariana Metso, *The Serekh Texts* (2007)

Another series is the Eerdmans Commentaries on the Dead Sea Scrolls (16 volumes are planned).

1. James R. Davila, *Liturgical Works* (2000)

Yet another series is The Literature of the Dead Sea Scrolls (London/New York: Routledge).

1. Daniel J. Harrington, *Wisdom Texts from Qumran* (1996)
2. John J. Collins, *Apocalypticism in the Dead Sea Scrolls* (1997)
3. James C. VanderKam, *Calendars in the Dead Sea Scrolls: Measuring Time* (1998)

CHAPTER 3

The Identification of the Qumran Group

W ho wrote the scrolls found in the eleven caves at Qumran? The issue has been discussed at great length from the earliest days of
scholarship on the Scrolls and has remained a matter of debate.

A. THE CASE FOR THE ESSENE HYPOTHESIS

Eleazar Sukenik, who purchased three scrolls from a Bethlehem antiquities dealer in November and December 1947, was the first scholar to pro-
pose that the scrolls might have a connection with the Essenes (see
chap. 1). The Essenes were one of the three ancient Jewish groups or
"philosophies" named and described by the historian Josephus; the other
two (or three if we include the Zealots) were the more famous Pharisees
and Sadducees, who also figure prominently in the New Testament Gospels and Acts. Josephus first mentions these three groups as he describes
the reign of Jonathan (152-142 B.C.); they remained active until the destruction of Jerusalem in A.D. 70.

1. THE EVIDENCE FROM PLINY THE ELDER

Sukenik suspected a connection between Qumran and the Essenes when
he read the Rule of the Community, which defined the way of life for a
wilderness sect. He wrote already in 1948 that he thought of the Essenes
because he knew that ancient sources placed a band of Essenes on the

west side of the Dead Sea near En-gedi. Although he did not name it spe-cifically, he was undoubtedly referring particularly to a passage in the work *Natural History* issued by the Roman geographer Pliny the Elder (A.D. 23-79) in approximately A.D. 77. In this book Pliny compiled a de-tailed account of places and items of interest throughout the Roman world and beyond (from Spain to India). When his survey reached the Syro-Palestinian area, he naturally included some words about the Dead Sea, the lowest point on the surface of the earth. In the course of describ-ing the area he wrote:

> On the west side of the Dead Sea, but out of range of the noxious exhalations of the coast, is the solitary tribe of the Essenes [*Esseni*], which is remarkable beyond all the other tribes in the whole world, as it has no women and has renounced all sexual de-sire, has no money, and has only palm-trees for company. Day by day the throng of refugees is recruited to an equal number by nu-merous accessions of persons tired of life and driven thither by the waves of fortune to adopt their manners. Thus through thou-sands of ages (incredible to relate) a race in which no one is born lives on for ever; so prolific for their advantage is other men's wea-riness of life!
>
> Lying below the Essenes [literally: these] was formerly the town of Engedi, second only to Jerusalem in the fertility of its land and in its groves of palm-trees, but now like Jerusalem a heap of ashes. (5.73)

Pliny locates the tribe *(gens)* of the Essenes on the west side of the Dead Sea, between its northern end and En-gedi, which he seems to place to the south of ("lying below") their residence. Scholars have often pointed out that the area Pliny describes has no archeological evidence of any communal center other than the one at Qumran. Some have argued that Pliny's words "lying below" imply that the Essene settlement should be sought on the hills above En-gedi, but his words appear to mean "to the south of." Furthermore, the hills above En-gedi have no traces of com-munal occupation.

Sukenik indirectly drew Pliny's account into the debate about the Scrolls, and to this day it remains one of the two pillars on which the widely accepted theory of Essene ownership of the Scrolls is based. One has in the writings of Pliny the witness of a non-Jewish author who had, as far as one can tell, no reason to invent his story. According to him, Essenes were living on the west side of the Dead Sea in an area that seems to be right around Qumran where the scrolls were found.

The argument from Pliny's seemingly clear testimony has not, however, gone unchallenged. Obviously, he makes some mistakes in the paragraphs quoted, or perhaps the mistakes have entered the manuscripts of his book through copyists' errors. For example, the text says that En-gedi was second only to Jerusalem in fertility and palm trees, but it seems quite unlikely that En-gedi would be compared with Jerusalem. The text should probably read "Jericho" at this point, unless the writer had not actually visited these places and thus was confused about them.

But a larger problem concerns the date at which Pliny wrote. As noted above, he finished his work *Natural History* in the year 77 or near to it. One can infer this date from the fact that he knows about events such as the destruction of Jerusalem in 70 (mentioned in the second paragraph quoted above) and perhaps even the capture of Masada (A.D. 73) and because he dedicated the book to Titus before Titus became emperor in 79 (Pliny himself died in 79, when his curiosity drew him too close to the erupting Mount Vesuvius). If Roland de Vaux's theory that the Qumran settlement was destroyed in A.D. 68 is correct, then Pliny published his *Natural History* about nine years after the Romans had ended the sect's history at Qumran. That in itself would be no problem, but, as various people have commented, Pliny describes the Essene settlement in the present tense: "the throng of refugees *is recruited* . . . a race in which no one is born *lives* on for ever; so prolific for their advantage *is* other men's weariness of life" (other present-tense verbs in the translation are not expressed but are implied by the syntax). The text states, then — so the argument goes — that at the time when Pliny wrote, the Essenes were living on the west side of the Dead Sea — that is, in approximately A.D. 77. From this evidence it would follow that either Pliny's Essenes were not at Qumran, the structures of which no longer existed; or, if they were, the community was not destroyed by the Romans in A.D. 68 or 70, as the standard theory holds.

An objection of this kind is hardly a convincing counterargument to the claim that Pliny described Essenes who lived around Qumran. Clearly, it does not follow that if Pliny wrote about something in the present tense it had to be existing at the very time he published his book. We have no way of ascertaining whether Pliny would have known, when he recorded his notes for publication, about the destruction of the

Qumran settlement, if that is what he was describing. Qumran was an out-of-the-way place, not even remotely as famous as Jerusalem or Masada. Thus, Pliny's writing about Essenes on the west side of the Dead Sea in the present tense may say nothing about whether the Essene community of which he writes was in existence when his book appeared. It says something about the circumstances when he visited the area (if he had) and compiled his notes, not necessarily about its condition when he issued the *Natural History.* It may be, too, that in this case he simply followed his normal pattern of describing people, places, and things in the present tense.

A more telling response to the counterargument has to do with the way in which Pliny compiled his *Natural History.* He was an avid reader who drew heavily on other sources for the information that he chose to record. He himself acknowledges that he did so and names some one hundred sources from which he derived the data compiled in the book. For book 5, in which the Essene paragraph appears, he admits to employing fifty-nine sources. The *Natural History* apparently contains far more information drawn from sources than original words from Pliny himself. His source-oriented procedure entails the likelihood that Pliny cited from another writer in his section on the Essenes. If this is true, then the date at which the book appeared would have no relevance for determining whether he could have been describing the Qumran group. If he quoted from an older source, the author of that source could have been the one who used the present tense in speaking of the Essenes and actually observed the Qumran group. Furthermore, if the mistake about Jerusalem and En-gedi belongs in the text, one could infer that Pliny himself may not have visited the area because he would have known better if he had. That mistake does not, however, occur in the paragraph on the Essenes, about whom Pliny seems quite well informed — presumably from a source. It is highly likely, therefore, that the *Natural History* speaks about the residents of Qumran.

Only one other ancient text places Essenes on the shores of the Dead Sea. Dio Chrysostom (about A.D. 40 to at least 112) is said to have written about them, although the report does not survive in any of his works. But in a biography of Dio, Synesius of Cyrene (about A.D. 400) writes: "Also somewhere he praises the Essenes, who form an entire and prosperous city near the Dead Sea, in the centre of Palestine, not far from Sodom." Since the words attributed to Dio differ significantly from those of Pliny, they were probably not taken from Pliny's *Natural History* but constitute an independent verification that Essenes lived close to the Dead Sea.

Pliny, then, says the following about the Essene population of Qumran: (1) they are located some distance from the smelly seashore (and perhaps isolated); (2) they are without women; (3) they have renounced all sexual desire; (4) they have no money; (5) they have only palm trees for company (that is, they are isolated); (6) refugees from life's trials join them daily; (7) in this way, though no children are born (see no. 2), the group continues forever. To this list Dio Chrysostom adds that theirs was a prosperous city.

If one could show that the Qumran texts also favor identifying their authors/copyists with the Essenes, then one would have two very different kinds of evidence on which to establish the case for the Essene hypothesis.

2. THE CONTENTS OF THE QUMRAN TEXTS AND ESSENE BELIEFS AND PRACTICES

The second principal argument for identifying the inhabitants of Qumran as Essenes is that the beliefs and practices of the Essenes, as reported in ancient sources (Josephus, Pliny, Philo, and others), agree remarkably well with the beliefs and practices presented and reflected in the Dead Sea Scrolls. What the texts originating in the community say coincides far more closely with Essene thought and action than with what the sources say about the Pharisaic and Sadducean views or those of any others. The most important text for this argument has been the Rule of the Community — the large Cave 1 copy of which was one of the first scrolls to be made available and also one of the best preserved. It describes, among other topics, the initiation processes and ceremonies for new members, some fundamental beliefs of the group, and the rules by which it governed its daily life and communal gatherings. Since it functions as a kind of constitution for the community, one can understand that it would be the primary source for identifying the members of the group. The next paragraphs compare the ancient accounts of the Essenes with several aspects of Qumran theology and practice.

a. Theology

Josephus and other ancient writers, whatever their sources of information may have been, noted Essene beliefs on several topics, many of which occur in the Scrolls. A few of them are listed here to illustrate the nature of the evidence.

(1) Determinism

One point on which the descriptions of the Essenes and the contents of the Rule of the Community and other Qumran texts show striking harmony is the doctrine of fate or predeterminism. According to Josephus the three Jewish parties held differing opinions on the matter. He has been accused of distorting their views to make them more comprehensible to his non-Jewish audience, but, however that may be, he describes their theologies in this way:

> As for the Pharisees, they say that certain events are the work of Fate, but not all; as to other events, it depends upon ourselves whether they shall take place or not. The sect of the Essenes, however, declares that Fate is mistress of all things, and that nothing befalls men unless it be in accordance with her decree. But the Sadducees do away with Fate, holding that there is no such thing and that human actions are not achieved in accordance with her decree, but that all things lie within our own power, so that we ourselves are responsible for our well-being, while we suffer misfortune through our own thoughtlessness. (*Antiquities* 13.171-73)

The third and fourth columns of the Cave 1 copy of the Rule of the Community articulate a thoroughly predestinarian theology of world history and human endeavor — one that immediately reminds the reader of Josephus's words. The lines are not in some Cave 4 copies of the text, but their presence in 1QS demonstrates the existence of such a view at an early time in the group's history.

> From the God of Knowledge comes all that is and shall be. Before ever they existed He established their whole design, and when, as ordained for them, they come into being, it is in accord with His

glorious design that they accomplish their task without change. (3.15-16; p. 101)

A few lines later the writer adds:

> The Angel of Darkness leads all the children of righteousness astray, and until his end, all their sin, iniquities, wickedness, and all their unlawful deeds are caused by his dominion in accordance with the mysteries of God. (3.21-23; p. 101)

Such sentiments put the Qumran group in direct contradiction with the Sadducean position, as described by Josephus, somewhat nearer though clearly distant from the Pharisaic theory, and in full agreement with that of the Essenes. Thus, the doctrine of determinism separates the people behind the Rule from all known Jewish parties except the Essenes.

The doctrine of fate or predestination is not confined to the Rule of the Community. If it were, one could argue that an Essene author may indeed have written the Rule but not the other Qumran texts. Other well-preserved texts express the same belief, as do a number of more fragmentary texts. The former category includes the Hymn (Thanksgiving) Scroll and the War Rule. Especially the ninth column of the large Cave 1 Hymn Scroll is replete with predestinarian sentiments.

> By Your wisdom [all things exist from] eternity,
>   and before creating them You knew their works for ever
>   and ever.
> [Nothing] is done [without You]
>   and nothing is known unless You desire it.
>
> (9.7-8; p. 253)

In the same column are these lines:

> You have allotted it to all their [humanity's] seed
>   for eternal generations and everlasting years. . . .
> In the wisdom of Your knowledge
>   You established their destiny before ever they were.
> All things [exist] according to [Your will]
>   and without You nothing is done.
>
> (9.18-20; p. 254)

Moreover, the whole scenario in the War Rule presupposes a doctrine of predestination: God had long ago arranged how history would transpire. The final war will simply follow his eternal blueprint because he is in full control. To these witnesses we may add the Damascus Document, which says of those who stray:

> They shall have no remnant or survivor. For from the beginning God chose them not; He knew their deeds before ever they were created and He hated their generations, and He hid His face from the Land until they were consumed. For He knew the years of their coming and the length and exact duration of their times for all ages to come and throughout eternity. He knew the happenings of their times throughout all the everlasting years. (2.6-10; p. 128)

Nor are such references confined to the texts from Cave 1. Copies of the Rule of the Community, the Thanksgiving Hymns, the War Rule, and the Damascus Document have been found in Cave 4. Copies of the Rule and the Damascus Document were also uncovered in Cave 5 and of the Damascus Document in Cave 6. Other works evidence similar thinking. One example is the Ages of the Creation (4Q180), in which two passages use almost the same words as in some of the statements quoted above: "Interpretation concerning the ages made by God, all the ages for the accomplishment [of all the events, past] and future. Before ever He created them. He determined the works of . . ." (1.1-2; p. 520; see also 2-4 ii 10). The theory behind the interpretation in the commentaries at Qumran depends on the same kind of thinking: the secrets of the last days are encoded in the scriptural prophecies by the God who not only knows the future but makes it happen as he designed it from the beginning. A number of texts from the caves mention the heavenly tablets on which all of history is written beforehand. This notion, too, is an expression of a deterministic theology.

The passages cited or mentioned above do not exhaust the evidence for a deterministic theology at Qumran. They do, however, show that this manner of thinking is present in various works represented in different caves. It is not confined to a single text or one place.

(2) The Afterlife

A second theological tenet on which one may favorably compare the Scrolls and ancient descriptions of the Essenes concerns the afterlife. What happens to a person when the earthly life ends? The Old Testament (Hebrew Bible) says little about the question. Only toward the end of the Old Testament period do a few references to resurrection of individuals occur (see Dan 12:2 for an example). This was another point on which, Josephus says, the three Jewish parties differed. The Pharisees believed that the dead would be raised, while the Sadducees denied any such miracle would occur. As for the Essenes:

> It is a fixed belief of theirs that the body is corruptible and its constituent matter impermanent, but that the soul is immortal and imperishable. Emanating from the finest ether, these souls become entangled, as it were, in the prison-house of the body to which they are dragged down by a sort of natural spell; but once they are released from the bonds of the flesh, then, as though liberated from a long servitude, they rejoice and are borne aloft. Sharing the belief of the sons of Greece, they maintain that for virtuous souls there is reserved an abode beyond the ocean. (*Jewish War* 2.154-55)

This description has peculiar features, not least of which is that the Essenes, who otherwise are pictured as opposed to pagan teachings, are compared with the Greeks and even resemble later body-condemning groups like the Gnostics. Furthermore, Josephus elsewhere attributes the same belief to the Pharisees, who, according to other texts, believed there would be a resurrection of the dead (see *Antiquities* 18.14; *Jewish War* 2.163).

The ancient sources for Essene theology happen to oppose one another on the matter of the postmortem fate of the body. Although Josephus claims that the Essenes embraced the immortality of the soul and dissolution of the body, Hippolytus of Rome (about 170-236) characterizes their eschatological notions differently. A presbyter and perhaps bishop in the Roman church, Hippolytus wrote *Refutation of All Heresies*, in which he pictures the Essenes much as Josephus does except for the Essene belief regarding the destiny of the body: "The doctrine of the resurrection has also derived support among them, for they acknowledge both that the flesh will rise again, and that it will be immortal, in the same manner as the soul is already imperishable" (9.27). No obvious mechanical or scribal explanation accounts for the disagreement between Josephus and Hippolytus, both of whom may have drawn from a common source of information. Who is more accurate?

It is understandable that Essene eschatological beliefs might not be crystal clear to external observers because some expressions in their writings could be taken in various ways. One passage that may be adduced in connection with Josephus's report comes from 1QH^a (the large Hymn Scroll):

> I thank You, O Lord,
>> for You have redeemed my soul from the Pit,
> and from the hell of Abaddon
>> You have raised me up to everlasting height.
> I walk on limitless level ground,
> and I know there is hope for him
>> whom You have shaped from dust
>> for the everlasting Council.
> You have cleansed a perverse spirit of great sin
>> that it may stand with the Host of the Holy Ones,
> and that it may enter into community
>> with the congregation of the Sons of Heaven.
> You have allotted to man an everlasting destiny
>> amidst the spirits of knowledge,
> that he may praise Your name in a common rejoicing
>> and recount Your marvels before all Your works.
>
> (1QH^a 11.19-23; p. 261)

The association with heavenly beings that is expressed here could be understood as reflecting the life of the soul with the angels after the body has died. It seems more likely, however, that the poet is talking about the present experience of the members of his group.

Jubilees, a document well represented at Qumran, speaks in a way that could also be confusing:

> Then the Lord will heal his servants. They will rise and see great peace. He will expel their enemies. The righteous will see (this), offer praise, and be very happy forever and ever. They will see all

their punishments and curses on their enemies. Their bones will rest in the earth and their spirits will be very happy. They will know that the Lord is the one who executes judgment but shows kindness to hundreds and thousands and to all who love him. (23:30-31)

The author mentions the rising of God's servants but also that their bones rest in the earth while their spirits are happy.

A belief about resurrection is attested in texts found in the caves. 4Q521 (Messianic Apocalypse), mentions a messiah and later deals with what the Lord will do. It is not possible to determine with certitude who is acting in the pertinent line — the messiah or God — but the context favors the latter: "For He will heal the wounded, and revive the dead and bring good news to the poor" (2.12; p. 392). The phrase "revive the dead" need not be taken in the sense of resurrection but it is probably meant that way in the context. 4Q385 2.2-9, based on Ezekiel's vision in the valley of dry bones (Ezekiel 37), speaks of bones and joints reviving when the heavenly spirit blows on them (paralleled by 4Q386 1 i 1-10; 4Q388 7.3-7). On the basis of these texts, then, it is likely that Hippolytus was correct about this article of Essene theology and that Josephus expresses an interpretation of their belief which is a misleading but understandable inference from some expressions in the texts as related in his sources. It is also possible that even Josephus's language does not deny to the Essenes a belief in physical resurrection. Some experts have argued that 4Q521 and 4Q385, 386, and 388 are not sectarian and therefore should not be seen as expressions of the sectarians' views. There is no decisive evidence against their being sectarian; moreover, their presence in the Qumran caves suggests their teachings were acceptable to the group.

b. Practice

Beyond the series of theological beliefs common to Josephus's Essenes and the authors of the Qumran texts is another set of agreements that focuses on conduct. Several kinds of behavior that for Josephus characterize the Essenes are also mandated in the Scrolls.

(1) Nonuse of Oil

Josephus draws attention to the Essenes' avoidance of the sorts of oil that people applied to their bodies: "Oil they consider defiling, and anyone who accidentally comes in contact with it scours his person; for they make a point of keeping a dry skin and of always being dressed in white" (*Jewish War* 2.123). The historian observes the trait but does not explain satisfactorily why the Essenes refused to apply oil to their skin.

The Qumran texts are more helpful. They indicate that the Qumranites believed liquids were ready transmitters of ritual impurity from one item to another. In Some of the Works of the Torah (4QMMT) we learn that they believed a liquid stream carried ritual defilement from one container to another. Hence, by wearing oil on the skin, one increased the danger of defilement from unclean objects and persons. To avoid contamination, then, they refrained from covering their skin with oil. The Damascus Document seems to deal with this issue: "(As for) all wood, stones, and dust which are defiled by human impurity, with stains of oil on them, the one who touches them will be impure according to their impurity" (Damascus Document 12.15-17 [my translation]). The point seems to be that oil itself is not impure; it simply conducts impurity easily and hence should not be used.

(2) Property

A second point on which the Scrolls and the ancient descriptions of the Essenes coincide has to do with the property of individual Essenes. Pliny mentions that the Essene group on the west side of the Dead Sea "has no money." Like the Jewish philosopher Philo (ca. 25/20 B.C.–A.D. 50; see *Every Good Man Is Free* 76-79, 84-87; *Hypothetica* 4-13), Josephus talks admiringly about the Essenes' common ownership of property:

> Riches they despise, and their community of goods is truly admirable; you will not find one among them distinguished by greater opulence than another. They have a law that new members on admission to the sect shall confiscate their property to the order, with the result that you will nowhere see either abject poverty or inordinate wealth; the individual's possessions join the common stock and all, like brothers, enjoy a single patrimony. (*Jewish War* 2.122)

On this topic the Rule of the Community specifies for the novice:

> Then when he has completed one year within the Community, the Congregation shall deliberate his case with regard to his understanding and observance of the Law. And if it be his destiny, according to the judgement of the Priests and the multitude of the men of their Covenant, to enter the company of the Community, his property and earnings shall be handed over to the Bursar of the Congregation who shall register it to his account and shall not spend it for the Congregation. . . . But when the second year has passed, he shall be examined, and if it be his destiny, according to the judgement of the Congregation, to enter the Community, then he shall be inscribed among his brethren in the order of his rank for the Law, and for justice, and for the pure Meal; his property shall be merged and he shall offer his counsel and judgement to the Community. (6.18-23; pp. 106-7)

Deliberate lying with regard to property was punished by a year's exclusion from the "pure Meal" and by a one-fourth reduction in rations (6.24-25). One should note that neither Josephus nor any other writer says the Essenes were poor. Rather, they shared their goods for the benefit of the community instead of amassing private property. The Rule of the Community mentions the same principle several other times (1.11-12; 5.2).

Alongside such statements, however, the Rule has some indications that the individuals whose conduct it legislates did in fact have some private property: "But if he has failed to care for the property of the Community, thereby causing its loss, he shall restore it in full. And if he is unable to restore it, he shall do penance for sixty days" (7.6-8; p. 107). The possibility of reimbursing lost communal property suggests that the member had some private means on which to call in order to repay the debt. Perhaps the same follows from 7.24-25; p. 108: "Moreover, if any member of the Community has shared with him [[an expelled member]] his food or property which . . . of the Congregation, his sentence shall be the same; he shall be ex[pelled]." It may be that when a new member contributed his property to the common purse, he retained some control over its use, although the first concern was to meet the needs of the community and its members.

This ambiguity in the Rule is not inconsistent with Josephus's testi-

mony about the Essene community of goods. Josephus also writes about
the Essenes:

> In all other matters they do nothing without orders from their su-
> periors; two things only are left to individual discretion, the ren-
> dering of assistance and compassion. Members may of their own
> motion help the deserving, when in need, and supply food to the
> destitute; but presents to relatives are prohibited, without leave
> from the managers. (*Jewish War* 2.134)

Their ability to give alms implies that they had the means to do so.

The point becomes more explicit in the Damascus Document. This
document envisages a community different from the fellowship as it is
reflected in the Rule of the Community. In the Damascus Document the
members belong to "camps" and are apparently located in various towns
in Israel. It has laws about lost or stolen property:

> When anything is lost, and it is not known who has stolen it from
> the property of the camp in which it was stolen, its owner shall
> pronounce a curse, and any man who, on hearing (it), knows but
> does not tell, shall himself be guilty.
>
> When anything is returned which is without an owner, who-
> ever returns it shall confess to the Priest, and apart from the ram
> of the sin-offering, it shall be his. (9.10-14; p. 138)

A few columns later, the text adds:

> No member of the Covenant of God shall give or receive anything
> from the sons of Dawn [or: of the Pit] except for payment.
>
> No man shall form any association for buying and selling
> without informing the Guardian of the camp.... (13.14-16; p. 142)

The principle is then explained:

> *This is the Rule for the Congregation by which it shall provide for all*
> *its needs*
> They shall place the earnings of at least two days out of every
> month into the hands of the Guardian and the Judges, and from it
> they shall give to the fatherless, and from it they shall succour the

poor and the needy, the aged sick and the man who is stricken
with disease, the captive taken by a foreign people, the virgin with
no near kin, and the ma[id for] whom no man cares. . . . (14.12-16;
p. 143)

Consequently, the sources do indicate an unusual sharing of goods but
not a total abolition of private property or ownership.

(3) The Pure Meal

Josephus saw fit to record the way in which the Essenes ate their communal meals. They would work until the fifth hour of the day (about 11
a.m.),

> when they again assemble in one place and, after girding their
> loins with linen clothes, bathe their bodies in cold water. After this
> purification, they assemble in a private apartment which none of
> the uninitiated is permitted to enter; pure now themselves, they
> repair to the refectory, as to some sacred shrine. When they have
> taken their seats in silence, the baker serves out the loaves to them
> in order, and the cook sets before each one plate with a single
> course. Before meat the priest says a grace, and none may partake
> until after the prayer. When breakfast is ended, he pronounces a
> further grace; thus at the beginning and at the close they do hom-
> age to God as the bountiful giver of life. (*Jewish War* 2.129-31)

Josephus knows more about the Essene meals than the Scrolls divulge.
Yet, on a number of particulars the two agree in a way that is not true for
what is reported about any other group. Scholars often compare
Josephus's reference to pre-meal bathing with the evidence, both written
and archeological, for bathing at Qumran. One sentence in the Rule of
the Community connects bathing and the pure meal of the group. When
describing the wicked, it declares, among other criticisms: "They shall
not enter the water to partake of the pure Meal of the men of holiness,
for they shall not be cleansed unless they turn from their wickedness; for
all who transgress His word are unclean" (5.13-14; p. 104). The Rule also
emphasizes repeatedly the varied ranks that the different members of the
group had achieved; status had important consequences in group activi-

ties, as Josephus notes. The sixth column of the Cave 1 copy of the Rule has several points of instruction about conduct of the communal meal. "They shall eat in common" (6.2; p. 105; this line comes immediately after "the man of lesser rank shall obey the greater in matters of work and money").

> Wherever there are ten men of the Council of the Community there shall not lack a Priest among them. And they shall all sit before him according to their rank and shall be asked their counsel in all things in that order. And when the table has been prepared for eating, and the new wine for drinking, the Priest shall be the first to stretch out his hand to bless the firstfruits of the bread and new wine. (6.3-6; p. 105; I have omitted parts of the section where the scribe has accidentally repeated them)

Josephus's comment that only members partake of the meal is verified by the procedure for admission to the group as described in the same column of the Rule. The candidate is not allowed to touch the food at the meal until he has completed a full trial year and has passed an examination. Only after another year is he permitted to have the wine as well (6.13-23). One of the punishments listed for several offenses in the Rule is exclusion from the meal for a stipulated time. The Rule of the Congregation (1QSa) also depicts a meal, one that characterizes the last days. At that meal, too, the author stresses, all must sit in their appropriate rank, and the priest blesses the bread and wine before anyone eats (1QSa 2.11-22).

(4) Bodily Functions

The parallels extend from such lofty principles as a community of goods to the exceedingly mundane such as toilet habits. Josephus relates that the Essenes

> are stricter than all Jews in abstaining from work on the seventh day [something that is easily documented in several scrolls]; for not only do they prepare their food on the day before, to avoid kindling a fire on that one, but they do not venture to remove any vessel or even to go to stool. On other days they dig a trench a foot deep with a mattock — such is the nature of the hatchet which

they present to neophytes — and wrapping their mantle about them, that they may not offend the rays of the deity, sit above it. They then replace the excavated soil in the trench. For this purpose they select the more retired spots. And though this discharge of the excrements is a natural function, they make it a rule to wash themselves after it, as if defiled. (*Jewish War* 2.147-49; cf. 4Q472)

While just such a hatchet may have been found in Cave 11 and a toilet in Locus 51 has been identified — next to a ritual bath, more helpful evidence comes from the War Rule, where the purity required of the soldiers among the sons of light receives attention. "And no man shall go down with them on the day of battle who is impure because of his 'fount,' for the holy angels shall be with their hosts. And there shall be a space of about two thousand cubits between all their camps for the place serving as a latrine [literally: the place of the hand], so that no indecent nakedness may be seen in the surroundings of their camps" (7.5-7; p. 170). The writer derived some but not all of these instructions from Deut 23:12-14. For instance, the distance at which the facilities were to be placed, the point Josephus makes, goes beyond the biblical givens.

The Temple Scroll offers legislation on the same subject but in connection with the holy city of the sanctuary. "You shall make for them latrines outside the city where they shall go out, north-west of the city. These shall be roofed houses with holes in them into which the filth shall go down. It shall be far enough not to be visible from the city, (at) three thousand cubits" (46.13-16; p. 206). It has often been noted that, as the sabbath limit for a journey was two thousand cubits (one thousand according to CD 10.21), the Essenes had to plan carefully so as not to defile the seventh day. Yigael Yadin has argued that the Essene Gate in Jerusalem was so situated that it would be at an appropriate distance from the communal "place of the hand."

(5) Spitting

Finally, both Josephus and the Rule of the Community mention a small detail. The historian writes: "They are careful not to spit into the midst of the company or to the right" (*Jewish War* 2.147). The Rule stipulates: "Whoever has spat in an Assembly of the Congregation shall do penance for thirty days" (7.13; p. 108). Why both mention this minor but practical rule is not known, although it must have been sufficiently unusual to call attention to itself. A prohibition of this kind is attested in rabbinic literature (Jerusalem Talmud, Berakhot 3.5), but it applied only during prayer.

B. PROBLEMS WITH THE ESSENE HYPOTHESIS

More could be said, but enough evidence has been assembled to show that the Scrolls reflect a series of beliefs and practices which the ancient sources (especially Josephus) characterize as Essene. Todd Beall, a professor at Capital Bible Seminary in Lanham, MD, after analyzing the comparative material, has reached the following conclusions: there are 27 parallels between Josephus and the Scrolls, 21 probable parallels, 10 cases in which Josephus makes claims about the Essenes that have no known parallel among the Scrolls, and six "apparent discrepancies" between them. In two of these six discrepancies the Scrolls do not offer unanimous testimony. An example of this last category, on Beall's reading, is the issue of common ownership of property. As argued above (A.2.b.2), however, the data entail no discrepancy on this point. It is worthwhile, nevertheless, to consider two of the disagreements, one of which falls among Beall's "apparent discrepancies," and the other of which some also consider to be problematic for identifying the Qumran community as Essene.

1. ENTRY PROCEDURES

The first has to do with the entrance requirements for candidates: it seems as if the initiatory procedure is longer by one year in Josephus's report than in the Rule of the Community. According to Josephus:

> A candidate anxious to join their sect is not immediately admitted. For one year, during which he remains outside the fraternity, they prescribe for him their own rule of life, presenting him with a small hatchet, the loin-cloth already mentioned, and white raiment. Having given proof of his temperance during this probationary period, he is brought into closer touch with the rule and is allowed to share the purer kind of holy water, but is not yet re-

ceived into the meetings of the community. For after this exhibition of endurance, his character is tested for two years more, and only then, if found worthy, is he enrolled in the society. But before he may touch the common food, he is made to swear tremendous oaths. (*Jewish War* 2.137-39)

Thus Josephus knew of a three-year initiatory procedure. But some have argued that the Rule of the Community presents a different picture in column 6 of the Cave 1 copy, parts of which were already cited:

Every man, born of Israel, who freely pledges himself to join the Council of the Community shall be examined by the Guardian at the head of the Congregation concerning his understanding and his deeds. If he is fitted to the discipline, he shall admit him into the Covenant that he may be converted to the truth and depart from all falsehood; and he shall instruct him in all the rules of the Community. And later, when he comes to stand before the Congregation, they shall all deliberate his case, and according to the decision of the Council of the Congregation he shall either enter or depart. After he has entered the Council of the Community he shall not touch the pure Meal of the Congregation until one full year is completed, and until he has been examined concerning his spirit and deeds; nor shall he have any share of the property of the Congregation. Then when he has completed one year within the Community, the Congregation shall deliberate his case with regard to his understanding and observance of the Law. And if it be his destiny, according to the judgement of the Priests and the multitude of the men of their Covenant, to enter the company of the Community, his property and earnings shall be handed over to the Bursar of the Congregation who shall register it to his account and shall not spend it for the Congregation. He shall not touch the Drink of the Congregation until he has completed a second year among the men of the Community. But when the second year has passed, he shall be examined, and if it be his destiny, according to the judgement of the Congregation, to enter the Community, then he shall be inscribed among his brethren in the order of his rank for the Law, and for justice, and for the pure Meal; his property shall be merged and he shall offer his counsel and judgement to the Community. (6.13-23; pp. 106-7)

It is reasonable to interpret the evidence in such a way that the sources do not conflict. One may sketch the stages of initiation for the novice as follows:

Josephus
1. one year outside the group but living by its rules
2. two more years of testing
3. enrollment

Rule of the Community
1. period from examination by the Guardian to examination by the Congregation
2. one year in the Council of the Community but with limited rights to the meal
3. after another year, he is again tested and becomes a full member with full rights to the meal

The procedure seems to move through the same stages, with one or the other source supplying different details. A question has been raised about the position of the oath: one could argue that Josephus puts it after the entire three-stage rite, while the Rule, in another passage (5.8), may locate it at the beginning of the process. But does Josephus place the oath at the end of the novitiate? That is not clear. He says only that it comes before the candidate may touch the common meal. The Rule states that the candidate may not partake of the meal until one year is completed, which is the first stage of the initiatory rite, during which the oath is taken. Thus the discrepancy here is not certain; it is more likely that in the case of the entry process, Josephus and the Rule once again agree.

2. MARRIAGE

Some have objected that the evidence regarding women and marriage is a roadblock in the way of identifying the Qumran group with the Essenes of Josephus, Pliny, and the other ancient writers. As already noted, according to Pliny the Essene community on the west side of the Dead Sea "has no women and has renounced all sexual desire." Josephus speaks in several places about the Essene attitude toward women and marriage. For example, he explains:

They shun pleasures as a vice and regard temperance and control of the passions as a special virtue. Marriage they disdain, but they adopt other men's children, while yet pliable and docile, and regard them as their kin and mould them in accordance with their own principles. They do not, indeed, on principle, condemn wedlock and the propagation thereby of the race, but they wish to protect themselves against women's wantonness, being persuaded that none of the sex keeps her plight trothed to one man. (*Jewish War* 2.120)

At the end of his long section about the Essenes, he adds further details:

There is yet another order of Essenes, which, while at one with the rest in its mode of life, customs, and regulations, differs from them in its views on marriage. They think that those who decline to marry cut off the chief function of life, the propagation of the race, and, what is more, that, were all to adopt the same view, the whole race would very quickly die out. They give their wives, however, a three years' probation, and only marry them after they have by three periods of purification given proof of fecundity. They have no intercourse with them during pregnancy, thus showing that their motive in marrying is not self-indulgence but the procreation of children. In the bath the women wear a dress, the men a loin-cloth. (*Jewish War* 2.160-61)

The Rule of the Community does not legislate about marriage; in fact, it does not even mention it. This omission would be surprising, if the Qumran group were celibate. Some rules would surely have been made about a subject of such practical significance. Moreover, the Qumran cemeteries, as noted in the first chapter (B.3.6), contain tombs with mostly male skeletons — at least so the available evidence implies. But there were skeletons of women and children — whether in the main cemetery or in the extensions and secondary burial areas. Their presence has led some scholars to argue that the Qumran community was not devoid of women and sex, contrary to Pliny's writing about his Essenes. He must have been describing a different community. Moreover, other texts found in the caves refer to women and children as part of the group. The best known of these is the Rule of the Congregation, which was copied on the same manuscript as the Cave 1 copy of the Rule of the Community. Also, the Damascus Document legislates explicitly for families and even offers rules for the special way in which children of members entered the community.

It is peculiar that the Rule does not legislate regarding marriage. One could object that the group had no need for such rules because it was not a problem, but we might expect at least a statement to that effect. A few points should be noted, however. First, the evidence of Pliny and Josephus is compatible with the two types of communities evident in the Rule and in the Damascus Document. The former governs a more isolated male society, while the latter legislates for "camps" of Essenes who live among non-Essenes and also have families. These would be the two types of Essenes that Josephus mentions. Second, as we saw in chapter 1, the evidence from the cemeteries is compatible with the thesis that the Qumran community consisted only of males.

3. The Name Essene

One often reads that a problem with the Essene hypothesis is that the word *Essene* never occurs in the Qumran texts. If the Qumranites were Essenes, would they not have mentioned their name at least once? This objection is illogical because the meaning of *Essene*, which occurs in Greek and Latin texts in various spellings, is a hotly disputed point, and no one knows for sure what the Hebrew or Aramaic term behind it was. To say that the name does not occur in the Scrolls presupposes that we would recognize it if we saw it. But if we do not know what the Hebrew or Aramaic term for *Essene* was, why should anyone claim that it is not in the Scrolls? Scholars offer different theories about the term and its derivation. Some relate it to a word for "pious one," others to a term for "healer," and both of these have some evidence behind them. Another possibility is that *Essenes* derives from a form of the word "doers." It would be an abbreviated form of a fuller name such as "doers of the Torah." If this explanation of the name is correct, then the word *Essene* does figure in the Qumran texts (an example is 1QpHab 7.10-12) and the objection falls.

The upshot of the whole investigation is that many strong arguments point to the residents of Qumran being Essenes, and no certain points tell against the identification. It is true that some aspects of Qumran thought find no place in the descriptions of the Essenes offered by the sources from antiquity. Among them are the special solar calendar of 364 days and the distinctive belief that two messiahs would come (see chap. 4 B.6). Nevertheless, in such cases the sources are silent, not opposed. Unless we are to believe that the sources give us exhaustive treatments of the Essenes — all their beliefs and practices — their failure to mention some tenets of their faith is not necessarily damaging to the Essene hypothesis. Indeed, Josephus says nothing about the calendar of any Jewish group that he describes, nor does he specify what, if anything, they thought would be the nature of the messiah(s).

C. OTHER THEORIES

A few other theories have attracted attention in the history of Qumran research. The suggestion, defended in one way or another, that the Qumran group was Christian can be dismissed as contrary to the archeological and paleographical evidence that it existed well before the time of Jesus. Two others deserve more serious consideration. One is that the residents of Qumran were Sadducees; the other is that Qumran had no permanent residents and that the scrolls found in the caves were placed there by residents of Jerusalem who concealed them for safekeeping during the first revolt against Rome.

1. SADDUCEES

A few experts suggested, in an earlier period of study, that the people of Qumran were Sadducees, but the idea never won much support. It was revived, however, after 4QMMT was published. Lawrence Schiffman of New York University has proposed that the Qumranites were Sadducees. His evidence is that several of the legal views on purity defended in Some of the Works of the Torah (4QMMT; on this text, see chap. 2 C.3.d) as those of the authors have significant overlaps with positions that rabbinic literature attributes to the Sadducees. If he is correct and if 4QMMT is a sectarian text that dates from near the time of Qumran beginnings, it would imply — in his opinion — that the sect at its inception was Sadducean or at least exhibited heavy Sadducean influences on its legal positions.

An important element in Schiffman's case is the series of Pharisaic-Sadducean disputes recorded in the Mishnah (Yadayim 4.6-7). On his reading, the four disputed legal points raised there have echoes in 4QMMT. What the Mishnah terms the Sadducean positions are the ones defended by the authors of the Qumran text. Since the interpretation of the full mishnaic passage is complicated, I cite only the clearest example:

> The Sadducees say, We cry out against you, O you Pharisees, for you declare clean an unbroken stream of liquid. The Pharisees say, We cry out against you, O you Sadducees, for you declare clean a channel of water that flows from a burial ground. (Yadayim 4.7)

This controversy between the Pharisees and Sadducces — the third in a series — offers a clear case of agreement between a legal stance in 4QMMT and the opinion of the Sadducees. It concerns the problem of a stream of liquid that, the Sadducees say, transmits the uncleanness of an impure vessel into which it is poured to the clean vessel from which it was poured. When the liquid forms a continuous stream from one container to the other, it is a conduit for ritual impurity. The form of the Hebrew word for a liquid stream is not identical in the two texts, but the legal stance is the same. The Pharisees took the opposite opinion: impurity was not conveyed in this manner. The next sentence adduces a counterexample to the Sadducean position on the previous point: the Pharisees charged that the Sadducees were inconsistent because in the case of a stream of water that comes from a burial ground the Sadducees seem not to have applied their principle that a liquid stream conveys impurity.

In this case the agreement is unmistakable between an exact legal stance that the Mishnah attributes to the Sadducees and the position of the author(s) in 4QMMT. Sadducean and Qumran views also coincide in other instances. What is the implication of this fact?

The Sadducees and the Essenes may well have agreed with one another on many laws and other points; they presumably did not disagree about everything. From a historical perspective, one would expect Sadducees and Essenes to share some views because both had deep priestly roots. The Qumran group may have been founded and led by priests who called themselves sons of Zadok (the leading priest in the time of David and Solomon), while the term *Sadducee* seems to be derived from the name *Zadok,* and some influential priests are known to have been Sadducees. Both parties opposed what they understood to be the Pharisaic tendency to soften some laws and to modify the related penalties.

That is, one reason why they shared some legal views is that both were strongly conservative on matters relating to the law.

The nature of the data from the Mishnah (which was compiled about A.D. 200) hardly matches the amount and character of the earlier information from Josephus, Pliny, and others that has led so many to identify the Qumranites as Essenes. That Qumran views and those attributed to the Sadducees correspond for a few individual laws does not entail that the Qumran group was Sadducean in any sense in which that name is commonly employed today. After all, the Qumran manuscripts teach such prominent anti-Sadducean doctrines as the existence of multitudes of angels and the all-controlling power of fate. How could Sadducees develop such teachings, which are diametrically opposed to what ancient writers said about them? Also, the fact that an *early* document such as the Cave 1 copy of the Rule of the Community (copied about 100 B.C.) enunciates thoroughly Essene, anti-Sadducean theology makes it most improbable that the Qumran residents arose from Sadducean origins. If they did, they succeeded in reversing themselves on fundamental theological tenets within a few years — from nonpredestinarians to all-out determinists, to name just one example. Such a scenario is thoroughly implausible.

Schiffman is aware that the Qumran texts express non-Sadducean theological points. He maintains that the Sadducees who are mentioned in the Mishnah are not the aristocratic ones whom Josephus and others describe; rather, they were a group that was conservative in its approach to law and were also called by a name derived from "Zadok." He may well be right about that point, but it is confusing to call two very different groups by the same name, even if ancient authors did so. Perhaps, for the sake of clarity in English, we could use *Zadokians* for the people to whom the Mishnah refers. They may have been very much like the Essenes or even identical to them. That they were Sadducees of the type known from the New Testament and Josephus is obviously wrong, and, despite the way it sounds, this identification is not what Schiffman claims. His studies suggest that there is much we do not understand about the variety of groups in early Judaism and the terms that the texts apply to them. In any case, Schiffman's theory is a challenge to the Essene hypothesis only in an indirect way and revolves more around proper terminology than the character of the Qumran community.

2. Jerusalem Origins

Some students of the Scrolls have maintained that the scrolls found in the caves were not the library of a community living at the site but were rather from libraries located in Jerusalem. K. H. Rengstorf, of the University of Munster, first made such a proposal in 1960 and Norman Golb of the University of Chicago has offered a revised version of it. Rengstorf thought the Scrolls "were the library — or part of the library — of the Temple at Jerusalem, which in view of some serious danger threatening it was hidden away in the Dead Sea caves — and perhaps elsewhere as well. . . ." The library, he thought, would have included the whole of Jewish literature, even heterodox works. For him, the Qumran buildings were "an outlying station of the Temple administration" to which the officials of the temple sent the treasures of the sanctuary — gold, silver, and the library — during the revolt against Rome. Norman Golb, in a somewhat different way, also connects the Scrolls with Jerusalem. He thinks the Qumran buildings were a fortress and that they had no direct connection with the caves. The scrolls found in the caves were not left there by the residents of Qumran but by people who fled from Jerusalem with their precious manuscripts in order to hide them from the approaching Romans around the time of the First Jewish Revolt. The remote area was thought to be suitable for depositing valuables, as other manuscript discoveries have shown (see the reports about Origen and Timotheus in chap. 1.A; there are other sites in the area as well). That copies of the Songs of the Sabbath Sacrifice were found at Qumran and at Masada shows that such works were not unique to Qumran but were found among people of different persuasions. The large number of Qumran texts makes it highly unlikely that they originated from a single small group; Jerusalem is the only likely candidate as the intellectual center from which so many texts could have come.

Golb has highlighted what he takes to be a series of anomalies in the Essene hypothesis (such as the marriage/celibacy issue) and has proposed his hypothesis as a more satisfactory way to account for all the evidence. If Golb were correct, disagreements and contradictions between the manuscripts would pose no problem because the texts would represent a cross section of Jewish literature, not the library of a single group. He rejects the inferences drawn from the paragraph about the Essenes in Pliny's *Natural History* on the grounds that Pliny, who published his work in A.D. 77, described the Essenes in the present tense (see the treatment given to this argument earlier in this chapter A.1), and the celibate Essenes who impressed him so could hardly have been the residents of Qumran. Thus Pliny wrote about a different place. Golb thinks that the chance discovery of the Cave 1 copy of the Rule of the Community, which does contain some Essene teachings, among the first batch of manuscripts has unduly influenced the rise of the Essene hypothesis, even after many more texts that did not fit the hypothesis were found. One can label only a small number of texts as sectarian; many more, however, either do not contain heterodox teachings or do not agree with what is known about the Essenes from classical sources.

Golb has also stressed that no documentary texts, that is, contracts, letters, business documents, and so on, were found at Qumran. The situation would be highly irregular for an organized community that was supposed to have lived at the site for some two hundred years (using de Vaux's chronology) and quite different from what we find in other manuscript collections. He thinks, too, that none of the texts at Qumran is autographic (or original, firsthand); all are scribal copies of earlier models, with the exception of the Copper Scroll, the treasures of which are incompatible with what he inaccurately calls "the wealth-eschewing Essenes" and clearly point to the practice of hiding valuables in the area of Jericho.

Golb has given clear, forceful expression to objections (some original with him, others of longer standing) that have, from time to time, been raised against the sundry forms taken by the Essene hypothesis. But his own theory is so beset by weaknesses, many of them shared by Rengstorf's hypothesis, that it has proved unacceptable to others in the field. In some ways it suffers from the fact that he formulated it before he (and most scholars) had a clear idea of what the unpublished material contained. Now we know, for example, of a number of documentary texts at Qumran (see the survey of the texts in chap. 2 C.8). But how Golb knows that no text from Qumran is an autograph is a mystery. Many scholars have pointed out that most of the commentaries (none of which appears in multiple copies) are probably autographs. It is likely that other manuscripts are as well. The poor state in which so many texts have survived precludes the certainty that Golb finds on this point. Moreover, Golb underestimates the extent and consistency of Essene teachings throughout the collection of manuscripts. Although he argues that the texts embody the beliefs of a broad spectrum of Jewish groups in the first century A.D., it is not obvious who they were or where their views come to expression in the Scrolls. If Golb were correct, we should be very surprised to see how widespread Essene views were in the supposedly haphazard collection of texts and how the distinctive views of other groups (such as the supposedly dominant Pharisees) appeared only in a negative light. As has often been proposed, one may explain the presence of the same work at Qumran and at Masada by assuming that someone from Qumran brought it to the fortress after the Romans destroyed the Essene settlement at Qumran.

Golb does not handle the evidence from Pliny in a convincing way. Indeed, in dissociating it from Qumran, he has no way to explain it. Pliny must have been describing some other place, he says; but what other place? None has been found along the west side of the Dead Sea either directly above or north of En-gedi. He has also not succeeded in locating any evidence for the group that Pliny might have been describing. Moreover, he is not able to account satisfactorily for the buildings at Qumran. The Qumran settlement was almost certainly not a fortress. This is the studied verdict of almost all the archeologists who have investigated the matter; casual visitors to the place have identified it as a fortress (see chap. 1 B.1.b). It is of some interest that Yigael Yadin, a general in the Israeli army and a professional archeologist who knew the Qumran site well, never thought it was anything but a communal center that had a smaller fortified area within it.

In sum, Schiffman's theory is not a genuine challenge to the Essene identification, and Golb's hypothesis fails to account adequately for the consistent character of the Qumran corpus, for Pliny's statement, or for the Qumran buildings. It is potentially misleading to call the people at Qumran Sadducees and there is no adequate reason to isolate the Scrolls from the people residing at the site or to think they are a cross section of Jewish literature of the time. One other theory, seemingly a safer one, posits that the people associated with the Qumran scrolls belonged to none of the Jewish groups named in the ancient sources. Shemaryahu Talmon of the Hebrew University of Jerusalem has argued that this Community of the Renewed Covenant, as he terms them, were "a socio-religious phenomenon *sui generis* of Judaism at the height of the Second Temple period." They regarded themselves as the only embodiment of the scriptural covenant people and believed they still lived in the age of prophetic inspiration. Talmon thinks the people at Qumran were a male group but that these men were there only temporarily and were not permanent residents of the site. His suggestions about their self-understanding may well be true, but it is difficult to avoid the force of the line of parallels linking the people at Qumran with the Essenes.

The Essene hypothesis (and it is only a hypothesis) accounts for the totality of the evidence in a more convincing way than any of its rivals. But once that point has been established, other questions arise. How did it happen that a group of Essenes decided to live at Qumran of all places, and what did they believe and do? The next chapter takes up these problems.

BIBLIOGRAPHICAL NOTES

The quotation of Pliny is from *Pliny, Natural History,* vol. II, *Books III-VII* (trans. H. Rackham; Loeb Classical Library; Cambridge: Harvard University Press; London: Wm. Heinemann, repr. 1969).

All quotations of Josephus are from *Josephus,* vol. II, *The Jewish War, Books I-III* (trans. H. St.-J. Thackeray; Loeb Classical Library; Cambridge: Harvard University Press; London: Wm. Heinemann, repr. 1976).

For Eleazar Sukenik's suggestion that the authors of the Scrolls were Essenes, see his *The Collection of the Hidden Scrolls in the Possession of the Hebrew University* (ed. Nahman Avigad; Jerusalem: Bialik Institute, 1954) 26 (Hebrew).

The passages from Synesius of Cyrene and Hippolytus are quoted from Geza Vermes and M. D. Goodman, *The Essenes According to the Classical Sources* (Oxford Centre Textbooks 1; Sheffield: Sheffield Academic Press, 1989).

The translation of a passage from the book of Jubilees is taken from my *The Book of Jubilees* (Corpus Scriptorum Christianorum Orientalium 510-11, Scriptores Aethiopici 87-88; 2 vols.; Louvain: Peeters, 1989) vol. 2.

Todd Beall's treatment of parallels between Josephus's descriptions of the Essenes and the evidence in the Scrolls is in his *Josephus' Description of the Essenes Illustrated by the Dead Sea Scrolls* (Society for New Testament Studies Monograph Series 58; Cambridge: Cambridge University Press, 1988).

For the Essene views about oil and other liquids, see Joseph Baumgarten, "The Essene Avoidance of Oil and the Laws of Purity," *Revue de Qumran* 6 (1967) 183-93.

For the section about bodily functions, see Jodi Magness, *The Archaeology of Qumran and the Dead Sea Scrolls,* 105-13.

One may read Lawrence Schiffman's arguments about the Sadducees and Qumran in, for example, "The New Halakhic Letter (4QMMT) and the Origins of the Dead Sea Sect," *Biblical Archaeologist* 53 (1990) 64-73, and in his *Reclaiming the Dead Sea Scrolls: The History of Judaism, the Background of Christianity, the Lost Library of Qumran* (Philadelphia: The Jewish Publication Society, 1994).

The parallels between the liquid stream law in 4QMMT and Mishnah Yadayim 4.7 were first spotted by Joseph Baumgarten, "The Pharisaic-Sadducean Controversies about Purity and the Qumran Texts," *Journal of Jewish Studies* 31 (1980) 157-70.

The citation from the Mishnah comes from Herbert Danby, *The Mishnah* (Oxford: Oxford University Press, 1933).

K. H. Rengstorf expressed his views in his German book of 1960, translated into English as *Ḥirbet Qumran and the Problem of the Library of the Dead Sea Scrolls* (Leiden: Brill, 1963).

Norman Golb's publications include "The Problem of Origin and Identification of the Dead Sea Scrolls," *Proceedings of the American Philosophical Society* 124 (1980) 1-24; "The Dead Sea Scrolls: A New Perspective," *The American Scholar* 58 (1989) 177-207; and *Who Wrote the Dead Sea Scrolls? The Search for the Secret of Qumran* (New York: Scribner, 1995).

One place in which Shemaryahu Talmon has published his theory is "The Community of the Renewed Covenant: Between Judaism and Christianity," in *The Community of the Renewed Covenant: The Notre Dame Symposium on the Dead Sea Scrolls* (ed. Eugene Ulrich and James VanderKam; Christianity and Judaism in Antiquity 10; Notre Dame, IN: University of Notre Dame Press, 1994) 3-24.

The organization indicated in the Qumran texts has been studied in relation to other associations in the Hellenistic world by Moshe Weinfeld, *The Organizational Pattern and the Penal Code of the Qumran Sect* (Novum Testamentum et Orbis Antiquus 2; Fribourg: Editions Universitaires/Göttingen: Vandenhoeck & Ruprecht, 1986).

CHAPTER 4

The Qumran Essenes

The Essenes who lived at Qumran were just a small part of the larger Essene movement in the land. Both Josephus and Philo put the number of Essenes at approximately four thousand. The estimates of how many people could have lived in the Qumran area range from about one hundred fifty to three hundred at the maximum. This total is only a rough guess derived from the number of tombs in the cemeteries, but the population is not likely to have exceeded three hundred. Thus about thirty-seven hundred Essenes lived elsewhere. Why would a small minority reject the way of life chosen by their fellow Essenes in order to pursue the same ends in the desert of Judea? What historical experience or experiences led to the formation of the Qumran group?

A. A SKETCH OF THE QUMRAN GROUP'S HISTORY

The archeological evidence caused Roland de Vaux to date the phases of Qumran occupation from some point in the second half of the second century B.C. to A.D. 68. Subsequent work has lowered the beginning of sectarian occupation to after 100 B.C. Those boundaries define the period within which one should look for Qumran origins and development. No work in the Qumran library offers anything resembling a history, but if we agree that the manuscripts belonged to one group and reflect its views, then we can take the sundry historical clues found here and there and from them sketch in broad strokes a history of the group that resided at Qumran.

1. The Pre-Qumran Period

The Damascus Document in particular furnishes some information about how the movement began, apparently sometime before any dissenters withdrew to Qumran. The first column defines two periods and even discloses how many years they lasted.

> And in the age of wrath, three hundred and ninety years after He had given them into the hand of King Nebuchadnezzar of Babylon, He visited them, and He caused a plant root to spring from Israel and Aaron to inherit His land and to prosper on the good things of His earth. And they perceived their iniquity and recognized that they were guilty men, yet for twenty years they were like blind men groping for the way.
>
> And God observed their deeds, that they sought Him with a whole heart, and He raised for them a Teacher of Righteousness to guide them in the way of His heart. (1.5-11; p. 127)

The numbers 390 and 20, which are confirmed by some of the copies found in Cave 4, have given rise to much debate. Are they meant literally or are they symbolic? The 390 years are the number of years prophesied by Ezekiel for the punishment of the house of Israel (Ezek 4:4-5). If one reads the numbers literally, then, according to the chronology of ancient Israel generally accepted today, the 390 years would have extended from about 587, when Nebuchadnezzar took Jerusalem, until 197 B.C. Jubilees and 1 Enoch also speak of one or more new movements of the same kind and in roughly the same period. The twenty years of groping would then follow, bringing us down to 177 B.C. Again we may wonder how to take the twenty years, which are half of the highly symbolic forty years. At this point the Teacher of Righteousness appeared on the scene and put an end to uncertainty by offering revealed guidance to the penitent group. Scholars often say that while one cannot press too literally the 390 + 20 years in Damascus Document column 1, they work out pretty well nevertheless. However this may be — and it is most uncertain — it is evident that before the Qumran settlement was built a new penitential movement came into being and that eventually the person known only by the epithet "the Teacher of Righteousness" became its leader.

Conflicts between the Teacher and others must have arisen from time to time. This situation is quite understandable when one realizes the force of the claims that he and his followers made for him: God revealed to him all the mysteries of the prophets. Also, if the Teacher is the one who wrote or spoke through some of the poems in the Hymn (Thanksgiving) Scroll (see chap. 2 C.4.b.1), then he felt an extraordinarily strong sense of divine call and election, a firm conviction that he occupied a unique place in God's plan for the latter days. It seems that someone (it is not clear they were part of the same group) refused to accept the Teacher's full claims and withdrew from him and his followers, taking a number of others with him. For his efforts he was branded as "the man of the lie" in the Damascus Document and in some of the commentaries. He is said to have led many people astray through the deceptive words that he spoke (Commentary on Psalms [4QpPs^a] 1-10 i 26, interpreting Ps 37:7).

Some evidence also suggests that the Teacher came into serious conflict with the authorities of the time. The Teacher may have lived around the time Judea endured a religious crisis in which the very existence of Judaism was threatened. It came about when, in response to a revolt in Jerusalem, Antiochus IV, the Seleucid king, banned what he perceived to be the cause of the unrest — the Jewish religion. The Maccabean/Hasmonean revolt was a native response to his prohibition of Judaism. When the revolt proved successful, Judaism was restored to its place as the religion of the land and the temple cult was purified of the abominations that had been practiced at the sanctuary by pagans. These events occurred between 167 and 162 B.C. For centuries before this time, the leading native official among the Jews had been the high priest who was descended from the line of David's priest Zadok. That family had lost the high priesthood shortly before the events of the 160s B.C. and never regained it. Instead, the kings of the Seleucid Empire appointed several high priests for what appear to have been largely political and financial reasons. Josephus, who with the authors of 1-2 Maccabees is one of our few sources of information for the period in question, maintains that there was no high priest in Jerusalem between 159 and 152 B.C. In 152, Jonathan, one of the Hasmonean brothers, was appointed high priest by another Seleucid king (Alexander Balas) because he needed Jonathan's military backing. In this way the Maccabean or Hasmonean high priesthood began. It lasted until 37 B.C., some 115 years in all.

The uncertain conditions surrounding the high priesthood may have had something to do with the Teacher. He was a priest (the Commentary on Psalms is explicit about this point), and his primary opponent is dubbed "the Wicked Priest." Scholars have long suspected that the epithet is a Hebrew wordplay on the title "the high priest" (*ha-kohen ha-ro'sh* = high priest; *ha-kohen ha-rasha'* = the wicked priest). If so, the Teacher's opponent was none other than the Jewish high priest of the time.

The Teacher of Righteousness and the (wicked) high priest apparently had some communication. The Commentary on Psalms mentions a Torah that the Teacher (the title has to be restored in a gap in the manuscript) sent to him.

> *The wicked watches out for the righteous and seeks [to slay him. The Lord will not abandon him into his hand or] let him be condemned when he is tried [Ps 37:32-33].*
>
> Interpreted, this concerns the Wicked [Priest] who [watched the Teacher of Righteousness] that he might put him to death [because of the ordinance] and the law which he sent to him. (1-10 iv 7-9; p. 490)

The editors of Some of the Works of the Torah (4QMMT) interpreted it as a letter, possibly from the Teacher to the Wicked Priest, in which the points at issue between them are listed and discussed. If this is the proper way in which to read the text (the matter is disputed), the irenic tone of the communication is noteworthy. At least one copy of the text begins with a full calendar of the year — 364 days with all the festivals known from other Qumran texts. It also mentions more than twenty legal issues, many concerned with ritual purity, about which the two sides disagreed. It closes with the hope that the recipient will recognize the truth of what is said so that he can rejoice in the end along with Israel.

If the two leaders ever had peaceful relations, they eventually soured. In the passage from the Commentary on Psalms quoted above, the expositor charges the Wicked Priest with attempting to kill the Teacher. A section in the Commentary on Habakkuk reads:

> *Woe to him who causes his neighbours to drink; who pours out his venom to make them drunk that he may gaze on their feasts! [2:15].*
>
> Interpreted, this concerns the Wicked Priest who pursued the Teacher of Righteousness to the house of his exile that he might confuse [[literally: swallow]] him with his venomous fury. And at the time appointed for rest, for the Day of Atonement, he ap-

peared before them to confuse [[= swallow]] them, and to cause them to stumble on the Day of Fasting, their Sabbath of repose. (11.2-8; p. 484)

That the Teacher was pursued to his house of exile should indicate that he had departed from his normal home to another place. It is tempting to surmise that the place was Qumran, but that is only a guess. Early in the study of this commentary, scholars noted that if the Wicked Priest was the reigning high priest and yet pursued the Teacher to his place of exile on the Day of Atonement, the two must have observed that most sacred day on different dates. The reason is that the Wicked Priest had a busy day's work officiating at the temple on this day and would have had no time to chase dissidents, nor would the ban on travel have allowed it (see Leviticus 16). The passage provided one of the first clues that a different calendar was one matter that separated the Teacher and the Wicked Priest.

Who were these two men? The honest answer is that no one knows. The Hasmonean Jonathan has received the strongest support for being the Wicked Priest. Some cause or series of causes must have made the Teacher separate physically from the larger Jewish community centered in Jerusalem and governed by the high priest. It is unlikely that the calendar difference alone was the cause for division. The 364-day calendar had been known and advocated already in 1 Enoch 72–82, a third-century-B.C. work. It is possible that this calendar was even older. If the calendar had not caused its adherents to separate from others for a century or more, why should it do so in, say, the second century B.C.?

A fundamental political dispute may have been the trigger that led to the exile of the Teacher and his followers, an exile that brought his followers to Qumran eventually. As noted above in this section, Josephus reports that there was no Jewish high priest from 159 to 152 B.C. Jonathan's accession ended this interlude and introduced a new family to the high priesthood. It is possible that one of the letters quoted in 1 Maccabees 10 mentions a high priest who was active during this period. If so, someone was occupying that office, whether officially or unofficially. Who was that person? One guess (and it is nothing more) is that it may have been the man known to us as the Teacher of Righteousness. The Qumran texts do not call him a high priest, but he may have been a very high-ranking priest who was an inspirational leader. When Jonathan was appointed high priest by the Seleucid monarch Alexander

Balas, military might seems to have been his major qualification for office (see 1 Macc 10:21). Did Jonathan with his army take the position by force from the Teacher? We do not know, but it is an intriguing possibility. It may be that with Jonathan's forceful arrival, an influential traditionalist such as the Teacher lost the opportunity to put his teachings into effect and, since he believed they were revealed to him by God himself, decided he had no choice but to separate from the powerful high priest who was now in charge.

Although Jonathan still appears to be a likely candidate for the role of Wicked Priest, the identification is disputed. In the history of Scrolls scholarship, virtually every high priest from the 170s B.C. on through the age of the Hasmoneans has been proposed for the dubious honor. The uncertainty reflects the ambiguity of the evidence. The so-called Groningen Hypothesis holds that the evidence is not decisive for any one high priest because "Wicked Priest" was an office, not a person. There were six successive high priests who received the epithet in the Commentary on Habakkuk: Judas, Alcimus, Jonathan, Simon, John Hyrcanus, Alexander Jannaeus. The theory has several implausible elements (Judas was not an official high priest, Aristobulus I is omitted from the list) and no text ever uses the plural Wicked Priests, but it does highlight how underwhelming the evidence is for determining which high priest received the title.

If Jonathan (152-142 B.C.) was the Wicked Priest, then the Teacher of Righteousness was active during his time and ran afoul of him. However, if it is true that the archeological data from Qumran point to sectarian use of the site after 100 B.C., it is unlikely that the Teacher led his followers there. We would have to posit a very long career for him if that were the case. The fact is we do not know whether the Teacher was ever at Qumran, though he was admired by the people who were there and who preserved texts about him and perhaps by him.

If the Teacher went into exile, he may have gone to Damascus — a city mentioned several times in the Damascus Document, although its meaning in it is disputed. That text also refers to a new covenant in the land of Damascus. It would probably have been some time after the Teacher's life ended that some of his disciples made their way to Qumran. It is very likely the Damascus Document refers to his death: "From the day of the gathering in of the Teacher of the Community until the end of all men of war who deserted to the Liar there shall pass about forty years [Deut 2:14]" (CD 20.13-15; see also 19.35-20.1; p. 135). Although scholars have interpreted the "gathering in of the Teacher" in different ways, it is reasonable to read it as referring to his death.

2. The Qumran Period

All of this is too speculative to provide any certainty, but something may have happened around 150 B.C. that triggered the exile of the Teacher and his disciples. It is possible that they went to Damascus, because the Damascus Document, which mentions the Teacher several times, speaks of a new covenant in the land of Damascus.

a. Phase I

In time a group settled at Qumran. Why did they choose a desolate spot overlooking the foul-smelling Dead Sea? The Rule of the Community provides an answer of sorts:

> And when these become members of the Community in Israel according to all these rules, they shall separate from the habitation of unjust men and shall go into the wilderness to prepare there the way of Him; as it is written, *Prepare in the wilderness the way of . . . , make straight in the desert a path for our God* [Isa 40:3]. This (path) is the study of the Law which He commanded by the hand of Moses, that they may do according to all that has been revealed from age to age, and as the Prophets have revealed by His Holy Spirit. (8.12-16; p. 109)

The group is called on to separate from those who are unjust and to go to the wilderness in fulfillment of Isaiah's command. The word *This* in the explanatory sentence "This (path) is the study of the Law" is feminine in gender and refers not to the general subject of separation but to one or both of the words *way* and *path* (both are feminine nouns), as Vermes's translation makes clear. Hence the text is saying that the people who had gone to the wilderness (this they read literally) understood Isaiah's words *way* and *path* in a figurative sense: they were not commanded to construct a real road but to study the law and in this manner to prepare for the Lord's coming. Thus, the group chose Qumran because it was a wilderness, exactly as Isaiah ordered, and there they studied the law, the divine way of life.

Removal from the temple community in Jerusalem entailed that no animal sacrifices were offered by the Teacher's disciples, who believed that the sanctuary was now under an impure administration.

We have no firm evidence on which to base a history of the Qumran community after it was founded. In the first phase, the buildings extended approximately one hundred meters from north to south and eighty from east to west. A fire and apparently an earthquake struck the buildings at a later time (or times) and caused considerable damage. Some decades after the structures were rebuilt in much the same shape they had before, the settlement was destroyed — in A.D. 68 or not far from it. We have reason to believe that as they were attacked, the Essenes defended themselves, perhaps thinking that the final war had come.

Scholars who have analyzed the major, well-preserved Qumran documents believe that they can detect in them successive stages of editing and expansion. Such literary-critical work is often highly subjective, and it rarely produces widespread agreement. Nevertheless, the Rule of the Community may have an ancient core that goes back to the earliest times of the Qumran community and perhaps earlier. Columns 8.1–9.26 speak about a pioneer community (the wilderness passage related to Isaiah 40 is from this section). A substantial part of these two columns is missing from some Cave 4 copies of the Rule. It is not certain, though, whether they preserve an earlier form of the evolving text or whether they are defective because a scribe skipped a section when his eye accidentally jumped from one statement to a similar one at a later line and omitted the intervening material. At any rate, the section is present in 1QS (ca. 100-75 B.C.).

In 8.1–9.26 of the Cave 1 copy of the Rule the exiled community presents itself as a holy of holies for Israel, that is, as the most sacred group within the larger holy community. Their task is to atone for the land and to serve as a pleasing offering to God. Deliberate violation of any Mosaic precept was punished by expulsion without hope of return; inadvertent violations earned the sinner a two-year sentence. Only then was he eligible, if he repented, for readmission. Two significant sentences read: "They shall atone for guilty rebellion and for sins of unfaithfulness, that they may obtain loving-kindness for the Land without the flesh of holocausts and the fat of sacrifice. And prayer rightly offered shall be as an acceptable fragrance of righteousness, and perfection of way as a delectable free-will offering" (9.4-5; p. 110). The life of the community was a substitute for the temple rituals of sacrifice and atonement. If this section is intact and is an early document of the community, then belief in two messiahs (mentioned in 9.11) was already held at this time (for more on this, see below, 4.B.6). The section also contains rules for the Master (Hebrew *maskil*), who was the leader of the group.

The history of the community in phase I has been related to an incident in the reign of Alexander Jannaeus (103-76 B.C.). Some Pharisees had tried to oust him by inviting King Demetrius, the Seleucid monarch, to Jerusalem to attack Jannaeus. In revenge he crucified eight hundred Pharisees in one day in the presence of their families. As already noted, the commentary on Nahum mentions this incident. Some scholars have proposed that Pharisees may have fled to Qumran, thus swelling its numbers after the gruesome executions of 88 B.C. That proposal seems unlikely, however. These Essenes ridiculed the Pharisees as "the seekers after smooth things" because of their failure to practice the stricter understanding of the law advocated by the Teacher and his disciples. It is not self-evident that the Qumranites would have found Jannaeus's barbarous action overly offensive. The Nahum commentary mentions it without passing judgment on the incident.

A text that may be relevant to this discussion is 4Q448 (Apocryphal Psalm and Prayer). It names King Jonathan (= Jannaeus) once for sure and perhaps another time and may contain the first positive reference to a Maccabean/Hasmonean king in the Qumran scrolls. The text says: "Holy City for King Jonathan and for all the congregation of Your people Israel" (2.1-4; p. 332). Another reading takes the word translated "city" as "rise" and "holy" as a reference to God: "Rise, Holy One. . ." A positive reference to Jannaeus would not be unthinkable at Qumran, since he had removed eight hundred of the Essenes' opponents. It would, however, raise the question why, if they felt positively about Jannaeus, they continued their separated existence. The answer may be that their beliefs about living in the last days and their stand on purity and separation from all impurity caused them to remain apart.

Although we have little information about the inhabitants of Qumran in phase I, we can safely say that a large number of manuscripts were copied during it. Some copies of the Rule of the Community, the Damascus Document, the Temple Scroll, the Hymn Scroll, the Songs of the Sabbath Sacrifice, the Daily Prayers, copies of other biblical books, works such as 1 Enoch and Jubilees — these and many others were copied during phase I.

De Vaux theorized that his phase I*b* was brought to a close when the earthquake of 31 B.C. shook Qumran and unleashed fires that destroyed the communal buildings. A nearly thirty-year gap in occupation (to the end of Herod's reign in 4 B.C.) ensued. The conclusion that the site lay uninhabited for several decades involves the interpretation of some coins and the sizable buildup of silt in one of the cisterns. As we have seen, not everyone has found de Vaux's explanation convincing. It surely does not take twenty-seven years for a thick layer of silt to accumulate. In addition, ten coins from Herod's reign have been found. We have no compelling reason for thinking the Essenes would not have soon rebuilt their settlement on the same spot.

b. Phase II

The second phase extends from some time around the turn of the eras to the final destruction of the buildings. The structures were rebuilt to roughly the same dimensions as in the previous phase, although some small changes occurred, such as the further strengthening of the tower. Like phase I, phase II was a period of intense scribal labor. Again biblical manuscripts and copies of other works appeared in abundance. The Cave 1 War Rule is from this phase, as are many of the biblical commentaries, and the fascinating first Psalms scroll from Cave 11. Whether one may draw any major conclusions from the dates when copyists prepared these manuscripts is open to question. For example, biblical interpretation certainly went on before phase II, and earlier manuscripts of an older version of the War Rule have been found. At any rate, when the Roman attack came, the Essenes hid their manuscripts and presumably attempted to defend themselves, with many perishing in the process. Widespread evidence of fire and the presence of iron arrowheads show the end was violent. We do not know whether any bodies in the cemeteries may date from this slaughter. It is possible that some Essenes escaped and went to places such as Masada. One piece of evidence that may support this theory is that a copy of the Qumranic Songs of the Sabbath Sacrifice was found at Masada. Perhaps a former resident of Qumran brought it there.

The later phases do not affect the history of the Qumran community and so may be left out of consideration here.

B. A SKETCH OF QUMRAN THOUGHT AND PRACTICE

It is useful to supplement the outline of Qumran history given above with a summary of the theology found in the Qumran texts and the conduct that flowed from it. The patterns of thought and practice that emerge from the texts and fragments cohere in a system: fundamental beliefs demand and take concrete form in particular kinds of conduct. While the theology and practice of the group rely heavily on biblical givens and thus share much with other Jewish systems of the time, they are sufficiently distinctive to define these Essenes as a group that diverged in important ways from other contemporary Jewish groups. An intriguing, overarching feature of Qumran thought is that it combines an intense awareness that the latter days are here with an equally intense conviction that conduct must accord with the most stringent legal precepts. It is oversimplifying to put it this way, but rabbinic Judaism as embodied in the Mishnah, Tosephta, and the Talmuds shows a strong interest in proper covenantal conduct. Early Christianity, at least in its Pauline forms, rejected that approach and placed a stronger accent on the eschatological side. Both aspects were underscored at Qumran.

It is not easy to provide a systematic account of a theology that is never set forth systematically in the texts, but a few basic principles may be formulated as follows.

1. Predeterminism

The eternal and omnipotent God created everything, but before he did he determined exactly what would happen in his creation. He not only predetermined all and then proceeded to create the universe in line with his plan; he also chose to communicate with his creatures and to scatter clues throughout his creation to the structure of the cosmos and the unfolding pattern of history. (For some of the texts expressing the predestinarian theology of Qumran, see chap. 3 A.2.a.1.) The central position given to predestination and providence in Essene theology is one feature that caught the eye of contemporary witnesses and set them apart from others. One of the expressions met frequently in the predestinarian statements is "before he created" or the like. It reminds one of verses in Second Isaiah where the anonymous prophet of the exile proclaims that the Lord knew from of old what was to happen. The

Essenes advanced beyond the prophetic assertion of foreknowledge to a confession that the deity had also arranged whatever would happen before there was a creation in which all the planned events would occur. The Qumran manuscripts apparently contain no extended attempt to deal with the logical perplexities that arise from a system of this kind. But several documents contain unmistakable statements of this characteristically Essene belief — one that, according to Josephus, set them apart from Pharisees and Sadducees.

2. THE TWO WAYS

In God's predestined plan there are two ways: the way of light and the way of darkness, the way of good and the way of evil. There is no mediating option. The entire universe is involved in this duality, which is ultimately under God's firm control. Angels, who are numerous, and humans belong in one or the other of the two camps. The two camps are engaged in constant warfare with one another, a conflict that will end only when God comes in final judgment and gives victory to the sons of light and their angelic allies.

The cosmic war between these two primal forces also played itself out in the lives of individuals. Each person had some amount of light and of darkness. Or, to put it another way, everyone is sinful, even the sons of light.

> The Angel of Darkness leads all the children of righteousness astray, and until his end, all their sin, iniquities, wickedness, and all their unlawful deeds are caused by his dominion in accordance with the mysteries of God. Every one of their chastisements, and every one of the seasons of their distress, shall be brought about by the rule of his persecution; for all his allotted spirits seek the overthrow of the sons of light. (1QS 3.21-24; p. 101)

The Rule goes on to enumerate the kinds of actions that result from the two spirits and to offer a programmatic declaration.

> The nature of all the children of men is ruled by these (two spirits), and during their life all the hosts of men have a portion of their divisions and walk in (both) their ways. And the whole re-

138

ward for their deeds shall be, for everlasting ages, according to whether each man's portion in their two divisions is great or small. For God has established the spirits in equal measure until the final age, and has set everlasting hatred between their divisions. Truth abhors the works of injustice, and injustice hates all the ways of truth. And their struggle is fierce in all their arguments for they do not walk together. (4.15-18; pp. 102-3)

The preferred explanation at Qumran for the muscular presence of evil in the life of humanity is the story about the fallen angels (see Gen 6:1-4) best known from the Enoch literature. When heavenly angels went astray and impregnated women, they and their offspring — the giants — introduced a superhuman element of evil into human society. The Adam-Eve story seems not to have played much of a role in Qumran thought. The angel (or Watcher) myth, in some of its forms, presupposes that evil existed beforehand in the heavenly realm but does not explain its origin.

3. THE COMMUNITY OF THE NEW COVENANT

In this state of affairs, God chose to enter into covenant with a people. These he selected and to them he revealed commandments at different times but especially at Mount Sinai when he disclosed the details of his will to Moses. Abraham and his descendants lived in covenantal relationship with God until their disobedience led him, many centuries later, to reject them and hand them over to Nebuchadnezzar. Nevertheless, with a surviving remnant of his people God renewed the covenant. It seems to be the old one but this time with a deeper understanding of what was required and a greater incentive to obey. The remnant with whom the new covenant was concluded considered themselves the true Israel. The people who lived in and around Qumran believed firmly that they were part of that remnant raised by God to be a plant of righteousness and truth. They enacted a ceremony of covenant renewal annually, at the festival of Weeks (see 4Q266 frg. 11.17-18). The first two and one-half columns of the Cave 1 copy of the Rule of the Community (with parallels in the Cave 4 copies) describe this ceremony.

The community organized itself in ways that recall biblical Israel's structure during its wilderness trek. That is, they continued to use the language of the tribes and distinguished between priests, Levites, and Israelites, with the Israelites divided into units of thousands, hundreds, fifties, and tens. While the organization of the community is treated most clearly in the Rule of the Community, the terms that it uses figure in other texts as well. A word that the members employed frequently for themselves is *yahad*, "unity" or "community." In the section that deals with the annual ceremony of covenant renewal, the writer pictures the "unity" in these words:

> Thus shall they do, year by year, as long as the dominion of Belial endures. The Priests shall enter first, ranked one after another according to the perfection of their spirit; then the Levites; and thirdly, all the people one after another in their Thousands, Hundreds, Fifties, and Tens, that every Israelite may know his place in the Community of God according to the everlasting design. No man shall move down from his place nor move up from his allotted position. For according to the holy design, they shall all of them be in a Community of truth and virtuous humility, of lovingkindness and good intent one towards the other, and (they shall all of them be) sons of the everlasting Company. (2.19-25; p. 100)

The group truly shared a communal life. Together they ate the pure meal, prayed, deliberated, and studied the scriptures (6.2-3, 7-8). The chief official was the Guardian (as Vermes translates *mevaqqer*) who was possibly the same official as the one called the Master *(maskil),* whose duties are enumerated in column 9. His tasks included teaching the true knowledge and the mysteries of God, assessing members according to their spirit, and presiding at group meetings. Moreover, candidates for admission had first to be examined by him; only if they passed the test were they allowed to continue the long process of becoming a member (6.13-15). The Guardian was to be zealous to do God's will and was to take delight in performing it. The Damascus Document, which legislates for different sorts of Essene communities (the camps), also speaks of a Guardian who is over them. It may be that the person whom Vermes calls the Bursar was an individual other than the Guardian, although that is not entirely clear. Whoever the Bursar was, he supervised the finances of the group, their common property. The Rule also refers to a Council of the Community, which had twelve men along with three priests (8.1-4). Whether this was an ongoing group or an early core of the community is not certain. The entire group is called "the Congregation" or "the many."

4. Scriptural Interpretation

The deeper awareness and commitment involved in the renewed covenant were closely related to scriptural interpretation. Every indicator points to the centrality of biblical study at Qumran, and from such study various kinds of information emerged.

a. The Latter Days

Study of God's revelation, made easier by the presence of the Teacher of Righteousness, who was regarded as an inspired expositor of prophetic secrets, disclosed that the latter days predicted by the prophets had arrived (see Some of the Works of the Torah C 21). The result was that special conditions now prevailed in this time when evil would reach its most potent level and the members of the renewed covenant would be subjected to severe tests. Various terms are used for these times, such as "epoch of wickedness" or "time of trial."

b. Special Laws

Scriptural interpretation not only uncovered the fact that the latter days had arrived; it also supplied the specific rules by which the covenanters were to live in the epoch of wickedness. The laws of the Torah were revealed, and of course one could not question their absolute authority. Violation of any of them merited expulsion from the community (1QS 8.21-23). But through their special techniques of interpretation the expositors of Qumran also derived from the revealed laws other laws and precepts that, they believed, lay hidden in the revealed words of the Torah. Everyone who had voluntarily earned the right to enter the community (for the procedure, see chap. 3 B.1) pledged to live by the divine will *as understood by the group*. The series of legal texts at Qumran proves the importance of the rules derived from their exegesis of the Torah. Strict adherence to the communal code of conduct was enforced by a series of penalties, the most serious of which was banishment from the community. The others varied, depending on the offense, between two years banishment for the most serious (if one has "betrayed the truth and walked in the stubbornness of his heart," 7.18-19; p. 108) and ten days for the most trivial (interrupting a companion while he is speaking, 7.9-10).

All members were ranked by the perfection or imperfection of their conduct, and they were assessed regularly. In fact, a record was kept so that the pertinent information would be available.

> They shall inscribe them in order, one after another, according to their understanding and their deeds, that every one may obey his companion, the man of lesser rank obeying his superior. And they shall examine their spirit and deeds yearly, so that each man may be advanced in accordance with his understanding and perfection of way, or moved down in accordance with his distortions. (5.23-24; p. 105)

Since purity was a primary concern, separation was demanded, whether the dramatic separation of the Qumran community or the limited but real one of the camps mentioned in the Damascus Document. Strict rules had as their goal to help the members achieve the requisite purity, free from contamination of any sort.

c. The Universe

Revelation and scriptural interpretation also conveyed information about the structure of the universe. Not only did the revelations disclose the course of history and one's location in it; they also communicated the true calendar and the properly ordered times in which to celebrate the festivals. Sun and moon operated according to strict, schematic laws that the covenanters understood but others, who followed the ways of the gentiles, did not.

The revealed calendar called for a solar year of 364 days *and a lunar one* of 354 days. When many of the Cave 4 texts remained unavailable, it appeared from the published texts that the Qumranites, like the author of Jubilees, accepted only a solar calendar of 364 days and rejected the lunar reckoning that the authorities in Jerusalem followed — a reckoning that was practically identical with the one used in the various Hellenistic kingdoms. In chapter 2, I enumerated those texts mentioning the 364-day solar calendar: Jubilees, 1 Enoch, the first Psalms scroll from Cave 11, the *mishmarot* texts (i.e., texts that use the rotation of the 24 priestly groups or "watches"), 4Q252, and 4QMMT. Now that all the calendrical texts are accessible, one can understand the complexity of the Qumran calendrical schemes to a greater extent. It is particularly interesting that one of the Cave 4 copies of the Rule of the Community (copy e) includes a long calendrical section that also deals with the priestly shifts or watches.

What we find often in the *mishmarot* texts is a chart correlating three entities: the date in the solar calendar, the corresponding date in the schematic lunar calendar, and the day of service in the week for the priestly shift that was then on duty. The first two items are simple enough to understand, but the third is more complicated. The priests in ancient Judah were divided into twenty-four shifts or watches (they are named in 1 Chr 24:7-18), and they rotated temple service among them. The priests from one of the twenty-four groups would serve for one week and then be replaced on a Sunday by the next one in the list. By correlating the priestly rotation with the solar and lunar dates, the calendarist added the element of the day in the week on which any event occurred. At times the calendars also name the festivals of the Hebrew Bible and those additional ones that the Essenes celebrated. Since the Torah specifies the dates for some of these festivals, one can calculate when the unfamiliar ones were celebrated. With this calculation, it is not too difficult to map out most details of these fairly complicated texts.

The importance of the Qumran calendrical system is that it differed from whatever one was used in the temple at the time. One result was that the residents of Qumran and some of their spiritual ancestors observed a unique festival cycle. That is, they did not celebrate on the same days those holidays they shared with other Jews. Moreover, they marked as festivals several occasions that other Jews seem not to have celebrated. The main additions to the list of biblical festivals are in bold print:

Passover (1/14)
Unleavened Bread (1/15-21)
Waving of the Omer (**1/26**) = the firstfruits of barley
Festival of Weeks (**3/15**) = the firstfruits of wheat
New Wine Festival (5/3)
New Oil Festival (6/22)
Wood Festival (6/23-30?)
Day of Remembrance (7/1)
Day of Atonement (7/10)

Festival of Booths (7/15-21, with an additional day on 7/22)

The extra holidays appear to have been a product of biblical interpretation. Dates for festivals are always according to the solar calendar.

The lunar calendar, which is now well attested for Qumran (Jubilees rejected any use of the moon for calendrical calculation, but the Astronomical Book in 1 Enoch accepted it), was not the same as the system used in Jerusalem. It is a purely schematic calendar and does not depend, strangely, on lunar observation. It has continually alternating months of thirty and twenty-nine days. In twelve months the total is 354 days, so that one month had to be added every third year to bring the lunar reckoning into harmony with the solar one. Another peculiar feature of the Qumran lunar calculations is that they may have regarded the full moon, not the new lunar crescent, as the time when the lunar month began. The advocates of this calendar traced it and the solar calendar back to the time of creation; they even dated the days of the creation week by the priestly shift that would have been on duty then had it existed. These careful exegetes of Genesis believed that God created the moon full, hence the first month began with a full moon. Since he made the sun, moon, and stars on the fourth day, the calendar began on the fourth day of the week (= our Wednesday).

The authors of the Scrolls seem to have been aware that their schematic solar calendar did not fit the actual length of the solar year. Some of the calendrical texts may hint at a complicated system of intercalation by means of which their 364-day calendar could be harmonized with the true solar year. The texts provide ample evidence that the calendars worked with larger units than just a year. There are references to weeks of years (as in Daniel 9) and jubilees of years (as in the book of Jubilees). The jubilees were reckoned as forty-nine-year units. The largest unit named is a jubilee of jubilees or forty-nine forty-nine-year entities. By means of such time units, the Essenes dated the past and predicted the future — both of which had, of course, been fixed in God's unalterable, predetermined plan.

5. Worship

As they lived in the epoch of wickedness leading up to the end, the covenanters felt called to offer worship and praise to God and sensed that, as they did so, they were in fellowship with the angels who partici-pated in the heavenly liturgy. The covenanters apparently did not offer animal sacrifice. One can interpret the animal bones found at Qumran as the remains of meals, not of sacrificial animals. Instead, the members sent up prayer and praise as sacrifices of the lips to the creating, sustain-ing, and saving God. As a passage already quoted puts it:

> They shall atone for guilty rebellion and for sins of unfaithfulness that they may obtain loving-kindness for the Land without the flesh of holocausts and the fat of sacrifice. And prayer rightly of-fered shall be as an acceptable fragrance of righteousness, and perfection of way as a delectable free-will offering. (Rule of the Community 9.4-5; p. 110)

6. THE END AND THE MESSIAHS

At the end of history, for which the covenanters were preparing by obey-ing God's revealed and hidden demands, the almighty Lord will inter-vene. He will then send the great leaders of the future — a prophet and the Davidic and priestly messiahs — who, along with the hosts of the sons of light, will take part in the ultimate divine victory over evil.

The Qumran belief about two messiahs has received much attention. As already mentioned, copies of the Damascus Document were found in Cairo in 1896 and published in 1910. The scholars who studied them no-ticed that four passages (CD 12.23-13.1; 14.18-19, 19.10 11; 19.33-20.1) used the phrase "the messiah of/from Aaron and Israel." They inevitably won-dered what it meant: did one messiah come from or represent all Israel, or was the writer referring to two messiahs, one from the priestly line of Aaron and another from the rest of Israel? No answer was forthcoming because the evidence was ambiguous, although in one passage a singular form of a verb has "the messiah of Aaron and Israel" as its subject. With this debate in the background, the discovery of the Cave 1 copy of the Rule of the Community caused great excitement because it employed the same phrase but with one additional letter so that it became: the messi-ah*s* of Aaron and Israel (9.11). The section of which this line is a part is missing from a copy of the Rule from Cave 4 (copy e), but its absence may have been caused by a scribal mistake. The plural form in 9.11 gave the first unambiguous evidence that the people of Qumran expected not one but two messiahs. The Rule of the Congregation (which calls itself a rule for the last days) added further data. It pictures a meal at which these two characters are present: the priest, who is not called a messiah in this text, presides over the meal with his blessings, and the messiah of Israel also plays an important role (1QSa 2.11-22).

The pattern of both a secular and a priestly leader of the end time is repeated in a relatively large number of Qumran texts of diverse types: rules, commentaries (continuous and thematic), and eschatological works. The messiah of Israel turns out to be a descendant of David, as one might have expected. He goes under several titles that are identified with one another: "branch of David" (a title from Isaiah), "messiah," and "prince of the Congregation." In language drawn from Isaiah, he is often described as one who will defeat Israel's foes and execute justice. But at his side we regularly find a priest who instructs him and carries out other sacerdotal duties. These two also play roles in the War Rule. One usually learns little about them, especially the priestly messiah, because the texts tend to be fragmentary; but atonement is listed as one of their functions.

At times the texts refer to just one messiah, it seems: 4Q521 (Messianic Apocalypse) reads, in a frustratingly broken section: ". . . the hea]vens and the earth will listen to His Messiah, and none therein will stray from the commandment of the holy ones" (2 i + 4.1-2). The spelling of the form translated "His Messiah" is most naturally taken as singular, although the parallel to it in the next line ("holy ones") is plural. The authoritative position of the messiah in this text is remarkable, as is that of the holy ones. Several lines below (line 12) is the passage about resurrection; it appears, however, that God, not the messiah, is the one who gives new life to the dead.

As already seen in chapter 3 A.2.a.2, the statements in the Scrolls about life after death are not always clear. Nevertheless, as noted there, there are texts mentioning that God will raise the dead. The resurrection happens apparently after the final war has been decided and cataclysmic destruction has occurred. At that time a new kind of communion with God and the angels will begin. That communion will be a continuation of the one that the members enjoyed in the present time, since they believed that in some way they joined with the heavenly hosts in their present worship of God. The Temple Scroll speaks of a new temple that God will create, while a series of other texts describe the layout of a new Jerusalem. Thus, the Qumranites envisaged a return to a purified Jerusalem with its new temple where the proper sacrificial and festival worship would be in effect.

C. THE QUMRAN ESSENES
AND THEIR PLACE IN JUDAISM

It is an interesting exercise to read a pre-1947 book about Judaism in the late Second Temple period and to compare it with one informed by the Scrolls discoveries. Much remains obscure about those times despite the increase in source material now available, but the picture is brighter and more nuanced because of what the Dead Sea Scrolls have shown.

Students of history knew from Josephus and other sources that there were several groups or factions (it is difficult to come up with an adequate term) among the Jewish people in the last century or two B.C. and the first A.D. While speaking about the time of the Hasmonean ruler Jonathan (152-42 B.C.), Josephus tells us that among the Jews there were three groups: Pharisees, Sadducees, and Essenes. He adds that the Zealots, who emerged later, were like the Pharisees other than in their political views (refusing to accept human rule). The New Testament, too, refers to Pharisees and Sadducees and it does mention Zealots without saying much about them. About these groups Josephus speaks at some length and gives us an idea concerning them, but the ones regarding whom he seems to have had the greatest amount of information were the Essenes. He (or his source or both) was quite interested in their unusual communal way of life and the ways in which they cared for members of the group. He pictures the Pharisees as influential with the masses and says they were regarded as very careful interpreters of the laws ("who are considered the most accurate interpreters of the laws" [*War* 2.162]), while the Sadducees appealed to the wealthier classes. Experts have wondered how complete or accurate Josephus's pictures of these groups are and how much he or his sources revised them so that they would be understandable and perhaps appealing to a wider, non-Jewish audience.

The Scrolls allow us to supplement the information found in such sources in what may be surprising ways. Let's begin with the Pharisees, a group relatively well known to many because Jesus encounters them in the Gospels where they are rarely presented in a positive light. For example, in Matthew, the Pharisees not only object when Jesus' disciples pluck grain on the Sabbath (12:1-8) but also have problems with his healing on the Sabbath, perhaps on the grounds that healing was work and all forms of work were prohibited on the seventh day (12:9-14), though no Jewish source of the time identifies healing as work. Later they accuse Jesus' disciples of breaking the tradition of the elders by not washing their hands before they eat, and he accuses them of breaking God's commandments to obey their tradition (15:1-9). Jesus warns his disciples about the yeast of the Pharisees and Sadducees, meaning their teaching (16:5-12). Jesus and the Pharisees debate laws of marriage and divorce (19:1-9). They try to trip him up with the question whether it is lawful to pay taxes to the emperor (22:15-22). All the conflicts between Jesus and the Pharisees build to a climax in chap. 23 where Jesus pronounces a long series of woes on the scribes and Pharisees. He accuses them right off of being hypocrites: "The scribes and the Pharisees sit on Moses' seat; therefore, do whatever they teach you and follow it; but do not do as they do, for they do not practice what they teach" (vv. 2-3). Perhaps the sum of his charges against them comes to clearest expression in these lines: "Woe to you, scribes and Pharisees, hypocrites! For you tithe mint, dill, and cumin, and have neglected the weightier matters of the law: justice and mercy and faith. It is these you ought to have practiced without neglecting the others. You blind guides! You strain out a gnat but swallow a camel!" (vv. 23-24). The picture is of leaders who major in minors and in doing so miss the point of the religion they lead.

Josephus commented on how the Pharisees were known as precise teachers of the laws. They disagreed with Sadducees about a number of points, he says. For one, the Pharisees, as indicated in the Gospels, had a tradition of legal teaching that they inherited from their predecessors and handed down to their followers. This was a tradition that offered interpretations of and expansions on the law of Moses to make it adaptable as social and political conditions changed.

The Scrolls give the clear impression that the chief conversation partners of the community were the Pharisees of their time. Actually, that is putting matters rather too politely. The Pharisees were their enemies, people they thought were terribly in the wrong, and the way in which they depict the Pharisees may come as a surprise to readers of the New Testament. The fact that the Pharisees are the major debaters with both Jesus and his disciples and the Qumran community probably reflects how influential they were and how they were active in many places in the land.

As we have had occasion to notice, a frustrating fact about studying the Dead Sea Scrolls is that they almost never name the individuals or groups they are discussing. They prefer to use code names that are often insulting. For example, the archenemy of the group in the early days of its existence they call the Wicked Priest. In a series of texts among the Scrolls a group of opponents is called "those who seek/look for smooth things." The word translated "seek" or "look" can be used for searching or investigating the scriptures, while the one rendered "smooth things" regularly has a negative connotation when it is connected with words and speaking. The term occurs in Prov 26:28 where it is a parallel of a lying tongue ("A lying tongue hates its victims, and a *flattering* mouth works ruin"), and Dan 11:32 attributes it to the enemy king who flatters with smooth words ("He shall seduce with *intrigue*"). It seems that the sense of the phrase "those who seek/look for smooth things" is not only that they are characterized by flattering or slippery speech but also that they are looking for easy things, the easy way out. When used with the verb "to seek" or "to search out," the label probably refers to people who are looking for a way to make obeying the commandments of scripture easier, smoother than a proper, rigorous interpretation of those laws requires. "Seekers of smooth things" is the name the Scrolls community gave to their opponents, who are almost certainly the Pharisees. The following passages illustrate the practice in the Scrolls of using code names and epithets and show what the group had to say about "those who seek smooth things." It is likely that the word for smooth things *(halaqot)* is a word play for the Pharisaic term *halakhot* (laws).

The epithet "those who seek smooth things" appears (with slight variations) in five texts found at Qumran. According to the Damascus Document, after the appearance of a "root of planting" (390 years after Nebuchadnezzar defeated the nation) and twenty years of uncertainty before the Teacher of Righteousness (an early leader of the group) emerged, an opponent of the new group and its leader came on the scene. The description of him and his community provides a revealing picture of who their opponents perceived them to be:

> . . . when the Scoffer arose who shed over Israel the waters of lies. He caused them to wander in a pathless wilderness, laying low the everlasting heights, abolishing the ways of righteousness and removing the boundary with which the forefathers had marked out their inheritance, that he might call down on them the curses of His Covenant and deliver them up to the avenging sword of His Covenant. For they sought smooth things and preferred illusions (Is. 30:10) and they watched for breaks (Is. 30:13) and chose the fair neck; and they justified the wicked and condemned the just,

149

and they transgressed the Covenant and violated the Precept. They banded together against the life of the righteous (Ps. 94:21) and loathed all who walked in perfection; they pursued them with the sword and exulted in the strife of the people. And the anger of God was kindled against their congregation so that He ravaged all their multitude; and their deeds were defilement before Him. (CD 1.14-2.1; pp. 127-28)

The dispute between the two sides transparently involved the law, with the author of the Damascus Document accusing the other side of breaking the covenant and misleading others to imitate their transgressions. Such charges show that the opponents were fellow Jews, people who should be keeping the covenant. Their quest for smooth things is just one criticism in a catalog of charges against them.

The Hodayot or Thanksgiving Psalms add to the picture in two poems that have been identified as hymns possibly coming from the Teacher of Righteousness. In 10.31-38 the poet thanks the Lord for saving him "from the zeal of lying interpreters, and from the congregation of those who seek smooth things" (10.31-32; p. 258). He claims they tried to murder him and calls them "seekers of falsehood" (line 34; p. 259). In the poem that begins at 12.5 he says "they, teachers of lies and seers of falsehood, have schemed against me a devilish scheme, to exchange the Law engraved on my heart by You for the smooth things (which they speak) to Your People" (12.9-11; p. 263). The opponents are condemned for their lying language which entailed rejecting the revealed law (understood in the correct way) for something else and for inducing others to do likewise. The issue is the proper interpretation and hence application of the law.

A few references to those who seek smooth things appear in broken contexts in fragmentary manuscripts; from these passages we learn little more about them. 4Q177 (Catena^a) 2.12-13 speaks of their hostility, while 4Q163 (4QpIsa^c) 23 ii 10-12 says they are in Jerusalem and, in the context, refers to the law.

We could draw several conclusions about the "ones who look for smooth things" from these references (e.g., they interpret the law in a way contrary to the manner advocated by the scroll community, reject the Teacher's claims, teach and mislead the people — all of which lead to their being punished by God), but the characteristics are too general to allow us to identify the group behind the label. As a consequence, the references to them in the fifth text, Pesher (or Commentary on) Nahum

(4Q169, one of the line by line, continuous commentaries), have been especially valuable because some of them are much more specific.

In the commentary we first encounter "the ones who look for smooth things" in the comment on Nah. 2:11b: *"whither the lion goes, there is the lion's cub, with none to disturb it";* about the passage the commentator writes: "[Interpreted, this concerns Deme]trius, king of Greece who sought, on the counsel of those who seek smooth things, to enter Jerusalem. [But God did not permit the city to be delivered] into the hands of the kings of Greece, from the time of Antiochus until the coming of the rulers of the Kittim. But then she shall be trampled under their feet" (3-4 i 2-3; p. 474). With this reference to two Greek, that is, Seleucid kings (Demetrius and Antiochus) — rare cases in which a Scrolls writer actually names historical individuals — and to the Kittim (that is, the Romans), we obtain a good idea of the time and circumstances which the commentator has in mind. It is very likely that Demetrius is Demetrius III Eucerus (95-88 B.C.), a king of the Seleucid Empire. He was invited by some Jewish people to invade their own land (ca. 88 B.C.) under circumstances we will examine shortly. Our text calls the people who issued this unusual invitation "seekers of smooth things." This passage indicates that the seekers of smooth things were very active in national affairs in the early first century B.C.

The following comment on Nah. 2:12b ("it fills] its caves [with prey] and its dens with victims") has for most scholars clinched the identification of the ones looking for smooth things as Pharisees because it also mentions crucifixion in a similar historical context: "Interpreted, this concerns the furious young lion [who executes revenge] on those who seek smooth things and hangs men alive, . . . formerly in Israel. Because of a man hanged alive on [the] tree, He proclaims, '*Behold, I am against [you, says the Lord of Hosts]'*" (3-4 i 4-8; p. 474).

The identification of the seekers as Pharisees, according to many experts, receives its strongest confirmation from a comparison of what Pesher Nahum says about them with Josephus's accounts of Alexander Jannaeus's relations with the Pharisees. Alexander Jannaeus was a Jewish king and high priest (103-76 B.C.) from the Hasmonean line. The versions of the story in Josephus's two histories — *War* and *Antiquities* — are not as specific as one might like, but there is enough in them to verify the identification of seekers of smooth things as Pharisees.

The storyline in Josephus's two works is largely the same, although he provides more detail in *Antiquities*. In *War*, the relevant passages are

1.88-98 and 1.110-14; in *Antiquities* the parallel parts are 13.372-83 and 13.398-415. In both works the historical sequence under discussion begins with a notice that after a number of his battles against external foes, the Jewish populace gave vent to their anger toward Alexander by taking advantage of the opportunity afforded by a festival when many of them had congregated at the temple. In *Ant.* 13.372, where the holiday is said to be the festival of tabernacles, the historian fills out the sparse givens of *War* by relating an incident in which the crowd pelted the high priest Jannaeus with fruit as he was about to officiate at the altar. Neither source names the opponents, other than calling them Jannaeus's own Jewish compatriots. Alexander was able to quash the uprising only through the use of his mercenary forces, an exercise that cost some six thousand Jews their lives.

After this incident, troubles continued as the ruler exhausted the nation's human and financial resources through his incessant wars. The internal opposition to him must have been strong and widespread because over a six-year period more than 50,000 Jews are said to have fallen victim to him (*War* 1.91; *Ant.* 13.376). When Jannaeus saw that his heavy-handed approach aroused only more hatred for him, he is supposed to have tried more conciliatory tactics, though the result was hardly what he intended: "But his change of policy and inconsistency of character only aggravated their hatred; and when he inquired what he could do to pacify them, they replied, 'Die; even death would hardly reconcile us to one guilty of your enormities.' They simultaneously appealed for aid to Demetrius, surnamed the Unready. Hopes of aggrandizement brought from him a prompt response. Demetrius arrived with an army, and the Jews joined their allies in the neighborhood of Sichem" (*War* 1.92; cf. *Ant.* 13.376). Again we should note that the opponents are not assigned a specific name; they are simply "the Jews."

Although Demetrius defeated Jannaeus in a battle, Josephus says that his Jewish allies soon abandoned the Seleucid monarch and that Alexander, who had fled to the hills, was joined by six thousand Jews who, for some reason, felt sorry for him. We do not know whether these six thousand were the same or even some of the same soldiers who had joined Demetrius and then left him. While these circumstances induced Demetrius to leave Judea, they did not improve relations between Jannaeus and parts of the Jewish population. Josephus tells of continued strife, with Alexander eventually killing large numbers of his enemies and confining the rest of them in a single city (identified differently in the two sources): "having subdued this town, he brought them up to Jerusalem as prisoners. So furious was he that his savagery went to the length of impiety. He had eight hundred of his captives crucified in the midst of the city, and their wives and children butchered before their eyes, while he looked on, drinking, with his concubines reclining beside him. Such was the consternation of the people that, on the following night, eight thousand of the hostile faction fled beyond the pale of Judaea; their exile was terminated only by Alexander's death" (*War* 1.97-98; see *Ant.* 13.380).

In *Antiquities* Josephus explains more fully why Jannaeus responded with such rage and cruelty to these opponents. In neither book does he name the foes, although in *Antiquities* he says they were among the most powerful of the rebels. He does, however, associate them specifically with the invitation to and invasion by Demetrius:

> This was the revenge he took for the injuries he had suffered; but the penalty he exacted was inhuman for all that, even though he had, as was natural, gone through very great hardships in the wars he had fought against them, and had finally found himself in danger of losing both his life and his throne, for they were not satisfied to carry on the struggle by themselves but brought foreigners as well, and at last reduced him to the necessity of surrendering to the king of the Arabs the territory which he had conquered in Moab and Galaaditis and the strongholds therein, in order that he might not aid the Jews in the war against him; and they committed countless other insulting and abusive acts against him. (*Ant.* 13.381-82)

Later in the *Antiquities* Josephus does provide enough information to identify the people he had crucified as Pharisees. On his deathbed Jannaeus acknowledged that his harsh treatment of the Pharisees was the root cause of his domestic troubles and that his wife, who was to succeed him as monarch, should allow the Pharisees to exercise power and even take revenge on his body, as he had abused the bodies of their deceased colleagues. And Pharisees figure in the story as the ones who were eager to win some belated justice for their fellows who had been hanged.

It is very likely that the incident of Alexander Jannaeus crucifying 800 of his opponents is the one to which the commentary on Nahum makes reference in speaking of hanging people alive. If this is true, then the historical evidence from Josephus, when combined with the statement in the commentary, allows one to identify the seekers of smooth things as Pharisees in a more secure way than the other Scrolls references do. Pharisees were the ones who induced Demetrius to invade Judea, and Pharisees were the ones Jannaeus crucified in such cruel fashion. These Pharisees are the ones the Commentary on Nahum calls "those who look for smooth things."

The identification of the Pharisees as the ones who look for smooth things receives confirmation elsewhere in the Scrolls. In at least one case they are accused of holding a legal position that the Pharisees seem to have held. According to the Damascus Document, a group it calls "the builders of the wall," another name for Pharisees, committed various offenses among which was fornication — a sin they considered one of the three traps of Belial. The text explains what the group meant by the charge of fornication: "And each man marries the daughter of his brother or sister, whereas Moses said, You shall not approach your mother's sister; she is your mother's near kin (Lev. 18:13). But although the laws of incest are written for men, they also apply to women. When, therefore, a brother's daughter uncovers the nakedness of her father's brother, she is (also his) near kin" (5.7-11; p. 131). The scroll forbids niece marriage, but later rabbis and presumably their predecessors, the Pharisees, permitted it. As a result, in attributing such a stance to a group called "builders of the wall" the Scrolls writer shows he is talking about Pharisees.

Comparing the way in which the Scrolls talk about the Pharisees with the way the Gospels present them, both bodies of literature are very critical of them but for different reasons. In the Gospels they are sticklers for legal detail, for putting their traditional understandings of the law above the weightier matters of religion; in the Scrolls they are criticized for not implementing the law in all its strictness, for looking for easy ways out of obeying it properly. The Pharisees could not win.

The legal stance of the Pharisees raises another point of importance in Scrolls studies. It is likely that they mention Sadducees (though not often) and call them by the code name "Manasseh." The group so designated appears to have been politically prominent (they have a kingdom). But what has interested experts in Jewish law to a greater degree than these few references is the fact that in rabbinic literature there are a small number of legal positions attributed to the Sadducees that agree with positions defended in the Scrolls. This has given rise to the suggestion that the community of the Scrolls were Sadducean in some sense (see chap. 2 C.1).

The evidence shows that the community of the Scrolls and the Sadducees took a similar, strict or severe approach to the law of Moses. Their approach may well have been a traditional one, while the Pharisees advocated a more flexible, milder approach, one more adaptable for practice by the wider population. If so, it is no wonder that the Pharisees are supposed to have been more influential in Jewish society than the Scrolls community or the Sadducees.

While it is important to recognize that the Scrolls community and the Sadducees took a similar stance on the law, they differed profoundly on theological matters. As we have seen. according to Josephus, the Sadducees denied what he calls fate or predetermination of events; the Scrolls indicate that the community had adopted a determinist theology. The Sadducees denied a resurrection would occur, whereas resurrection is mentioned in the Scrolls. And the Sadducees are supposed to have denied there were angels or spirits; the Scrolls refer to many of them. So, in theology the Scrolls group(s) were not Sadducees, though they may well have been akin to them in legal approach.

One conclusion worth stressing heavily is that the Scrolls have helped us to see in a clearer light that legal matters were of utmost importance for the different Jewish groups and were an integral part of their ways of being Jewish. They did arrive at their separate views on some theological points, but their stances on legal matters more clearly set them off from one another.

BIBLIOGRAPHICAL NOTES

For the history of the Qumran community, I have followed and modified aspects of the sketch appearing in my article "2 Maccabees 6,7A and Calendrical Change in Jerusalem," *Journal for the Study of Judaism* 12 (1981) 52-74. It is in part based on the work of Jerome Murphy-O'Connor, "Demetrius I and the Teacher of Righteousness," *Revue Biblique* 83 (1976) 400-420; and of Hartmut Stegemann, *Die Entstehung der Qumrangemeinde* (privately printed, Bonn, 1971).

The presence of King Jonathan in 4Q448 was proposed by E. and H. Eshel and A. Yardeni. They published the text in *Qumran Cave 4 VI Poetical and Liturgical Texts, Part 1* (ed. James VanderKam and Monica

Brady; Discoveries in the Judaean Desert 11; Oxford: Clarendon, 1998) 403-25.

Lawrence Schiffman analyzed the notions of the revealed and hidden commands in *The Halakhah at Qumran* (Leiden: Brill, 1975).

J. T. Milik first drew attention to the calendrical texts from Cave 4 in his *Ten Years of Discovery in the Wilderness of Judaea* (Studies in Biblical Theology 1/26; London: SCM, 1959).

The calendar texts were published in Shemaryahu Talmon, Jonathan Ben-Dov, and Uwe Glessmer, *Qumran Cave 4 XVI: Calendrical Texts* (Discoveries in the Judaean Desert 21; Oxford: Clarendon, 2001). See also my *Calendars in the Dead Sea Scrolls: Measuring Time* (The Literature of the Dead Sea Scrolls; London and New York: Routledge, 1998).

For messianism in the Scrolls and other texts, see John J. Collins, *The Scepter and the Star: The Messiahs of the Dead Sea Scrolls and Other Ancient Literature* (The Anchor Bible Reference Library; New York: Doubleday, 1995).

For a set of essays on central aspects of Qumran thought, see John J. Collins and Robert A. Kugler, eds., *Religion in the Dead Sea Scrolls* (Studies in the Dead Sea Scrolls and Related Literature; Grand Rapids: Eerdmans, 2000). Still useful is the older study, Helmer Ringgren, *The Faith of Qumran: Theology of the Dead Sea Scrolls* (Philadelphia: Fortress, 1963).

CHAPTER 5

The Scrolls and the Old Testament

One of the areas of study to which the Dead Sea Scrolls have made a profound contribution is the text of the Hebrew Bible (= Old Testament) and related issues. If the community of Qumran existed from about 100 B.C. until A.D. 68/70, its end came before most books of the New Testament were written. At that time, the only scriptures for those Jews who remained within their traditions as well as for those who believed Jesus to be the messiah were the books of the Hebrew Bible and perhaps a few other works also written by Jews. The Qumran community was dedicated to the daily study of scripture, and its library includes a number of commentaries on the biblical books. What have the Scrolls taught us about the Old Testament books that were so important to the community? The answer to that question can be divided into three parts: the text of the Hebrew scriptures; the development of some biblical books; and the issue of a canon.

A. THE TEXT OF THE HEBREW BIBLE/OLD TESTAMENT

The biblical scrolls have generated great excitement since the earliest days of Qumran studies. As already noted, among the first seven scrolls removed from Cave 1 were two copies of Isaiah. The one (called 1QIsa^a) was especially noteworthy as it contained the entire sixty-six chapters of the biblical book, minus a letter or two here and there. In fact, it is the most complete manuscript found in any of the caves. Once people had become convinced that the Qumran manuscripts came from the last three centuries B.C. and the first century A.D., they could hardly fail to recognize the immense potential of such finds for studying the wording of the biblical text. In order to understand the importance of the Scrolls in uncovering some of the history through which the Old Testament text has passed, we should examine the evidence for the wording of that text before the Qumran scrolls were found.

1. THE PERIOD OF THE HEBREW BIBLE/OLD TESTAMENT

There has been much debate about when different parts of the Old Testament were written. More conservative people, whether Jewish or Christian, have long believed that Moses wrote the first five books (Torah, Pentateuch). Even if one were to accept this conclusion (no direct evidence supports it), the matter of date would still not be settled because the time when Moses lived is also disputed. The two top candidates are the fifteenth and the thirteenth centuries B.C. The choice between these dates depends on how one interprets some biblical dates and various pieces of archeological evidence. While many people accept Mosaic authorship of the Pentateuch, many others (Jewish, Christian, or otherwise) hold that the first five books are composites written by various individuals at different times but that all these authors or editors lived long after the time of Moses. According to some who adhere to this latter view (often called the documentary hypothesis), the earliest of the major sources for the Pentateuch was written in the tenth-ninth and the latest in the sixth-fifth centuries B.C. It is likely — and this all admit — that some books (or parts of them) outside the Pentateuch such as Amos come from approximately the time when the prophets for whom they were named were active (the eighth century in Amos's case).

Another energetically debated point is which is the latest book of the Old Testament and when was it written. A traditional candidate has been Malachi, whose prophetic career is supposed to have taken place around 400 B.C. Many scholars, however, think that Daniel is the latest book and argue that the apocalyptic visions in Daniel 7–12 come from the 160s B.C. Whichever view one takes — whether the Old Testament was written between 1400/1200 and 400 B.C. or between 900/800 and 165 B.C. — all the books in it date from pre-Christian times and many of them from several centuries before the turn of the eras.

2. The Pre-Qumran Textual Witnesses

Even though the books of the Hebrew Bible were written well before the Christian or Common Era, we had no pre-Christian Hebrew copy of any of these books before the Dead Sea Scrolls were found. In fact, the territory of Israel had yielded hardly any manuscripts or fragments of any type that could be dated to that time. The Hebrew texts, which one would assume to be the most reliable witnesses to what the Old Testament books said originally, had been copied and recopied by hand through the centuries, but none of the earlier copies had survived.

a. The Masoretic Text

The traditional Hebrew text of the Bible is called the Masoretic Text. It is a carefully annotated product of a centuries-long tradition throughout which the sacred words were meticulously guarded, copied, and checked by Jewish experts. It includes two basic components: the consonants (almost all Hebrew texts were and still are written only with consonants) and vowels that were added to ensure correct reading of the words. Despite the respect and diligence with which it was transmitted, the earliest surviving copies of the Masoretic Text are the Cairo Codex of the Prophets from A.D. 895 and the Aleppo Codex (now partly destroyed), finished in approximately A.D. 925. Thus, if Daniel was completed in about 165 B.C., the Aleppo Codex was compiled some 1,090 years after the last book of the Hebrew Bible was written (Daniel, which is not classified among the Prophets in the Hebrew Bible, is not in the Cairo Codex of the Prophets). For the most ancient books of the Hebrew Bible the chronological gap is, of course, much greater. Depending on one's dating of the books, the most ancient copy of the Masoretic Text would range from about seventeen hundred to over two thousand years later than the time when the first book of the Hebrew Bible was composed. The time gap between composition and the earliest surviving copy was clearly enormous. In an age of hand copying, much could happen to a text in so many centuries — all of it bad.

b. The Septuagint

One set of textual witnesses does lie closer in time to when the books of the Hebrew Bible were composed than the Masoretic Text does, but it suffers from a different drawback — it is a translation. The books of the Hebrew Bible were translated into Greek, beginning apparently in the third century B.C. A story about the translation of the five books of Moses is preserved in a Greek work entitled the Letter of Aristeas. It tells how Ptolemy II Philadelphus (283-246 B.C.), the Greek king of Egypt, issued the appropriate commands and money to bring seventy-two Jewish scholars from Israel to Egypt to do the work of translating. The motive was to make the Law of Moses accessible to those who used the great library in Alexandria. The Letter of Aristeas contains too many improbable assertions for one to take it as literal history, but the time when it places the first translations may not be far from the truth, since we have evidence for Greek renderings of parts of the Bible by about 200 B.C. Over the next century or two all the books in the Hebrew Bible were translated into Greek and the whole was given the name Septuagint (= 70 in Latin, hence its abbreviation LXX) after the number of scholars who, according to the Letter of Aristeas, took part in the translation of the Law of Moses (two are omitted from the total of 72, presumably for the sake of convenience). As with the Hebrew Bible, the surviving copies of the Greek translation are much later than the times when the translating work was done. The earliest complete copies date from the fourth century A.D., although as noted above more ancient evidence exists for parts of it. Nevertheless, some of the Greek copies do bring us nearer to the time when the Hebrew texts were composed than the extant Hebrew copies do.

The Greek translations (there are several, all having their own histories of transmission and varieties of manuscripts) differ at times from the Masoretic Text. In fact, thousands of variations exist between them, but most of the differences are quite minor, ones that would not be noticed by the casual reader of the Bible. For example, the Greek might read the word *the* with a noun and the Hebrew lack it, or the two versions might spell a name somewhat differently. At other times they differ in more significant ways. A clear and consistent case is found in Genesis 5, the genealogy of the patriarchs who lived before the flood. They lived more than nine hundred years in most instances. If one compares the ages of each of these individuals at the birth of his first son as given in the

Hebrew and in the Greek versions, one notices that the Greek often gives a larger number, usually higher by one hundred years. The result is that for the period before the flood the Masoretic Text allows 1,656 years, but the Septuagint has 2,242 (other textual traditions have only 1,307). More examples of this type are that the Greek has an extra generation between Adam and Abraham in comparison with the Hebrew text (an extra Kenan in Gen 10:24; 11:12); and the Greek has 151 rather than 150 poems in the book of Psalms. The largest way in which the Hebrew and Greek differ is in having variant versions for entire books. The clearest one is Jeremiah. The fifty-two-chapter Hebrew version is much longer than the Greek translation, which reproduces a text equivalent to only about seven-eighths of the Masoretic text.

An obvious question raised by the many differences, large and small, between the two is: which text is better, the Hebrew or the Greek? One would naturally favor the Hebrew, since Hebrew is the original language of almost all books in the Old Testament (parts of Daniel and Ezra are in Aramaic). Indeed, the Hebrew often is at times preferable, although in some cases the Greek is clearly superior. Yet, to say that the Hebrew is often superior still leaves open the question of the source for the Greek (and Hebrew) deviations. Did the translator make a mistake? Or did he invent a reading that seemed better to him for one reason or another (perhaps he thought the text he was translating made no sense so he "corrected" it)? Did a copyist later misunderstand or mistranscribe the text? Or did the translator have in front of him a Hebrew text that differed somewhat from the reading preserved in the Masoretic Text? Before the Dead Sea Scrolls were found, there were few external data to offer controls for answering queries of these kinds and thus determine what was the preferred reading in a particular case.

c. The Samaritan Pentateuch

A third important textual witness is the Samaritan Pentateuch, the complete Bible of the Samaritan community. As the term *pentateuch* indicates, it contains only the five books of Moses. It is a Hebrew text that is often the same as the Masoretic Text; although it differs from the Masoretic Text in some six thousand readings, most of these are minor matters such as different spellings of words. For some nineteen hundred of these six thousand variants, the Samaritan Pentateuch agrees with the

Septuagint. It also contains a few extra statements that Samaritans obviously added for ideological reasons to provide authority for Mount Gerizim, their holy place. A glaring example is an addition to the two forms of the Ten Commandments (Exodus 20 and Deuteronomy 5): the Samaritan text has extra material, taken from Deut 27:2, 3a, 4-7, and 11:30, so that the command to build an altar on Mount Gerizim (Deut 27:4; this version names Gerizim, whereas the Masoretic Text has Ebal) becomes one of the Ten Commandments. It seems now that the Samaritan Pentateuch began its independent development in the second century B.C. The earliest existing copies of it are, however, from the Middle Ages.

3. QUMRAN CONTRIBUTIONS

Thus, before 1947 scholars had the Masoretic Text, the Septuagint, and the Samaritan Pentateuch, all of which are preserved in copies made well after the Common Era (that is, the A.D. years) began. The Qumran biblical manuscripts now furnish copies of scriptural books written in their original languages and dating from the last centuries B.C. or the first century A.D. They are consequently far and away the oldest copies of biblical books in our possession and, in most cases, are in the original language. What do they indicate about the text of the Hebrew Bible?

a. The Great Isaiah Scroll

Once scholars had had opportunity to study the great Isaiah scroll from Cave 1 (1QIsaᵃ, copied in approximately 100 B.C.) and to compare it with the Masoretic Text, they were impressed with the results. Despite the fact that the Isaiah scroll was about a thousand years older than the earliest surviving copy of the Masoretic version of Isaiah, the two were usually in very close agreement except for small details that rarely affect the meaning of the text. One interesting variant occurs in Isa 6:3. In the Masoretic Text, the seraphim in the heavenly throne room call to one another: "Holy, holy, holy is the Lord of hosts"; the Isaiah scroll reads: "Holy, holy is the Lord of hosts." In some instances the Isaiah scroll seemed superior, in others the Masoretic Text did. The results obtained from comparative studies of this kind have been repeated for many other scriptural books represented at Qumran. Many of the new scrolls do belong to the same textual tradition as the Masoretic Text. They are, however, centuries older and thus demonstrate in a forceful way how carefully Jewish scribes transmitted that text across the years.

b. Qumran Agreements with the Septuagint against the Masoretic Text

Nevertheless, in some cases the situation is different. Textual critics have catalogued a number of passages in which the Masoretic Text and the Septuagint disagree and where a Qumran Hebrew manuscript agrees with the Septuagint. Such instances are important for textual critics because they show that in these examples at least the Greek translators did not invent their variant readings. Rather, they were translating a Hebrew text that differed from the Masoretic Text. This is the case not only for small details that may interest textual critics alone but also for larger deviations. Which reading may be preferable is another matter. But just to have established that many Septuagint variants from the Masoretic Text reflect *Hebrew* variants is a noteworthy contribution. The next paragraphs provide a few examples of smaller and larger cases in which a Qumran manuscript agrees with one or more Greek witnesses against the Masoretic Text.

(1) Minor Examples

A clear case of a minor variant comes from a manuscript of Exodus. Exod 1:5 tells how many of Jacob's descendants came with him to Egypt. For the total the textual witnesses line up as follows:

Masoretic Text:	70 descendants
Septuagint:	75 descendants
4QExod[a]	75 descendants

Those who are familiar with the New Testament will recall that in his last speech the deacon and martyr Stephen recounted Israelite history and mentioned that Joseph invited Jacob and all his relatives to come to Egypt, 75 in all (Acts 7:14). A slightly different way of counting Jacob's family members may underlie the Acts passage, but the Qumran copy makes clear that at least one Hebrew text had the number 75 at Exod 1:5, as does the Septuagint (which may have been the Bible used by the writer of Acts).

A second illustration is found in Deut 32:8, where the Masoretic Text reads:

When the Most High apportioned the nations,
    when he divided humankind,
he fixed the boundaries of the peoples
    according to the number of *the sons of Israel.*
                              (NRSV, modified at the end)

For the italicized words most Greek manuscripts have "angels of God" and a few read "sons of God." 4QDeut[j] preserves the reading "sons of God." Here the reading in the Masoretic Text ("the sons of Israel") may represent a theologically motivated change from an earlier phrase: the reading "sons of God" refers in this context to divine beings, whom the uninformed reader might consider lesser gods — a thought precariously close to polytheism. As recent translators have recognized, the reading of the Septuagint, now supported by a Qumran copy of Deuteronomy, is preferable, since it is easier to explain why someone might change "sons of God" (a theologically suspect phrase) to "sons of Israel" than it would be to account for the reverse.

(2) Major Examples

Not only do the Qumran scrolls indicate that small variants in the Septuagint at times rest on different Hebrew models; a few of them do the same for larger ones, such as different versions of an entire section or even of a whole book.

(a) Jeremiah I indicated above that the book of Jeremiah is about one-eighth shorter in the Septuagint than in the Masoretic Text. Among the six copies of Jeremiah recovered from the caves, some manuscripts clearly have the longer form of the text as known in the Masoretic text, and one (the second copy in Cave 4) just as clearly has the shorter version as attested in the Septuagint. This last-named manuscript provides some words from, among other places, Jer 10:3-11. There the Septuagint lacks what the Hebrew has in verses 6-8, 10; enough of the Qumran copy survives to demonstrate that it lacks the same verses. Emanuel Tov of the Hebrew University of Jerusalem has provided a translation that indicates clearly what the situation is. The words printed in regular type are shared by the three witnesses (Masoretic Text, Septuagint, and 4QJer[b]); those in italics are not present in the Greek and in the Qumran copy (which must in part be restored).

3 For the laws of the nations are delusions. For one cuts down a tree in the forest, the work of a craftsman's hands, with an axe. 4 He adorns it with silver and gold; he fastens it with nails and hammer, so that it cannot totter. 5 They are like a scarecrow in a cucumber field, they cannot speak. They have to be carried, because they cannot walk. Be not afraid of them, for they cannot do evil, nor is it in them to do any good. 6 *There is none like You, O Lord. You are great, and Your name is great in might. 7 Who would not revere You, O king of the nations? For that is Your due. For among all the wise of the nations, and in all their kingdoms, there is none like You. 8 But they are altogether dull and foolish; the instruction of idols (?) is but wood!* 9 Beaten silver is brought from Tarshish, and gold from Uphaz, the work of a craftsman, and of the goldsmith's hands; violet and purple is their clothing; they are all the work of skilled men. 10 *But the Lord is the true God, he is a living God, and the everlasting king; at His wrath the earth trembles, and the nations cannot endure His rage.* 11 Thus shall you say to them: "The gods who did not make heaven and earth, shall perish from the earth and from under these heavens."

The contents of the verses that are in the Masoretic Text but not in the other two versions (the words in italics) suggest that the textual variation here is not a result of mere scribal negligence. The extra verses in the Masoretic version of the Hebrew text (other than v. 8) center on the praise of the Lord, while the part of the passage shared by all three witnesses attacks the idols of the nations. It is possible that the Masoretic version here is the product of literary expansion. If so, the shorter text in the Greek and the Qumran fragment would have a stronger claim to originality. In a case like this, however, we are not dealing with variant texts that grew casually — through copying errors — but probably with two versions of a passage that had their own literary histories. The statements praising the Lord seem to have been added purposefully by a writer as he was dealing with the words of Jeremiah. Those additions were not in the manuscript translated by the scholar who rendered this part of Jeremiah into Greek. The Qumran fragment now confirms that such shorter Hebrew copies did indeed exist.

(b) Samuel The books of Samuel are represented on four copies from Qumran, including 4QSam[b], which may be the oldest or second-oldest biblical manuscript from the caves (from the third century B.C.). These copies have received extensive study because they clarify some of the complicated history that the text of 1–2 Samuel has experienced in the different traditions. We need not enter into the details of that analysis here, but it is instructive to examine the evidence for the story about David and Goliath (1 Samuel 17). The form of the Hebrew found in the Masoretic Text devotes fifty-eight verses to the story; the Septuagint has only thirty-three verses: 1-11, 32-40, 42-49, and 50-54. The major section not found in the Greek — verses 12-31 — tells of Jesse's sending David to his brothers who were serving in Saul's army, his arrival there, his hearing Goliath's taunt to the Israelite soldiers, the reward promised by King Saul, and the embarrassment that David's boast caused to his brother Eliab. The other large difference is at the end, where the Greek version lacks the curious report in the Hebrew text that Saul, even though he had by this time met David at least twice, still did not know who he was.

Little from this chapter is preserved in the Samuel scrolls. One detail, however, is interesting. The Masoretic Text introduces Goliath thus: "And there came out from the camp of the Philistines a champion named Goliath, of Gath, whose height was six cubits and a span" (17:4). Since a cubit is roughly 18 inches and a span is a half cubit, Goliath's height was nine feet nine inches. In some of the major Greek manuscripts, Goliath shrinks to a mere four cubits and a span — six feet nine inches (no text gives David's height). The first copy of Samuel from Cave 4 also reads *four* as the number of cubits in Goliath's stature. Yet, though the Qumran manuscript agrees with the Greek reading for this detail, it apparently does not support the drastically shorter Greek text for the entire chapter. Calculations of how much text the manuscript would have contained if all of it had survived show that it read a longer version, such as the one in the Masoretic Text.

166

c. An Unusual Case

A further example involves a passage that may have disappeared from all biblical copies and is now preserved in one Qumran scroll. 1 Samuel 11 mentions Nahash, king of the Ammonites. He offered to make a treaty with the Israelite residents of Jabesh-gilead on the condition that he be allowed to gouge out the right eye of each person in the city. The men of the city requested assistance from the newly crowned King Saul, and he rescued them from a grisly fate. The Jewish historian Josephus, who provides so much information about the Essenes, wrote a lengthy history of his people entitled *Jewish Antiquities*. In the first half of it he summarizes the biblical story line, including the Nahash incident. But at this point he gives more information than the traditional text does.

> However, a month later, he [Saul] began to win the esteem of all by the war with Naas [Nahash], king of the Ammonites. For this monarch had done much harm to the Jews who had settled beyond the river Jordan, having invaded their territory with a large and warlike army. Reducing their cities to servitude, he not only by force and violence secured their subjection in the present, but by cunning and ingenuity weakened them in order that they might never again be able to revolt and escape from servitude to him; for he cut out the right eyes of all who either surrendered to him under oath or were captured by right of war. This he did with intent — since the left eye was covered by the buckler — to render them utterly unserviceable. (*Antiquities* 6.68-71)

The text then moves to the Jabesh-gilead episode. Some of the additional material recorded by Josephus has now been found in a Qumran manuscript of the books of Samuel (4QSam^a). It appears quite possible that the other ancient versions of the Bible lack the extra section because a mechanical or scribal error occurred at some point in the transmission of the text. If one compares the New Revised Standard Version — the first Bible translation to incorporate the extra paragraph — with any other translation of the end of 1 Samuel 10, the additional passage is immediately obvious, since it is set off from the context as a separate paragraph without a verse number:

> Now Nahash, king of the Ammonites, had been grievously oppressing the Gadites and the Reubenites. He would gouge out the

right eye of each of them and would not grant Israel a deliverer. No one was left of the Israelites across the Jordan whose right eye Nahash, king of the Ammonites, had not gouged out. But there were seven thousand men who had escaped from the Ammonites and had entered Jabesh-gilead.

The trigger for omission of this paragraph from the versions of 1 Samuel was the presence of two phrases, one coming just before this paragraph ("But he held his peace," 10:27) and one just after it ("About a month later," 11:1, lacking in the Masoretic Text but found in some Greek copies). In Hebrew the two phrases look almost the same. It appears that a scribe skipped from the end of the first to the end of the second, and in this way he omitted the paragraph that came between them. One can account for the situation in other ways, but the explanation presented here seems most likely. The extra material furnishes a suitable context for understanding what Nahash proposed to do to the residents of Jabesh in Gilead.

d. Theories about Textual Development

What is one to make of all the new textual evidence from Qumran? How should one assess its relation with the other ancient versions of the Bible? In the light of the Qumran texts, the experts have formulated several theories about the way in which the different textual traditions of the Hebrew Bible came into being. I note three here.

(1) A Theory of Local Texts

Following the lead of his mentor William Foxwell Albright (who recognized the antiquity of the Scrolls in 1948), Frank Moore Cross of Harvard University elaborated the thesis that the different traditions for the first five books of the Bible represented by the Masoretic Text, the Septuagint, and the Samaritan Pentateuch evolved naturally in geographically separated areas. The Hebrew Bible was written in Palestine (or at least most of it was), where it continued to be studied and copied over the centuries. The Samaritan Pentateuch (minus its specifically sectarian additions) is the prime representative of this Palestinian family of texts. Jews carried the scriptural texts to Babylon and later to Egypt — two places with large Jewish communities. In each of these localities, as the texts were copied by hand over the centuries, variations arose through normal scribal labors and mistakes. Although the sources have left no data about the history of the biblical text in Babylonia, it is reasonable, Cross thinks, to suppose that the Masoretic Text is the result of the process through which the Hebrew Bible passed within the large Jewish community in Babylon. The situation is quite different for Egypt, where information is more plentiful. The Septuagint was the work of some Jewish residents of Egypt who, beginning in the third century B.C., translated a Hebrew text that was available to them there. The base text came from Palestine. Not only do our sources indicate this provenance; the Septuagint itself implies it because it agrees with the Samaritan Pentateuch in many cases (about 1,900) in which both disagree with the Masoretic Text. Thus, the first five books of the Septuagint are more closely related to the Samaritan (a Palestinian representative) than to the Masoretic (Babylonian) Pentateuch. Examples of all three text types were eventually brought to Palestine and began to influence one another. The presence of the three kinds at Qumran is proof that the Babylonian and Egyptian types had arrived in Palestine before the Christian era (see the diagram below for a visual representation of these points).

Century B.C.

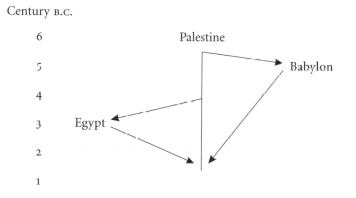

(2) A Theory of Textual Plurality and Variety

A second theory, which we may associate with Emanuel Tov, explains the evidence differently. Tov does not find only three basic types of texts for the Pentateuch as Cross does. Rather, he draws attention to the great diversity among the many manuscripts, no two of which are exactly alike. He believes there were few allied classes of manuscripts — that is, ones that were extremely closely related to one another and different from all others; we have many copies that differ more or less from one another and that do not fall neatly into the three categories of Cross's hypothesis.

Tov speaks of five groups of Qumran texts (note the restriction to Qumran), four of which — numbers 1, 3, 4, 5 — were not known to scholars before the Qumran biblical manuscripts became available.

1. Texts written in the special Qumran practice (that is, ones with the styles of spelling, grammatical formation, and writing characteristic of the Qumran texts and no other group). These texts tend to have numerous errors and corrections and may have been copied from texts that resemble the later Masoretic Text. (no percentage given)

2. Proto-Masoretic texts, which resemble very closely the consonants of the later Masoretic Text — 47% of the biblical manuscripts.

3. Pre-Samaritan texts, which are very similar to the later Samaritan Pentateuch but without the special Samaritan additions — about 6.5% (of scrolls with pentateuchal books).

4. Texts close to the presumed Hebrew source for the Septuagint. Tov finds the manuscripts classified here to be a less closely knit collection — about 3.3%.

5. Nonaligned texts, which exhibit no consistent patterns of agreement or disagreement with other witnesses — the remaining 47%.

(The percentages do not total 100 because the third category is calculated for only a part of the manuscripts.)

Tov's five groups are helpful in some respects but problematic in others. The first (texts written in the special Qumran practice) is not a textual type, only a manner of writing found in the manuscripts grouped here. The percentage of biblical scrolls falling in category 2 is inflated: he counts as specifically Proto-Masoretic the copies that agree with both the Masoretic Text and the Samaritan Pentateuch, but they could as well be placed in category 3 (Pre-Samaritan Texts) because the Masoretic Text and Samaritan Pentateuch almost always offer the same reading. As a result, the percentage for category 3 is correspondingly deflated; it contains scrolls that side with the Samaritan Pentateuch only when they agree with it in readings that differ from those in the Masoretic Text — a rather small number of readings.

(3) Successive Literary Editions

Eugene Ulrich has proposed a history of textual development involving what he calls successive literary editions of individual books — a development in stages that was different for each book or set of books. The literary editions of the individual works resulted when an author or scribe intentionally revised a text in light of his circumstances and times (see, for example, the differing editions of Jeremiah). Often a newer edition replaced older ones but not always. Ulrich calls the editions, as they changed over time, text traditions, unified by their agreements on patterns of textual variants. If one compares the editions with others available at the same time, they are text types.

Each of these theories has its strengths and all point to a fundamental fact: there were different forms of the texts of the scriptural books that circulated in antiquity. Much like modern translations of the Bible differ in wording from one another, ancient copies of the scriptural works were not the same. At times the differences could be sizable. Textual uniformity was not a feature of the Second Temple period. Variant editions of books could even be found in the same place (e.g., Qumran). There are indeed many variants between copies, but they are regularly not of a sort that affect the meaning of the text.

The scrolls found in the caves near Khirbet Qumran have provided the scholars who study the wording of the books in the Hebrew Bible with a vast amount of new information about those works and the early history of copying through which they passed.

B. NEW INFORMATION ABOUT THE HISTORY OF SOME TEXTS

The Qumran biblical manuscripts, then, show us a time when at least some books circulated in different versions, and the sundry copies of scriptural books had assorted variant readings. But they contribute more than text-critical details: they — and occasionally nonbiblical works — also give a rare glimpse into the development of some scriptural books and sections. Jeremiah could be discussed here, but for the sake of variety I describe two other examples in this section, one arising from data in biblical manuscripts, the other from information in an extrabiblical text.

1. THE BOOK OF PSALMS

One should recall that more manuscripts of the book of Psalms have been identified at Qumran than of any other scriptural work. The Scrolls now appear to have preserved two versions of the Psalter. One version, attested in most of the copies, belongs in the tradition that would culminate in the Masoretic Text. That is, in this version the psalms appear in the order and form that they have in the traditional Hebrew text and consequently in all the modern translations made from it. But the familiar form seems not to have been the only shape the Psalter took in antiquity. I have already noted that in the Septuagint the book has 151 psalms, not 150 as in the traditional Hebrew text. Psalm 151 has now been found among the Scrolls — in Hebrew. It is part of the large Psalms scroll removed from Cave 11 (11QPs^a). In that scroll the psalm occurs in the last position, just as it does in the Greek Psalter. It is a psalm that focuses on David — his selection by God, his work as a shepherd, and his defeat of Goliath. The Greek version of the psalm reads thus:

I was small among my brothers,
and the youngest in my father's house;
I tended my father's sheep.
My hands made a harp;
my fingers fashioned a lyre.
And who will tell my Lord?
The Lord himself; it is he who hears.
It was he who sent his messenger
and took me from my father's sheep,
and anointed me with his anointing oil.
My brothers were handsome and tall,
but the Lord was not pleased with them.
I went out to meet the Philistine,
and he cursed me by his idols.
But I drew his own sword;

> I beheaded him, and took away disgrace from the people
> of Israel.
>
> (NRSV)

The Qumran version has a somewhat different wording but the same contents. Because of Psalm 151, the scroll, which elsewhere also has a stronger Davidic emphasis than the Masoretic book of Psalms, ends with a poem about the dominant human character in the Psalter, the traditional author of the whole collection.

But the remarkable Psalms scroll from Cave 11 may provide more information about the growth of the Psalter than the relatively minor fact that it, like the Greek, has Psalm 151. Scholars have long debated what the Cave 11 Psalms scroll was intended to be. Is it a private or at least special collection of psalms that were chosen for a specific purpose (for example, private use, group study)? Or is the collection of poems on a par with the other manuscripts that attest the Psalter best known in the Masoretic Text? To put it differently, was it considered an authoritative, scriptural compilation of psalms, or did the person who collected the poems in it regard it as a different kind of psalm anthology? Another question is: how can we tell the difference? Such queries arise because the arrangement and even the contents of the psalms on the scroll are far different from any other version known from antiquity. The twenty-seven surviving columns contain passages in this order (using their Masoretic numbers; in some cases verses are missing because the scroll is damaged or lost in that place, not because they would have been lacking from the complete scroll):

101:1-8
102:1-2, 18-29
103:1
109:21-31
105:25-45
146:9-10
148:1-12
121:1-8
122:1-9
123:1-2
124:7-8
125:1-5

126:1-6
127:1
128:4-6
129:1-8
130:1-8
131:1
132:8-18
119:1-6, 15-28, 37-49, 59-73, 82-96, 105-20, 128-42, 150-64, 171-76
135:1-9, 17-21
136:1-16, 26b (?)
118:1, 15, 16, 8, 9, 29
145:1-7, 13-21
154 (attested previously only in a Syriac-language translation of the
    Bible)
Plea (Prayer) for Deliverance
139:8-24
137:1, 9
138:1-8
Sir 51:13-20b, 30
Apostrophe to Zion
93:1-3
141:5-10
133:1-3
144:1-7, 15
Psalm 155 (known only in Syriac)
142:4-8
143:1-8
149:7-9
150:1-6
Hymn to the Creator
2 Sam 23:7
David's Compositions (the only prose section)
140:1-5
134:1-3
151

Several features of the Psalms scroll are curious when compared
with the familiar Psalter. First, the order is different. Roughly speaking,
it is: 101–3, 109, 105, 146, 148, 121–32, 119, 135–36, 118, 145, 154, a new com-

position, 139, 137, 138, Sirach 51, a new composition, 93, 141, 133, 144, 155, 142–43, 149–50, a new composition, 2 Sam 23:7, a new composition, 140, 134, 151. It clearly shares some ordered clusters of psalms with the traditional Psalter (101–3, 121–32, 135–36, 142–43, 149–50), but the others vary greatly from the Masoretic arrangement. Such deviation comes in addition to many minor textual variants. Second, the Cave 11 Psalms scroll contains nine texts not present in the Masoretic Psalter: three were known from other versions of the Psalter (Psalms 151 and 154–55), two from other books (2 Sam 23:7, from the last words of David; and Sirach 51), and the other four are texts previously unattested (Plea for Deliverance, Apostrophe to Zion, Hymn to the Creator, and David's Compositions). All the new works appear in the second half of the scroll. One of them is not even a poem — the list of David's writings. How are we to assess the evidence?

One should keep in mind a few facts about the Cave 11 Psalms scroll. First, all the psalms preserved on it come from the last two of the five books that make up the Psalter (in the Psalter, book one is Psalms 1–42, book two Psalms 42–72, book three Psalms 73–89, book four Psalms 90–106, and book five Psalms 107–50 [or 151]). The Qumran Psalms scrolls in general show that the order of poems in the first three books was much more firmly fixed at the time of the community than the order for Psalms 90–150/151. Consequently, the difference in order in the Cave 11 Psalms scroll, taken by itself, is not a decisive argument against its official or authoritative character, since all these psalms appear in parts of the Psalter where greater sequential fluctuation is the norm. It could simply be one witness that testifies to the fact that the last two books of Psalms took different shapes in different copies. Second, there are other copies of this type of Psalms scroll — a second from Cave 11 and another from Cave 4. Hence, one should not dismiss the Cave 11 text as purely idiosyncratic. It has allies.

That the Psalter attested in 11QPs[a] is now available in more than one copy adds to the likelihood that it is indeed an official book of Psalms. It seems that the Psalms scroll allows us to be privy to a time in the development of the Psalter when the order of the units and, to some extent, even the units themselves in books four and five fluctuated considerably. The Psalms scroll from Cave 11 and its allies are prime examples of how much some Psalters disagreed with others in sequence and even in content.

Could an official Psalter have contained a prose section such as "David's Compositions"? It is certainly surprising to find it in the Cave 11 copy, but one could defend its presence as part of a scriptural collection of psalms. The focus on David in the scroll is stronger than in the Masoretic Psalter. Perhaps "David's Compositions" functioned like a general title, much as many of the psalms have titles (some of which appear in the Qumran text). Those titles are not poetic, just as "David's Compositions" is not.

The result is that the Scrolls show how a single community could have two versions of the Psalter in its possession. This circumstance would entail that much about the Psalter was not finalized by the mid-first century A.D. — the date of the first Cave 11 Psalms scroll. Variation in order existed almost exclusively in the last two books of the Psalter, while the first three appear to have been much more firmly fixed. We cannot determine whether other groups in Judaism at the time had variant Psalters because we have no evidence for their views on the matter.

2. DANIEL 4

The book of Daniel provides a different kind of example. It is well attested at Qumran, and all copies of it evidence the sort of text found in the Masoretic tradition. This is a point of some interest because Daniel appears in two or more forms in the ancient versions. The Masoretic Text has twelve chapters, while the Septuagint contains these and several additions: Susanna (sometimes numbered as chap. 13); the Prayer of Azariah and the Song of the Three Young Men (68 verses inserted between Dan 3:23 and 3:24); Bel and the Dragon (sometimes numbered as chap. 14). None of these extra passages has surfaced in a Daniel manuscript from Qumran or in any separate work. One or two texts appear to have points of similarity, but none of them is a copy of Susanna, Bel and the Dragon, or the Prayer/Song addition in chap. 3. They remain attested only in Greek manuscripts and in translations dependent on the Greek.

Nevertheless, Daniel stories were of great interest at Qumran. Eight copies of the book have been found. To these one should add some other Daniel tales, including four texts from Cave 4: 4Q243-45, designated as copies of a pseudo-Daniel text, and 4Q246, which also belongs in the orbit of Daniel literature. All four fragmentary manuscripts are written in the Aramaic language, as are large parts of Daniel in the Masoretic Text (2:4b–7:28).

While these texts are interesting in their own right, a fifth Danielic work (4Q242) has fascinated scholars ever since it was published in 1956. It was given the title "The Prayer of Nabonidus":

> The words of the prayer uttered by Nabunai [[Nabonidus]] king of the l[and of Ba]bylon, [the great] king, [when he was afflicted] with an evil ulcer in Teiman by decree of the [Most High God].
> I was afflicted [with an evil ulcer] for seven years. . . and an exorcist pardoned my sins. He was a Jew from [among the children of the exile of Judah, and he said], "Recount this in writing to [glorify and exalt] the name of the [Most High God." And I wrote this]:
> "I was afflicted with an [evil] ulcer in Teiman [by decree of the Most High God]. For seven years [I] prayed to the gods of silver and gold, [bronze and iron], wood and stone and clay, because [I believed] that they were gods. . . ." (p. 573)

The picture of a Jewish man who dealt directly with a Babylonian king and urged him to glorify the true God after the Lord had punished the king naturally reminded scholars of the roles Daniel plays in the book named after him. Scholars zeroed in on Daniel 4, in which Nebuchadnezzar himself reports about his experience of living like an animal away from Babylon for seven "times" until he was restored to his royal position.

Nebuchadnezzar (605-562 B.C.) was the great Neo-Babylonian ruler whose troops conquered Judah and Jerusalem, destroyed the temple and the city, terminated the Davidic dynasty, and led thousands of Judeans to exile in the east. He became the most famous or notorious Babylonian ruler in Jewish literature. The book of Daniel tells several stories about him. Among his successors, the one who ruled longest was Nabonidus (556-539 B.C.), a curious monarch whom ancient authors portrayed in opposing ways. One of his deeds that caught the attention of those who chronicled his activity was his absence from the capital city for a number of years (the sources mention seven or ten) when he remained with his troops in Teiman in Arabia. The reason(s) for his journey no one knows fully. Not long after he returned to Babylon, the city and empire were taken by Cyrus (in 539 B.C.), the first ruler of the Persian Empire.

All the evidence supports the belief that the Prayer of Nabonidus is a Judaized refraction of the story about Nabonidus's peculiar stay in Teiman. The names of both the king and the city appear in the little text, and the person responsible for his healing was Jewish. Scholars have long suspected that Daniel 4 is another Jewish version of Nabonidus's stay in Teiman. Important changes took place, however, between the event and the form it takes in Daniel 4. For one, the king's name became *Nebuchadnezzar,* a much more famous monarch than Nabonidus; and the nature of his removal from Babylon is considerably different. The change of royal names reflects a commonly attested feature of folklore: a more famous individual tends to attract to him- or herself the traits or stories associated with less well-known people. Both the Prayer of Nabonidus and Daniel 4 offer a theological reason for the king's experience in Teiman: it was by decree of God. Yet the two describe that period of absence from Babylon in very different terms.

The Prayer of Nabonidus suggests the following development. Historical sources relate that King Nabonidus of Babylon was away from his capital city for seven or ten years. His opponents saw in the king's conduct an offense to the god Marduk and regarded the loss of his kingdom as Marduk's punishment on him. Nabonidus's controversial behavior soon became famous and served as the trigger for folkloric and native theological adaptations by subject peoples such as the Jews. The Prayer of Nabonidus reflects this stage in the evolution of the story. When its version of the story was fashioned, it was still tied to the last Neo-Babylonian king. But the God involved was already the deity whom Jews worshiped. Nabonidus's fame soon faded, however, and he was forgotten by the Jews, who had more reason to remember Nebuchadnezzar and what he had done to Jerusalem and Judah. The adaptable story about the less-familiar Nabonidus in Teiman became associated with the more-famous Nebuchadnezzar. This is the stage represented in Daniel 4. That is, the Prayer of Nabonidus may well show an earlier version of the story that eventually found its place in Daniel 4. The biblical version of the tale would, then, embody a later series of changes. Much of this reconstruction is hypothetical, but it does provide a plausible explanation for how the story in Daniel 4 came into being.

C. A CANON OF SCRIPTURE

One could distinguish several issues under this rubric, but the focus here is on what Second Temple literature and the Qumran texts tell us about the process through which different Jewish groups went in order to define the books that constituted their Bible. We should remember that speaking of *books* of the Bible is misleading since, in the Second Temple period, there were no books in the modern sense of the term. Texts had to be consulted on scrolls, and scrolls rarely contained more than one composition. Among the biblical scrolls found at Qumran, only a few preserve evidence that they contained two books: 4QGen-Exod[a], 4QpaleoGen-Exod[l], 4QExod-Lev[f], 4QLev-Num[a]; besides these there are copies of the Twelve Prophets (perhaps eight of them, though none of them contains fragments from each book). As a result, in thinking about a Bible one should imagine a collection of many scrolls, not a single book with numerous compositions between its two covers. Moreover, there were probably few scrolls in circulation. The time-consuming processes of procuring and preparing the writing material and having a text copied made scrolls expensive so that few could afford them, and not many people could have read them if they had them. It is likely that there were larger collections of scrolls in very few places. As a result, one would rarely have seen in one place all of the scrolls that might have constituted a full collection of sacred scriptures.

1. Evidence outside Qumran

No Jewish texts roughly contemporary with the Dead Sea Scrolls employ the word *canon* in the sense of an official, unchanging list of books that serve as the fundamental authority for a community. Beginning in the fourth century A.D., Christians used the Greek term in this sense. Although *canon* was not used earlier, we have strong reasons for thinking that most or all Jewish people considered some books divinely revealed and hence uniquely authoritative. The evidence does not permit one to say exactly which books those might have been in, say, 100 B.C., but a significant number elicited widespread agreement. Our information comes from a small series of texts that almost exhaust the explicit surviving evidence about the development of a Bible in Jewish circles.

a. The Prologue to Sirach (the Wisdom of Jesus ben Sira)

The wisdom book Sirach was written in Hebrew perhaps in 190 or 180 B.C. The grandson of the author translated Jesus ben Sira's tome into

Greek not long after 132 B.C. The translated form of the book is part of what Protestants call the Apocrypha and is in the Catholic Old Testament. The original composition furnishes some evidence about which works Jesus ben Sira considered authoritative. He commends devotion to the law of the Most High and study of wisdom, prophecies, parables, proverbs, and the like (39:1). More importantly, the sage composed a long poem in praise of famous men from biblical times (chaps. 44–50). The order in which he lauds the ancients discloses the sources from which he drew and the sequence in which he found them: he borrows from the five books of Moses, Joshua, Judges, 1–2 Samuel, 1–2 Kings (he offers some parallel material from Chronicles and Isaiah), Jeremiah, Ezekiel (Sir 49:9 may mention Job, but the text is problematic), the Twelve Prophets, and the books of Ezra and Nehemiah. If Chronicles (and possibly Job) were removed from the list, it would coincide with the order of the books in the Hebrew Bible. The only difference is that some books later accepted as canonical are absent (for example, Ruth, Song of Solomon, Esther). Since the famous heroes are the models admired by the writer, he seems to have attached a particular authority to the books in which he found records of their exploits and piety.

The first two paragraphs from the Prologue to the grandson's translation contain what seem to be three categories of books in which great teachings, worthy of diligent study, are found.

> Many great teachings have been given to us through the Law and the Prophets and the others that followed them, and for these we should praise Israel for instruction and wisdom. Now, those who read the scriptures must not only themselves understand them, but must also as lovers of learning be able through the spoken and written word to help the outsiders. So my grandfather Jesus, who had devoted himself especially to the reading of the Law and the Prophets and the other books of our ancestors, and had acquired considerable proficiency in them, was himself also led to write something pertaining to instruction and wisdom, so that by becoming familiar also with his book those who love learning might make even greater progress in living according to the law.
>
> You are invited therefore to read it with goodwill and attention, and to be indulgent in cases where, despite our diligent labor in translating, we may seem to have rendered some phrases imperfectly. For what was originally expressed in Hebrew does not have

exactly the same sense when translated into another language. Not only this book, but even the Law itself, the Prophecies, and the rest of the books differ not a little when read in the original.

In the late second century B.C., the grandson knows of a threefold division (some view it as a twofold division: Law and Prophets, Others) that constitutes the authoritative source for wisdom and instruction. He expresses this division in slightly different ways: (1) "the Law and the Prophets and the others"; (2) "the Law and the Prophets and the other books"; (3) "the Law itself, the Prophecies, and the rest of the books." While the first two categories are familiar and clear (though he does not say specifically which books belong in them), the third is remarkably imprecise ("the others," "the other books," "the rest of the books"). The last sentence quoted may imply that the translator put his grandfather's work on a level with those in the three divisions ("Not only this book, but even the Law . . ."). The same sentence also implies, incidentally, that Greek translations of all these books, including the grandfather's, were then available.

b. 2 Macc 2:13-15

Another of the apocryphal or biblical books, 2 Maccabees, contributes a statement that may have some significance for the question of what was thought to be authoritative literature. In the second letter that appears at the beginning of the book (written not much after 100 B.C.), the residents of Judea write to a certain Aristobulus and the Egyptian Jews (after mentioning biblical episodes in which fire descended from heaven):

> The same things are reported in the records and in the memoirs of Nehemiah, and also that he founded a library and collected the books about the kings and prophets, and the writings of David, and letters of kings about votive offerings. In the same way Judas [Judah the Maccabee] also collected all the books that had been lost on account of the war that had come upon us, and they are in our possession. So if you have need of them, send people to get them for you.

According to the writer, Nehemiah collected books in his time (the mid-fifth century B.C.) and Judah did the same in his day (about 166-161 B.C.).

What this collecting means is not said, but Nehemiah is credited with assembling particular kinds of books: "the books about the kings and prophets, and the writings of David, and letters of kings about votive offerings." It is tempting to see in these groupings the historical and prophetic books (Joshua, Judges, 1–2 Samuel, 1–2 Kings, and the prophets), the Psalms, and Ezra (which contains royal letters having to do with offerings in the temple). The author is, however, not explicit on the point.

c. Philo, *On the Contemplative Life* 25

Philo was a Jewish philosopher who lived in Alexandria, Egypt, from about 25/20 B.C. until around A.D. 50. In his treatise *On the Contemplative Life,* he describes a Jewish group in Egypt called the Therapeutae. They have been of particular interest to students of the Scrolls because they share a number of traits with the Essenes. Philo says of them:

> In each house there is a consecrated room which is called a sanctuary or closet and closeted in this they are initiated into the mysteries of the sanctified life. They take nothing into it, either drink or food or any other of the things necessary for the needs of the body, but laws and oracles delivered through the mouths of prophets, and psalms and anything else which fosters and perfects knowledge and piety.

Philo seems to be familiar with the categories mentioned by Jesus ben Sira's grandson: Philo's "laws" and "oracles . . . of prophets" sound very much like the grandson's "Law and Prophets," while Philo's "psalms and anything else" could correspond with the grandson's even less specific "the others." That "psalms" are mentioned before "anything else" may indicate that the book of Psalms was considered the most important or at least the first of the nonlegal, nonprophetic works.

d. Luke 24:44

In a section of Luke that is not paralleled in the other synoptic Gospels, the writer depicts a scene in which the resurrected Jesus appears to his eleven disciples, the travelers to Emmaus, and other friends. Once he had convinced them that he was not a ghost by eating some fish in their presence, he declared to them: "These are my words that I spoke to you while I was still with you — that everything written about me in the law of Moses, the prophets, and the psalms must be fulfilled." Jesus' intent here is to teach that all the scriptures spoke of the messiah's suffering, death, and resurrection. The sequel says as much: "Then he opened their minds to understand the scriptures" (v. 45). He was able to call to their attention all the scriptures by naming three categories: the law of Moses, the prophets, and the psalms. It is possible that the term *psalms* included more than the book of that name, although we have no proof that the writer of Luke intended it in this more inclusive sense.

e. Matt 23:35

Some have claimed that the way in which Jesus speaks of the unending history of righteous martyrdom implies that the first (Genesis) and last (2 Chronicles) books of the Hebrew Bible already occupied those positions in official lists late in the first century A.D. when Matthew was written. The text reads: "so that upon you may come all the righteous blood shed on earth, from the blood of righteous Abel to the blood of Zechariah son of Barachiah, whom you murdered between the sanctuary and the altar." Jesus mentions two examples: Abel's death is recorded in Gen 4:8, while that of Zechariah *son of Jehoiada* occurs in 2 Chr 24:20-22 (the Bible has no martyrdom of a Zechariah *son of Barachiah*; Zechariah son of Berechiah is the prophet whose words appear in the book that bears his name). Proponents of the view that Jesus' words have canonical significance insist that he selected examples from the first and last books of the Bible to imply that such conduct permeated the scriptures. This argument has some plausibility, especially since Jesus makes explicit that he is choosing cases from the beginning and the end ("all the righteous blood . . . , from . . . to"). If he wished to find examples from the earliest and latest points on the biblical *time line,* he would not have selected Zechariah, for there were later instances (for example, Gedaliah in 2 Kings 25:22-26). But, even if we were to grant the point, the statement in Matthew still does not say which books came between Genesis and 2 Chronicles in such lists.

f. 4 Ezra 14:23-48

4 Ezra, a Jewish book not in the Apocrypha but classified as one of the Pseudepigrapha, was written after A.D. 70, the year in which the Romans destroyed Jerusalem and the temple. It contains an extended meditation on the profound issues raised by the destruction. According to the author, the scriptures were also lost in the calamitous event so that they would have to be revealed once again if Israel was to enjoy their guidance. Ezra, the putative hero of the book, prayed that the Holy Spirit would inspire him to write all that had been recorded in God's law (used in a comprehensive sense for all of scripture). He prepared materials for the task, downed a powerful drink, and, with his spirit and mouth thus loosened, he dictated ninety-four books to five scribes without a break over a Mosaic forty-day period.

> And when the forty days were ended, the Most High spoke to me, saying, "Make public the twenty-four books that you wrote first, and let the worthy and the unworthy read them; but keep the seventy that were written last, in order to give them to the wise among your people. For in them is the spring of understanding, the fountain of wisdom, and the river of knowledge." And I did so. (14:45-48)

Much is implied in a few words. The number twenty-four is one enumeration of the books in the Hebrew Bible/Old Testament (modeled after the twenty-four letters in the Greek alphabet). Therefore, it is highly likely that the author is referring to the full Hebrew Bible when he speaks of the twenty-four books that Ezra wrote first. That they were transcribed at the beginning gives them a literal priority, but they are meant for a general audience ("the worthy and the unworthy"), not for the righteous alone. What, though, are the seventy books written later but intended for an exclusive audience, the ones described as sources of understanding, wisdom, and knowledge? It seems that in a sense the author gives them a higher status than the first twenty-four, that is, the scriptural books. It may be that the number seventy is a general one expressing the writer's conviction that many more books are inspired than the scriptural twenty-four but that special expertise is needed to interpret them properly. At the very least, the author did not limit the inspired writings to the twenty-four found in the Hebrew Bible.

g. Josephus, *Against Apion* 1.37-43

The historian wrote *Against Apion* in the 90s A.D. In it he defended the veracity of the ancient records in which one could read the history of his people and contrasted these records with those of the Greeks, which contradicted one another.

> Our books, those which are justly accredited, are but two and twenty, and contain the record of all time.
>
> Of these, five are the books of Moses, comprising the laws and the traditional history from the birth of man down to the death of the lawgiver. This period falls only a little short of three thousand years. From the death of Moses until Artaxerxes, who succeeded Xerxes as king of Persia, the prophets subsequent to Moses wrote the history of the events of their own times in thirteen books. The remaining four books contain hymns to God and precepts for the conduct of human life.
>
> From Artaxerxes to our own time the complete history has been written, but has not been deemed worthy of equal credit with the earlier records, because of the failure of the exact succession of the prophets. (1.38-41)

The number twenty-two is another of the more widely attested ways of counting the books in the complete Hebrew Bible (perhaps based on the Hebrew alphabet, which has twenty-two letters). The books of Moses are easily recognizable in Josephus's description — from Genesis through Deuteronomy, the last chapter of which recounts "the death of the lawgiver." The "prophets," in normal Jewish style, are the historical as well as the strictly prophetic works (Joshua–Kings, Isaiah–Malachi). The mention of Artaxerxes as the end point of the prophetic succession suggests strongly that Ezra and Nehemiah are included in these prophetic texts, since he is the latest Persian ruler named in them. The thirteen books may be: Joshua, Judges, 1 Samuel, 2 Samuel, 1 Kings, 2 Kings, Ezra-Nehemiah (one book?), Esther, Isaiah, Jeremiah, Ezekiel, Daniel, and the Twelve (Minor) Prophets (one book). The "remaining four books," containing "hymns and precepts," presumably include Psalms and Proverbs, possibly Job and Ecclesiastes.

These seven texts are the ones that speak most directly to the history of the canon. They indicate that their authors divided the sacred books into three categories: law, prophets, and the rest, the most famous of which was Psalms. A number of other texts not surveyed here mention just two categories: law and prophets. Only 4 Ezra and Josephus specify a number for the books (both apparently conforming to the number of letters in the alphabet), and Josephus alone furnishes enough hints to allow the reader to name practically all of his twenty-two books. Some uncertainty remains, nevertheless, about exactly which books are included for all the authors cited. Do any of them, for example, presuppose the Song of Solomon was among the sacred books? They indeed concur to a degree about a core of books (law and prophets with Psalms and perhaps some others), but unanimity about all details of a canon is not evident from the sources. One should also not forget that Judaism comprised different groups during the centuries covered by the texts quoted above. Pharisees and Sadducees may have disagreed about the precise contours of their scriptures, and the same may have been the case for other groups as well. We do not know when disputes regarding the canon ended generally in the Jewish communities. It has been customary to maintain that a so-called Council of Jamnia — a rabbinic gathering — made the final decisions about A.D. 90. Contemporary experts on canonical matters have, however, disproved that notion and have emphasized that the only canonically related discussions among the Jamnian leaders involved whether a book or two (Esther, for example) should actually be considered biblical. We have no evidence that the Jamnian rabbis either defined a canon or issued any authoritative decree about one. Some uncertainty about books such as Esther and the Song of Solomon seems to have continued well past A.D. 100.

2. Evidence from Qumran

The texts that were available before 1947 cast some light, however dim, on the growth of a canon of scripture, but they left many problems unresolved. Could books still be added to the scriptures in the last century B.C. and the first century A.D., and, if so, were they in fact added? Or did the process of defining a canon involve only excluding some books (such as Sirach) from a solid core that all accepted? Did all Jews agree with what the texts quoted above say, or do the authors reflect the views of smaller groups (or even private opinions)? More germane to the present purpose, do the texts from Qumran make any contributions to clarifying the murky history of canonical development? To the last question we can reply: they do make several contributions and at the same time raise some new questions. One of the scrolls — Some of the Works of the Torah (4QMMT) — has been thought to mention a threefold division of books that should by now be familiar: "[And furthermore] we [have written] to you that you should understand the Book of Moses and the Book[s of the Pr]ophets and Davi[d and all the events] of every age." (C 9-10; p. 227).

Eugene Ulrich, however, has made a convincing case that the full reading in this fragmentarily preserved context lacks a firm basis in the manuscript evidence. The words translated "the Book of Moses" / "and the Book[s" / and "of the Pr]ophets and Davi[d" are located on three separate pieces (4Q397 frgs. 18, 17, and 15). The question is whether they belong together. Fragment 17, which is small and has only the words "]in the Book[," is very uncertainly located. Consequently, the assertion that 4QMMT attests the three divisions of books — Moses, Prophets, David — rests on an insecure foundation.

a. Criteria

The first matter to resolve is to establish some criteria by which to tell whether the Qumranites considered a book scriptural. None of the Scrolls states flatly that a document is canonical, since no equivalent word is used. Whether there was a word corresponding to our term *Bible* is also not clear. In lieu of such markers, we are reduced to assembling clues that a book was considered especially *authoritative*. One way in which to do that is to check whether it is cited or named as an authority and how it is cited. For example, "thus says the Lord" is a helpful pointer. Another is to ask how the work in question presents itself. If a Qumran text quotes from book *X* as an authority and book *X* presents itself as a revelation from God, then we have a likely candidate for a book that the Qumran author considered ultimately authoritative. Another criterion is whether book *X* became the subject of a commentary of the *pesher* sort, that is, the ones whose authors find in the prophetic text God's blueprint for the last days. It is improbable that someone would comment on a book in *pesher* fashion if he thought it was just a good book, nothing out of the ordinary. One should also not forget that the commentaries may contain the inspired interpretations taught by the Teacher; if so, they would have claimed a particular authority.

b. Authoritative Books

Employing the criteria set forth above, we can identify a number of books that were considered supremely authoritative at Qumran.

(1) Books Quoted as Authorities

We find quotations from many of the biblical books in the Qumran corpus, although not from all. Words from them are at times introduced with formulae such as "for it was written in this way." One should note, however, that such introductions also occur with some books that did not become part of the Hebrew Bible (see below b.2).

A quick survey of the more completely preserved texts from Qumran provides a rough but apparently accurate picture of which books were believed to possess the greatest authority. The Rule of the Community (most fully preserved in 1QS), the Damascus Document (CD), the War Rule (1QM), the Florilegium (4QFlor), the Testimonia (4QTestim), and the Melchizedek text (11QMelch) *cite as authorities* the following books that eventually made up the Hebrew Bible (the books are listed in their order in many Hebrew Bibles; the lines separate the three major divisions: Law, Prophets, Writings):

Genesis	CD
Exodus	1QS, CD (2), 4QFlor, 4QTestim
Leviticus	CD (4), 11QMelch (2)
Numbers	CD (4), 1QM, 4QTestim
Deuteronomy	CD (8), 4QTestim (2), 11QMelch

Joshua	4QTestim
Judges	
1–2 Samuel	CD (?), 4QFlor (2)
1–2 Kings	
Isaiah	1QS (2), CD (6), 1QM, 4QFlor, 11QMelch (3)
Jeremiah	
Ezekiel	CD (3), 4QFlor
Hosea	CD (3)
Joel	CD

Amos	CD (2), 4QFlor
Obadiah	
Jonah	
Micah	CD (4)
Nahum	CD
Habakkuk	
Zephaniah	
Haggai	
Zechariah	CD
Malachi	CD, 4QFlor, 11QMelch (3)

Psalms	4QFlor (2), 11QMelch (3)
Proverbs	CD
Job	
Song of Solomon	
Ruth	
Lamentations	
Ecclesiastes	
Esther	
Daniel	4QFlor, 11QMelch
Ezra	
Nehemiah	
1–2 Chronicles	

The Damascus Document makes the most extensive use of scriptural passages, but the other texts have enough examples to make the survey more representative. The results are instructive: all the books of the Law serve as proof texts, Isaiah does so more than any other book, and other prophetic books serve in a similar capacity (Ezekiel, Hosea, Amos, Micah, Zechariah, and Malachi). The historical books are rarely used in such contexts, while the shortest prophetic books and most of the Writings (other than Psalms and Daniel, with Proverbs) do not function as sources for proof texts. Surprisingly, Jeremiah is not cited as an authority, although the Damascus Document (col. 8) mentions him and texts dealing with Jeremiah turned up in Cave 4. The absence of other books from the list does not mean that they were unimportant or that the writers did not refer to them. It means only that they are not quoted in support of points that these particular authors were making. But the fact that, apart from one use of Proverbs, only the Psalms, the most popular biblical book at Qumran, and Daniel, also well known there, serve as proof texts among the Writings suggests that if a writer wished to find strong support for his case, he was more likely to turn to the Law and Prophets than to the Writings.

A few of the formulae that introduce the quotations merit mention. Damascus Document column 3 cites Deut 9:23 with the words "He said to them." In the sequel the "He" is identified as "their Maker." Damascus Document 6.13 quotes from Mal 1:10 and prefaces it with "as God said." The same work (19.11-12) has a passage from Ezekiel accompanied by "which [He] said by the hand of Ezekiel" — where the "He" is obviously God (in Vermes's translation "God" is the subject). Damascus Document 8.9-10 adduces words from Deut 32:33 with "of whom God said." In a poem addressed to God, the author of the War Rule (col. 11) considers Num 24:17-19 and Isa 31:8 God's revelation.

Next, one should recall that several biblical books were the subjects of commentaries at Qumran: Isaiah (6 commentaries), Psalms (3), Hosea (2), Micah (2), Zephaniah (2), Nahum (1), and Habakkuk (1). Thus, one could add Zephaniah and Habakkuk to the list of works whose texts were clearly authoritative at Qumran.

At least for those books that served as scripture at Qumran, we can say that they present themselves explicitly as divine revelation (the prophetic books, for example) or contain substantial amounts of material identified as the words of God (the books of the Law, the historical books).

If other criteria were used, one would perhaps have to add more books to the list. For example, some have said that Chronicles was probably regarded as scriptural at Qumran because the group accepted the division of the priests into twenty-four shifts, as stipulated in 1 Chr 24:7-18. The conclusion may not follow, however, because the twenty-four groups had certainly become traditional by this time (War Rule 2.2 refers to twenty-six of them, not twenty-four).

(2) Other Authoritative Books

While many of the books that came to be regarded as biblical prove to have been authoritative at Qumran and some do not, other compositions among the Scrolls may also have been considered revealed and therefore authoritative. In this section I assemble evidence for the thesis that, judging by the criteria listed above, one would number works such as 1 Enoch, Jubilees, and the Temple Scroll among the scriptural works that the Qumran community preserved.

(a) **Jubilees** Fragments from fourteen or perhaps fifteen copies of Jubilees have been found in five of the Qumran caves. That in itself is a telling indicator of how important the book was to the community. The total of fourteen or fifteen copies places it behind Psalms, Deuteronomy, Isaiah, Genesis, and Exodus among the biblical books. Furthermore, Jubilees blatantly advertises itself as divine revelation. The setting for the book is Mount Sinai. God summons Moses to the mountain on the sixteenth day of the third month (cf. Exod 19:1) and there sketches Israel's past and future. All of the book's contents are either the directly revealed words of God (chap. 1) or the message that he instructed an angel of the presence to dictate to Moses from the heavenly tablets. Any use of the book would, as a consequence, bring the reader face-to-face with the claim for inspiration that it makes for itself.

Jubilees is also cited as an authority at Qumran. Damascus Document 16.2-4 (p. 137) says: "As for the exact determination of their times to which Israel turns a blind eye, behold it is strictly defined in the *Book of the Divisions of the Times into their Jubilees and Weeks*." The italicized title of the book is the name given to Jubilees in a number of ancient sources, including itself. For the writer of the Damascus Document, Jubilees, which claims to be revealed, is the place in which to find exact statements about historical periods. That the word *perush* ("the exact determination") is employed is probably also significant: elsewhere it is associated with biblical books. The term translated "strictly defined" is used in the first line of the same column in connection with the Law of Moses.

The Damascus Document may base another point on Jubilees. In the tenth column, the age limits for judges are defined as between twenty-five and sixty years. "No man over the age of sixty shall hold office as Judge of the Congregation, for 'because man sinned his days have been shortened, and in the heat of His anger against the inhabitants of the earth God ordained that their understanding should depart even before their days are completed'" (10.7-10; p. 139). The writer may have Jub 23:11 in mind here, although he does not quote it exactly.

One other possible appeal to Jubilees as an authority is present in 4Q228 which uses some of the language characteristic of Jubilees: "for this is the way it is written in the divisions of the days." Elsewhere the fragment has two other references to "the division of its time," both of which could also be allusions to Jubilees.

To summarize the evidence regarding Jubilees: the book is represented on more copies than all but five biblical books at Qumran; it presents itself as divine revelation; and reference is made to it as an authority in perhaps three places in Qumran literature. In addition, several other texts have been called "Pseudo-Jubilees" because they employ Jubilees-like language or concepts (4Q225-27), although they diverge somewhat from it. Jubilees, then, has all the traits that mark a book as authoritative at Qumran except the quality of having a commentary based on it. Later, the book became canonical for some Christian groups, including the Abyssinian Church in Ethiopia. The high esteem it enjoyed in Ethiopia insured its preservation after the original Hebrew and the Greek translation based on it had disappeared. One complicating fact in the discussion of the status of Jubilees at Qumran is that 4Q252 (Commentary on Genesis A) shows that not every detail of Jubilees' chronology of the flood was accepted in all the pertinent documents at Qumran. Moreover, some calendrical texts set forth the schematic lunar calendar that Jubilees condemns. Consequently, while most indicators demonstrate that Jubilees was a highly regarded source, not everyone at Qumran agreed with everything in it.

(b) 1 Enoch I noted earlier (chapter 2 B.2.a), in the survey of the texts found in the caves, that much of 1 Enoch, which is composed of five booklets, has surfaced in Cave 4. No trace of the second booklet, the Similitudes of Enoch, has, however, been found to date. Instead, a text called the Book of Giants appears to be closely associated with the other Enochic booklets and may even have been copied on the same scroll as several of them. Seven manuscripts contain parts of three of the Enochic booklets, four others preserve sections of the Enochic Astronomical Book, and nine or ten (one each from Caves 1, 2, and 6, and six from Cave 4) offer the Book of Giants. If one considers all of these as part of one (possibly two) large composition, the number of copies is twenty — a very high total for any work at Qumran. This work, so generously represented in the caves, also makes revelatory claims for itself throughout. Enoch reports frequently that the contents of his writings come from visions which God's angels showed to him or from God himself. Some of Enoch's information derives from the heavenly tablets, as in Jubilees.

Qumran literature does not seem to name the work that we know as 1 Enoch as an inspired or revealed source, unless one views Jub 4:17-24 in this capacity. The author of Jubilees obviously knows the booklets of Enoch, since he summarizes their contents in these verses and traces them to angelic revelation. But the book of Enoch did serve as a powerful source in other, related ways. Jubilees and a number of Qumran texts make use of the so-called Watcher story that appears to have its origin in 1 Enoch 1–36, appropriately called the Book of the Watchers. The text interprets Gen 6:1-4 in the sense that some of God's good angels (= the sons of God) left their natural heavenly home and descended to earth — either because they lusted after women (= the daughters of men) or because they wished to do good but strayed after catching sight of the women. The children born to the unnatural marriages between angels and women were giants whose violence ravaged the earth and eventually led to cannibalism. In order to punish the horrible evil that arose in this way, God sent the flood. This story in various forms permeates the Enoch literature, is reproduced in Jubilees, and can be found in a number of Qumran texts such as the Damascus Document and the Genesis Apocryphon. It, more than the story of Adam and Eve in the garden, served as the standard account for the virility of evil on the earth before the flood. The widespread acceptance of the Watcher story at Qumran is testimony to the authority of 1 Enoch. In addition, 1 Enoch's use of the schematic solar and lunar calendars served as a model for the calendrical texts from Qumran. 1 Enoch became a canonical book for a number of early Christians, including the writer of the New Testament Epistle of Jude, who quoted 1 Enoch 1:9 as the authentic words of the seventh man (see Jude 14-15 where Enoch is said to prophesy).

(c) **The Temple Scroll** The Temple Scroll is a different sort of example. It is attested in fewer copies than either Jubilees or the various parts of 1 Enoch: two (possibly three) copies from Cave 11 — one preserving a large percentage of the original text, the other very fragmentary — and one fragmentary copy from Cave 4. Nevertheless, the text lays a powerful claim to its own inspiration in a noteworthy way: its contents are cast as the direct speech of God to Moses on Mount Sinai. The same is the case, of course, for much of Exodus 19–Numbers 10 — the long stretch of biblical material devoted to the Sinai legislation. But the Temple Scroll at times goes farther than the biblical authors in packaging its contents as God's words. The writer changes what in the Bible is in the third person

(Moses relaying God's instructions to the people) to a first-person address by the Lord to Moses. One of several examples is in column 56, which reproduces the law of the king from Deut 17:14-20. Compare these lines in the two works:

> Deut 17:14-15a: "When you have come into the land that **the Lord your God** is giving you, and have taken possession of it and settled in it, and you say, 'I will set a king over me, like all the nations that are around me,' you may indeed set over you a king whom **the Lord your God will choose**."

> 11QTemple 56.12-14; p. 212: "When you enter the land which I give you, take possession of it, dwell in it and say, 'I will appoint a king over me as do all the nations around me!', you may surely appoint over you the king whom **I** will choose."

The claim to be revelation is, then, blatant in the Temple Scroll, which reworks and at times quotes large parts of Exodus, Leviticus, Numbers, and especially Deuteronomy.

Does any Qumran text refer to the Temple Scroll as an authority? The answer to that question is debated. But no other work from the caves makes a clear reference to the Temple Scroll to support an argument. The contents of the scroll are reflected elsewhere (for example, its calendar, its teaching about hanging a criminal), but the writers of the other texts do not name the scroll under any recognizable title as their authoritative source. Yet, it is difficult to imagine that a text which offers itself to the reader as God's very speech to Moses and whose contents had authority at Qumran was not itself regarded as an authoritative work. There is no evidence that any Jewish group later considered the Temple Scroll a canonical writing.

The Qumran literature is the only example that we have of a Jewish library from the last centuries B.C. and the first century A.D. in which we can examine the evidence for a "canonical" consciousness. The texts prove that the books of the Law and Prophets were paid high honor there, as were Psalms and Daniel. They show little or no evidence that several of the books in the later category of the Writings were held in such regard. They also demonstrate that other books were authoritative: Jubilees and parts of 1 Enoch in particular but also the Temple Scroll and probably others such as the commentaries. Thus, one gets the impression that the Qumranites did not have a closed, precisely defined list of books that constituted a Bible; or, perhaps more accurately, we sense that the residents of Qumran included in their category of authoritative books several works that never became parts of the Hebrew Bible. The community certainly believed that revelation continued to be given in their time (the Teacher was inspired). Perhaps they embraced something akin to the broader view of the revealed books expressed in 4 Ezra 14.

BIBLIOGRAPHICAL NOTES

Eugene Ulrich of the University of Notre Dame, editor of many of the biblical scrolls from Qumran, has supplied some of the information found in this chapter. The essay in which he stressed the uncertainty of the editors' reading at 4QMMT C 9-10 is "The Non-attestation of a Tripartite Canon in 4QMMT," *Catholic Biblical Quarterly* 65 (2003) 202-14. The new paragraph in 1 Samuel 10–11 was first treated by Ulrich in *The Qumran Text of Samuel and Josephus* (Harvard Semitic Monographs 19; Missoula, MT: Scholars Press, 1978). For his theory of multiple or successive literary editions of scriptural books, see several of the essays collected in his *The Dead Sea Scrolls and the Origins of the Bible* (Studies in the Dead Sea Scrolls and Related Literature; Grand Rapids: Eerdmans, 1999).

Frank Moore Cross explained his theory of local texts in "The Evolution of a Theory of Local Texts," in *Qumran and the History of the Biblical Text* (ed. F. M. Cross and Shemaryahu Talmon; Cambridge, MA: Harvard University Press, 1976) 306-20.

For the views of Emanuel Tov, see his *Textual Criticism and the Hebrew Bible* (second revised edition; Minneapolis: Fortress/Assen: Royal Van Gorcum, 2001), especially 325-26 for Jeremiah, 114-17 for his classification of the Qumran biblical manuscripts, and 342-44 for the extra paragraph in 1 Samuel 10–11. For a later revision of the percentages of scrolls falling into his categories, see "The Biblical Texts from the Judaean Desert — an Overview and Analysis of the Published Texts," in *The Bible as Book: The Hebrew Bible and the Judaean Desert Discoveries* (ed. Edward D. Herbert and Emanuel Tov; London: The British Library/ New Castle, DE: Oak Knoll Press, 2002) 139-66.

The analysis of 11QPsalms[a], the first Psalms scroll from Cave 11, is dependent on Peter Flint, *The Dead Sea Psalms Scrolls and the Book of*

Psalms (Studies on the Texts of the Desert of Judah 17; Leiden: Brill, 1997).

The quotations of Philo and Josephus are from the editions in the Loeb Classical Library (Cambridge: Harvard University Press; London: Wm. Heinemann): *Philo,* vol. IX, *On the Contemplative Life* (trans. F. H. Colson; repr. 1985); *Josephus,* vol. I, *The Life, Against Apion* (trans. H. St.-J. Thackeray; repr. 1976); *Josephus,* vol. V, *Jewish Antiquities, Books V-VIII* (trans. H. St.-J. Thackeray and R. Marcus; repr. 1988).

The section on canon is dependent upon my essay "Revealed Literature in the Second Temple Period," in my *From Revelation to Canon: Studies in the Hebrew Bible and Second Temple Literature* (Supplements to the Journal for the Study of Judaism 62; Leiden: Brill, 2000) 1-30. Many helpful essays on a range of related topics may be found in *The Canon Debate* (ed. L. M. McDonald and J. A. Sanders; Peabody, MA: Hendrickson).

CHAPTER 6

The Scrolls and the New Testament

A. INTRODUCTION

Some of the greatest excitement and hottest controversies about the Scrolls have revolved around their possible relations with the New Testament and earliest Christianity, including Jesus himself. From the first wave of Qumran studies to the present, some scholars have either spotted extraordinarily close parallels between the Scrolls and the books of the New Testament or identified the Qumranites as Christians. Most would agree that such claims go too far — there are also blatant differences between the two groups and the literatures they penned. In this chapter I examine the various sorts of evidence on this question. At the outset one should note that the Scrolls never mention Jesus or any other New Testament character. If any New Testament personages are present in the Qumran texts, they would have to be hidden behind symbolic names. It is also highly probable that no part of any New Testament book or other early Christian text is included among the innumerable scraps from the eleven caves (the issue is examined below in B.1.b.1). As a result, any relations that may exist between the Scrolls and the New Testament would have to be more indirect. It is quite possible that some Essene works influenced early Christian writers and that Qumranites and a character or characters mentioned in the New Testament had some contact. For the most part, however, the connections between them are in the realm of ideas and resulting practices. The members of the two movements were, nevertheless, distinguishable from one another, as their literatures demonstrate. To name just one contrast: the New Testament is centered on Jesus the messiah, while the Scrolls never mention him.

One of the most famous and influential of the early writers on Qumran was the French scholar André Dupont-Sommer. His studies of the first published Qumran texts led him to assert a remarkable series of parallels between the Teacher of Righteousness — the founder and original leader of the movement — and Jesus (watch which pronouns are capitalized in this 1952 English translation of his book):

> The Galilean Master, as He is presented to us in the writings of the New Testament, appears in many respects as an astonishing reincarnation of the Master of Justice [= the Teacher of Righteousness]. Like the latter He preached penitence, poverty, humility, love of one's neighbour, chastity. Like him, He prescribed the observance of the Law of Moses, the whole Law, but the Law finished and perfected, thanks to His own revelations. Like him He was the Elect and the Messiah of God, the Messiah redeemer of the world. Like him He was the object of the hostility of the priests, the party of the Sadducees. Like him He was condemned and put to death. Like him He pronounced judgement on Jerusalem, which was taken and destroyed by the Romans for having put Him to death. Like him, at the end of time, He will be the supreme judge. Like him He founded a Church whose adherents fervently awaited His glorious return.

Although some of his claims rested on serious misreadings of texts, Dupont-Sommer's writings about and translations of the Scrolls reached a broad audience, including both experts in the field and interested observers outside the discipline. A member of the latter category was Edmund Wilson, who wrote the widely read article published in the 1955 *New Yorker*, "The Scrolls from the Dead Sea." According to Wilson, the relation of the Essenes of Qumran to Jesus and the first Christians could be characterized as "the successive phases of a movement." More rhetorically, he declared about Qumran: "The monastery, this structure of stone that endures, between the bitter waters and precipitous cliffs, with its oven and its inkwells, its mill and its cesspool, its constellation of sacred fonts and the unadorned graves of its dead, is perhaps, more than Bethlehem or Nazareth, the cradle of Christianity." He anticipated later accusations by charging that Jewish and Christian scholars were reluctant to admit the full extent of what the Scrolls implied because it would unsettle their coveted religious assumptions. Jewish scholars, he averred, were too anxious to protect the authority of the Masoretic Text and were hardly willing to admit that Christianity was a natural development from any sort of Judaism. The Christians, of course, were nervous lest the uniqueness of Christ be abrogated. In an oft-quoted line Wilson concluded: "it would seem an immense advantage for cultural and social intercourse — that is, for civilisation — that the rise of Christianity should, at last, be generally understood as simply an episode of human history rather than propagated as dogma and divine revelation. The study of the Dead Sea scrolls — with the direction it is now taking — cannot fail, one would think, to conduce to this." Precisely how such large conclusions would follow from the limited evidence of the Scrolls is not immediately obvious, nor, it seems, has the great benefit to "social and cultural intercourse" envisaged by Wilson taken place.

Still today some scholars draw Christianity and the Scrolls into much closer proximity than the mainline view allows, but they have convinced few if any and are generally taken more seriously by the media than by their colleagues. They tend to reject the paleographical and archeological evidence that has been used to date the Scrolls to earlier times than their hypotheses demand. One contemporary example is Robert Eisenman, who has posited a "Zadokite" movement that existed for centuries and included Ezra, Judas Maccabeus, John the Baptist, Jesus, and his brother James; it became sectarian only in the first century A.D. Another example is Barbara Thiering, who has identified John the Baptist as the Teacher of Righteousness and Jesus as the Wicked Priest of the Qumran texts. She also has determined that the Gospels and Acts are *pesher*-like documents that can be read on the simplistic literal level (apparently the way almost all have read them for the last 1,900 years) and on another, more profound level that she has at last decoded.

While a series of writers have drawn controversial conclusions about Qumran in relation to Christianity, more scholars have quietly, patiently engaged in the work of establishing precisely the points of contact and the differences between the two literatures and how one might explain their interrelations. The results of their labors appear in almost all the introductions to the Scrolls written over the last four decades. Millar Burrows of Yale, one of the first scholars to see the Scrolls, wrote about similarities between John and the covenanters, Jesus and the Teacher, and the messages that each proclaimed. But he thought that the more convincing resemblances were to be seen in matters such as communal structure (12 nonpriests in the Qumran council parallel the 12 apostles), forms of worship (baptism, meals), practices (community of goods), doctrines (dualism of light and darkness, a righteousness conferred by grace), and interpretation of scripture (without a fixed notion of what constituted the Bible). From his sustained, intensive study he concluded: "For myself I must go farther and confess that, after studying the Dead Sea Scrolls for seven years, I do not find my understanding of the New Testament substantially affected. Its Jewish background is clearer and better understood, but its meaning has neither been changed nor significantly clarified."

The sorts of kinship noted by Burrows (and a few other parallel items such as eschatology) have remained the areas in which scholars have perceived the greatest likeness between the two communities and what they wrote. The simple fact of a substantial list of parallels between them showed, if it needed showing, that Christianity in many ways emerged from Judaism and borrowed much of Judaism's heritage in shaping its own life and doctrine. As Krister Stendahl, former dean of the Divinity School at Harvard, has remarked: "It is true to say that the Scrolls add to the background of Christianity, but they add so much that we arrive at a point where the significance of similarities definitely rescues Christianity from false claims of originality in the popular sense and leads us back to a new grasp of its true foundation in the person and the events of its Messiah."

Any survey of Qumran–New Testament studies will reveal that most have adopted a moderate position: although the two literatures and communities had major differences, they were also remarkably similar in theological vocabulary, some major doctrinal tenets, and several organizational and ritual practices. One can explain the parallels in different ways, but at the least one may say that the Qumranites and the early Christians, both of whom considered themselves members of a new covenant (2 Cor 3:6; Damascus Document 20.12), were children of a common parent tradition in Judaism.

B. SIMILARITIES BETWEEN THE SCROLLS AND THE NEW TESTAMENT

The remainder of this chapter contains a selective survey of the specific pieces of evidence that document the nuanced kinship between aspects of the New Testament and of the Qumran literature. For ease of comparison I subsume the material under six headings. One should remember that listing parallels is not the same exercise as explaining how they arose. If we could show that early Christianity and Essenism shared a trait, we would still not be sure that one got it from the other and certainly not that the Christians, say, took it from the Qumran covenanters. Nevertheless, if we can isolate a large number of cases in which the early Christians agreed with the residents of Qumran or the Essenes in general and disagreed on these points with other Jewish groups, we would be taking a big step toward explaining the sort of Judaism that bequeathed the most to Jesus and his first followers.

1. LANGUAGE AND TEXT

Before the Dead Sea Scrolls came on the scene, very little Hebrew or Aramaic literature from the last centuries B.C. and the first A.D. was extant. Almost all the books of the Hebrew Bible were, of course, much older (although they were available only in medieval copies), while the vast rabbinic literature was not recorded until a much later time. Virtually all that survived from the period between these two bodies of Hebrew and Aramaic texts were a few inscriptions. The picture has changed dramatically since 1947. Now scholars have at their disposal a considerable body of Hebrew and Aramaic manuscripts — from Qumran and elsewhere — that supply valuable information about the written and even the spoken languages of Palestine during the centuries in question.

a. Language

All of the New Testament is written in Greek (a couple of Aramaic words are transliterated into Greek characters here and there, such as *talitha cum* in Mark 5:41), but Jesus himself spoke Aramaic and perhaps Hebrew, and all the first disciples were Semitic-speaking Jews of Galilee or Judea.

Thus, the earliest preaching of Jesus' followers and the preserved words of Jesus himself do not survive in their original language but only in edited translations. Naturally, it would often be helpful, in interpreting the Gospels, to know what the original words and sentences were. We still do not have anything close to that ideal, but the Semitic originals of a number of New Testament words and phrases (at times with specialized meanings) are now attested for the first time in the Scrolls.

(1) The Many

One example that is often cited is the expression "the many/majority" — a general term that became a special designation for entire groups of believers in several New Testament passages. It is possible that in Jesus' eucharistic words as given in Matthew and Mark the term is employed with reference to the band of disciples, while in the parallel passage Luke felt the need to clarify the meaning for his readers.

Matt 26:27-28	Mark 14:23-24	Luke 22:20
Then he took a cup, and after giving thanks he gave it to them, saying, "Drink from it, all of you; for this is my blood of the covenant, which is poured out for many for the forgiveness of sins."	Then he took a cup, and after giving thanks he gave it to them, and all of them drank from it. He said to them, "This is my blood of the covenant, which is poured out for many."	And he did the same with the cup after supper, saying, "This cup that is poured out for you is the new covenant in my blood."

It is possible, though hardly certain, that Jesus referred to his disciples as "many" and that Luke, who surmised the intent, rendered the expression as "you." A clearer case appears in Paul's second letter to the Corinthians. There he writes to the church that had aroused such a variety of emotions in him: "But if anyone has caused pain, he has caused it not to me, but to some extent — not to exaggerate it — to all of you. This punishment by the majority [*tōn pleionōn*] is enough for such a person" (2 Cor 2:5-6; see also, for a possibly synonymous word, Acts 6:2, 5; 15:12, 30).

At Qumran the full membership is designated by the Hebrew word that lies behind Paul's "the many/majority." The Rule of the Community lays down regulations regarding who may speak and when during general meetings of the entire group: "And in an Assembly of the Congregation [*ha-rabbim* = the many] no man shall speak without the consent of the Congregation [*ha-rabbim*], nor indeed of the Guardian of the Congregation [*ha-rabbim*]" (6.11-12; p. 106). The word appears in this sense twenty-six times in columns 6-8, once in column 9, and three times in the Damascus Document. In some of these instances "the many" clearly had judicial functions, just as they do in 2 Corinthians: "And furthermore, let no man accuse his companion before the Congregation [*ha-rabbim*] without having admonished him in the presence of witnesses" (6.1; p. 105).

(2) The Guardian

The Hebrew word that Geza Vermes renders as "the Guardian" (*ha-mevaqqer*) may be another case in point. It is the translational equivalent of *episkopos* (bishop/overseer) in the New Testament (Phil 1:1; 1 Tim 3:1-7; Tit 1:7-9) and refers to a man who has similar supervisory roles in the Qumran community. There he may be the one who examines aspiring members at the beginning of their novitiate (1QS 6.13-15), though a different word is used here. He is said to be (literally) "over the many" (6.12). Much of the ninth column treats his qualifications; the power to teach and virtuous personal qualities are highlighted, as they are in the job description of the bishop in 1 Timothy and Titus.

(3) Other Examples

Besides terminological similarities of the kind detailed above, the Scrolls reveal the Semitic original also for other expressions here and there in the New Testament. Joseph Fitzmyer, a scholar of the New Testament and of the Scrolls, has listed a number of Pauline expressions that belong in this category. Among them are: "the righteousness of God," "works of the law," "the church of God," and "sons of light." While it would have been possible, if we did not have the Scrolls, to ascertain the Hebrew or Aramaic equivalents of the Greek phrases, they do demonstrate that these expressions were being used in Semitic languages at the time when the New Testament books were being written.

b. Text

(1) New Testament Papyri in Cave 7?

José O'Callaghan, a Spanish Jesuit, caused a sensation in the 1970s when he argued that Qumran Cave 7, where Greek fragments were found, contained several scraps with parts of the text of Mark, Acts, Romans, 1 Timothy, James, and 2 Peter. If he could have proved his case, scholars would have had to revamp the dominant theory about the residents of Qumran, at least during the later phases of the settlement. If copies of New Testament books were in the caves, then it would be reasonable to suppose that Christians were at Qumran. Had O'Callaghan been right, New Testament scholars would also have had to revise drastically their dating of books such as 2 Peter, which is often thought to be the latest book in the New Testament. While some New Testament experts place it in the early second century, O'Callaghan's thesis would entail that it was composed before the Qumran community was destroyed in A.D. 68 or 70. As it turns out, his novel view has not carried the day. A few have accepted O'Callaghan's identification of one of these papyri (7Q5) as containing a few letters and one word from Mark 6:52-53, but the texts that he identified are very small and in no case did every letter on any fragment agree exactly with the New Testament passages they are supposed to contain. It is quite improbable, therefore, that any New Testament (or other early Christian) text has been found in any of the eleven caves at Qumran.

(2) Qumran Words and Phrases in the New Testament

While virtually no one who works with the Scrolls believes that copies of New Testament books have surfaced at Qumran, more think it likely that parts of some New Testament books may have been based on Qumran (or more generally Essene) sources that were perhaps revised and edited into their present contexts. The section that has attracted the greatest attention in this regard is 2 Cor 6:14–7:1.

Do not be mismatched with unbelievers. For what partnership is there between righteousness and lawlessness? Or what fellowship is there between light and darkness? What agreement does Christ have with Beliar? Or what does a believer share with an unbeliever? What agreement has the temple of God with idols? For we are the temple of the living God; as God said,

"I will live in them and walk among them,
    and I will be their God,
    and they shall be my people.
Therefore come out from them,
    and be separate from them, says the Lord,
and touch nothing unclean;
    then I will welcome you,
and I will be your father,
    and you shall be my sons and daughters,
says the Lord Almighty."

Since we have these promises, beloved, let us cleanse ourselves from every defilement of body and of spirit, making holiness perfect in the fear of God.

These six verses contain various Qumran-sounding words and phrases: no association between the righteous and the wicked; the dualism of light and darkness with no middle ground; the name Beliar = Belial, extremely common in a wide variety of Qumran texts, for the evil one (the only time it occurs in the New Testament). Here, too, Paul exhorts the Corinthians to purity, which is related to holiness; purity was, of course, a central concern at Qumran. It is not possible to prove that Paul took these words from a Qumran or even an Essene work, but in 2 Cor 6:14–7:1 he does indeed employ language that is best known from Qumran texts.

(3) The Sermon on the Mount

Another section that offers several Qumran-sounding words and phrases is the Sermon on the Mount in Matthew 5–7. One of these expressions is "poor in spirit" (Matt 5:3; 1QM 14.7). Among the actions encouraged in the Sermon are avoiding the use of oaths (5:33-37), which, according to

Josephus (*Antiquities* 15.371), was an Essene trait, and the duty to turn the other cheek (5:38-39; 1QS 10.17-18). Moreover, the antitheses in the Sermon ("you have heard that it was said . . . , but I say to you . . .") remind one of the way in which Some of the Works of the Torah = 4QMMT introduces disagreements between the sect and its opponents: "you know. . . . we think/say."

A familiar section of the Sermon on the Mount, the Beatitudes (Matt 5:1-12), has found a parallel in 4Q525 (Beatitudes). The wisdom text from Cave 4 also contains a list of sentences, each introduced by "Blessed . . ." and naming a virtuous type of individual or group of persons. An example is: "Blessed is the man who has attained Wisdom, and walks in the Law of the Most High" (2.3-4; p. 424). There is no extensive verbal overlap between the two texts, but they share a form (see Ps 1:1).

2. CHARACTERS

For a long time people have been attracted to the idea that individuals who appear in the New Testament may have had something to do with Qumran. Some have even claimed to find New Testament characters disguised behind epithets such as "the Teacher of Righteousness" and "the Wicked Priest," but these theories have failed to gain much of a following. Is there any reason to believe that some New Testament figures had contact with Qumran and the group there, even if they are not mentioned by name or title?

a. John the Baptist

From the beginning of comparative studies, scholars have underscored the resemblances between John and his teachings and the Qumran residents and their doctrines. John seemed an especially fitting candidate for possible contacts with Qumran for several reasons. First, his father was a priest (Luke 1:5, 8-23), and when he was born his father said about him:

> "And you, child, will be called the prophet of the Most High;
>   for you will go before the Lord to prepare his ways,
>   to give knowledge of salvation to his people
>   by the forgiveness of their sins.

206

By the tender mercy of our God,
   the dawn from on high will break upon us,
to give light to those who sit in darkness and in the
      shadow of death."

(Luke 1:76-79)

In the immediate sequel Luke adds: "The child grew and became strong in spirit, and he was in the wilderness until the day he appeared publicly to Israel" (1:80). John was, then, in the wilderness even before his ministry began, and there the word of God came to him in the fifteenth year of Emperor Tiberius (3:1-2).

The three synoptic writers introduce John's public ministry in similar fashion by characterizing his work as a preaching of repentance (Matt 3:2; Mark 1:4; Luke 3:3 [where it is called "proclaiming a baptism of repentance for the forgiveness of sins"]). His labors served a larger purpose in the divine plan for the latter days because they implemented the prophetic words of Isaiah: John was

the voice of one crying out in the wilderness:
"Prepare the way of the Lord,
   make his paths straight.
Every valley shall be filled,
   and every mountain and hill shall be made low,
and the crooked shall be made straight,
   and the rough ways made smooth;
and all flesh shall see the salvation of God."

(Luke 3:3-6 = Isa 40:3-5; see also Matt 3:3;
Mark 1:2-3, both of whom cite only Isa 40:3)

John's preaching was marked by an eschatological urgency, by a necessity for repentance before the great day dawned and the Lord came. Matthew and Mark also append a description of John's unusual clothing and diet (Matt 3:4-5; Mark 1:6), and they, joined by Luke, report that he baptized people in the Jordan River (Matt 3:5-6; Mark 1:5; Luke 3:3 [here Luke says that "he went into all the region around the Jordan"]). His forceful, blunt message stirred the people, and John did not hesitate to confront his audience with their sin and its possible consequences (Matt 3:7-10; Luke 3:7-14). Luke reports that John himself became the object of his audience's interests: "As the people were filled with expectation, and all were questioning in their hearts concerning John, whether he might be the Messiah" (3:15). In response he announced the coming of a greater one who would baptize not with water as John did but with the Holy Spirit and with fire, and who would come for judgment (Luke 3:16-18; see also Matt 3:11-12; Mark 1:7-8; John 1:19-28). Of course, John eventually baptized Jesus in a memorable scene and was later imprisoned and beheaded.

Much in the New Testament picture of John reminds one of the Qumran community and texts. At times John may have operated fairly close to Qumran. The Gospel of John locates his baptizing ministry "in Bethany across the Jordan" (1:28) and "at Aenon near Salim because water was abundant there" (3:23). Neither of these sites has been securely identified, but they seem to have been farther to the north than Qumran. Yet his activity in the wilderness near the Jordan could well have brought him to the vicinity of or even to Qumran. John's baptism for the purpose of repentance parallels the Qumran teaching about washing in water for cleansing and sanctification (1QS 3.4-5, 9). The Rule also says: "They shall not enter the water to partake of the pure Meal of the men of holiness, for they shall not be cleansed, unless they turn from their wickedness: for all who transgress His word are unclean" (5.13-14; p. 104). The Qumran complex is dotted with cisterns, some of which have stairways leading down into the water — a fact showing that they were used for the regular ritual baths of those who belonged to the community. The baptism of John and the Qumran rituals probably differed in some ways. For example, John's baptism seems to have occurred just once for each penitent. The Qumran ablutions were almost certainly more frequent, even daily. Nevertheless, both types of washing — that of John and that of Qumran — are intimately connected with repentance and, unlike proselyte baptism, were meant for Jews. One should also remember that the texts explain the missions of both the Qumran community and John the Baptist by means of the same scriptural citation — Isa 40:3. The Rule of the Community (1QS 8.12-15) quotes this verse to indicate that the group believed it was fulfilling the prophet's words by going literally to the wilderness, there to prepare the way of the Lord through study of Moses' Torah. All of the Gospels relate it to John's ministry as forerunner to Jesus.

The series of similarities between the Qumran sect and John amount to something less than an identification of John as an Essene or Qumranite, but they are certainly suggestive and have led some to make strong claims for the Essene connections of John the Baptist. Yet, if he ever was a member of the Qumran community or visited the site, he must have later separated from it to pursue his independent, solitary ministry. In fact, however, there is no evidence that John was associated with the Qumran community.

b. Others

No other person in the New Testament is as likely a candidate for being associated with the Qumran community as John the Baptist. But, using the word *characters* in a wider sense to include Old Testament individuals who play a role in the New, one could include Adam, Enoch, Noah, David, and many others. Another such personality with whom some Qumran texts deal is Melchizedek. He plays a prominent role, of course, in the Letter to the Hebrews as a priest to whose order Jesus belonged and who prefigured him in a number of ways. The genealogies in Matthew and Luke show that Jesus was not descended from the tribe of Levi — the tribe from which the priests came. Since it was important for his christology that Jesus be a perfect high priest, the author of Hebrews elaborates traditions about the enigmatic priest-king of Salem who met Abram in Gen 14:18-20 and blessed the patriarch.

> This "King Melchizedek of Salem, priest of the Most High God, met Abraham as he was returning from defeating the kings and blessed him"; and to him Abraham apportioned "one-tenth of everything." His name, in the first place, means "king of righteousness"; next he is also king of Salem, that is, "king of peace." Without father, without mother, without genealogy, having neither beginning of days nor end of life, but resembling the Son of God, he remains a priest forever. (Heb 7:1-3)

By combining Gen 14:18-20 with Ps 110:4 ("You are a priest forever according to the order of Melchizedek") and drawing inferences from them, the writer created a remarkable portrait of an obscure but mysterious person.

A text from Cave 11, labeled 11QMelchizedek, furnishes at least something of a parallel to the exalted status and characteristics of Melchizedek in Hebrews. In 11QMelchizedek, he figures as an angel who proclaims liberty, judges, and takes divine vengeance on the wicked. His superhuman status, his heavenly activity within the divine council, and his acts of salvation for the just are of special interest here, though in 11QMelchizedek the priest-king of Salem is hardly presented as he is in the Letter to the Hebrews. In fact, this heavenly Melchizedek more nearly resembles Jesus in the Epistle to the Hebrews. Another text may mention Melchizedek: the Songs of the Sabbath Sacrifice (4Q400-407; other copies come from Cave 11 and Masada) may present him as the heavenly high priest, as the Letter to the Hebrews presents Jesus. Caution is in order, however, because the relevant parts of the text are poorly preserved.

3. Practices

As the experts have long recognized, some of the truly impressive and convincing parallels between the covenanters of Qumran and the New Testament Christians have been found in the area of conduct or practices. Here I give a selection of the similarities.

a. Shared Property

After describing the events of Pentecost, the first church historian, Luke, wrote: "All who believed were together and had all things in common; they would sell their possessions and goods and distribute the proceeds to all, as any had need" (Acts 2:44-45). Acts 4:32 offers a programmatic statement: "Now the whole group of those who believed were of one heart and soul, and no one claimed private ownership of any possessions, but everything they owned was held in common." Later, in Acts 5:1-11 Luke tells of Ananias and Sapphira, who sold land but presented to the community a percentage of the proceeds as if it were all. Acts 5:4 indicates that such donations were voluntary and that the communal sharing of all goods was not compulsory. There Peter asks: "While it remained unsold, did it not remain your own? And after it was sold, were not the proceeds at your disposal?" While Acts pictures a community of goods as the practice of the first Christians in Jerusalem, it seems not to have been a universal one in the ancient church, since Paul writes as if members of the churches that he founded had private means with which to contribute to the needs of others (see, for example, 1 Cor 16:2).

From the early days of Scrolls studies, scholars detected the similarity of this famous practice to what the Rule of the Community, Josephus (*War* 2.122), and Pliny the Elder (*Natural History* 5.73) say about the Essenes. The Rule alludes several times to the merging of members' private property with the possessions of the group, but the theme is especially prominent in the section that describes initiatory procedures for aspiring members. At first the novice was not allowed to participate in the pure meal of the congregation, "nor shall he have any share of the property of the Congregation" (1QS 6.17; p. 106). Once he had completed a full year within the group and the decision was made that he could stay, "his property and earnings shall be handed over to the Bursar of the Congregation who shall register it to his account and shall not spend it for the Congregation" (6.19-20; p. 106). Once he had successfully passed the test at the end of an additional year, "his property shall be merged" with the community's possessions (6.22). The discussion of this practice in chap. 3 (A.2.b.2) showed that Qumran also had a place for some private control of property. The communities reflected in the Damascus Covenant, though they contributed a percentage of their monthly earnings to the communal treasury, also held private property. Thus, the practices at Qumran and in the Jerusalem church appear to be the same with regard to sharing and ownership.

b. The Meal

The Gospels present the last supper that Jesus shared with his immediate followers in two different ways. In the synoptic Gospels (Matthew, Mark, and Luke), it is a Passover meal; hence it includes bread and wine and other features of that festal ceremony, although on this occasion it was also tinged with sadness. John, the unique Gospel, places the last meal on the night before Passover, mentions neither bread nor wine, and makes foot washing prominent. In the Passover version of the supper, the bread and wine take on sacramental significance:

> While they were eating, Jesus took a loaf of bread, and after blessing it he broke it, gave it to the disciples, and said, "Take, eat; this is my body." Then he took a cup, and after giving thanks he gave it to them, saying, "Drink from it, all of you; for this is my blood of the covenant, which is poured out for many for the forgiveness of sins. I tell you, I will never again drink of this fruit of the vine un-

til that day when I drink it new with you in my Father's kingdom."
(Matt 26:26-29 // Mark 14:22-25 // Luke 22:17-20)

These words assign profound significance to the bread and wine and place the ceremony within a context of expectation for "that day when I drink it new with you in my Father's kingdom."

Some Qumran texts speak about a meal, and they, too, refer to the basic elements of bread and wine. The Rule of the Community refers to the meals of the group: "And when the table has been prepared for eating, and the new wine for drinking, the Priest shall be the first to stretch out his hand to bless the firstfruits of the bread and new wine" (1QS 6.4-6 [lines 5-6 repeat some words, which Vermes has not translated; p. 105]). We have met their "pure Meal" on several occasions in previous chapters. The Rule stipulates that only those who had spent a full year within the community were permitted to eat the food (6.16-17), while even these were not allowed to partake of the "drink of the Congregation" until a second year had transpired, that is, until they had attained full membership (6.20-21). Those who were guilty of slandering another were excluded from this meal for one year (7.16). Such concern for limiting admission to the meal is reminiscent of Paul's words to the Corinthian church:

> Whoever, therefore, eats the bread or drinks the cup of the Lord in an unworthy manner will be answerable for the body and blood of the Lord. Examine yourselves, and only then eat of the bread and drink of the cup. For all who eat and drink without discerning the body, eat and drink judgment against themselves. For this reason many of you are weak and ill, and some have died. (1 Cor 11:27-30)

By "discerning the body" Paul seems to mean "understanding the nature and unity of the group, the body of Christ." The Rule of the Community shows the same concern for grasping what the group is, what its requirements are, with regard to the meal.

The most extended description of a meal at Qumran occupies much of the second column in the Rule of the Congregation, which was copied on the same manuscript as the Cave 1 copy of the Rule.

> [*This shall be the ass*]*embly of the men of renown* [*called*] *to the meeting of the Council of the Community.*

When God engenders (the Priest-) Messiah, he shall come with
them [at] the head of the whole congregation of Israel with all
[his brethren, the sons] of Aaron the Priests, [those called] to the
assembly, the men of renown; and they shall sit [before him, each
man] in the order of his dignity. And then [the Mess]iah of Israel
shall [come], and the chiefs of the [clans of Israel] shall sit before
him, [each] in the order of his dignity, according to [his place] in
their camps and marches. And before them shall sit all the heads
of [family of the congreg]ation, and the wise men of [the holy
congregation,] each in the order of his dignity.

And [when] they shall gather for the common [tab]le, to eat
and [to drink] new wine, when the common table shall be set for
eating and the new wine [poured] for drinking, let no man extend
his hand over the firstfruits of bread and wine before the Priest;
for [it is he] who shall bless the firstfruits of bread and wine, and
shall be the first [to extend] his hand over the bread. Thereafter
the Messiah of Israel shall extend his hand over the bread, [and]
all the congregation of the Community [shall utter a] blessing,
[each man in the order] of his dignity.

It is according to this statute that they shall proceed at every
me[al at which] at least ten men are gathered together. (2.11-22;
pp. 159-60)

The meal is messianic in the most literal sense because it is eaten in the
presence of the messiah of Israel and his priestly colleague (who is called
a messiah in the Rule of the Community but not in the preserved portions of the Rule of the Congregation, though Vermes imports the title
between brackets into his translation). The text stresses that the meal is
only for those who are ritually pure. It is also explicitly eschatological, as
the first words of the composition state: "*This is the Rule for all the congregation of Israel in the last days*" (1.1; p. 157). One might think that the
meal described in this text is unusual, one celebrated rarely; yet the last
words of the document indicate otherwise: "It is according to this statute
that they shall proceed at every me[al at which] at least ten men are gathered together" (2.21-22, p. 160). The word translated *meal* is actually more
general, meaning "arrangement," but it is used to refer to the arrangement of the meal that is described in the immediately preceding lines.
Lawrence Schiffman argues that the Qumran meals were noncultic in
nature: "These meals, conducted regularly as part of the present-age way

of life of the sect, were preenactments of the final messianic banquet which the sectarians expected in the soon-to-come end of days. Again, the life of the sect in this world mirrored its dreams for the age to come." However one interprets the meal of the Essenes (e.g., who played the role of the messiah of Israel in these recurring meals?), its messianic character, the prominence of bread and wine, the fact that it was repeated regularly, and its explicit eschatological associations do recall elements found in the New Testament treatments of the Lord's Supper.

c. Calendar

In the early 1950s a French scholar, Annie Jaubert, wrote a series of articles in which she argued that the 364-day calendar of the Qumran scrolls solved an old problem in Gospel studies. The synoptic Gospels (Matthew, Mark, and Luke) on the one hand and John on the other describe the last days of Jesus' ministry in great detail. Those days were obviously an essential element in what the writers chose to present to their readers, and presumably early Christians would have been well informed about what happened on those days of all days. Nevertheless, if one reads the Gospels carefully, one discovers that even for the final days of Jesus' life the Gospels have chronologies that differ. The synoptics place the last supper on a Passover, whereas John puts it on the day before Passover. His dating of the final meal entails that Jesus was crucified at the time when the Passover lambs were being slaughtered. How could early Christians assign the same pivotal event to different days? The Qumran texts indicate that their calendar was not the same as the one followed elsewhere in Judaism. Thus, at least two calendars were practiced at that time. The existence of these two calendars — the official lunisolar one of the temple and the 364-day solar calendar of the Qumran community — suggested to Jaubert the possibility that Matthew, Mark, and Luke calculated the days according to one system (the solar) and John according to the official one (the lunisolar calendar).

This solution is attractive and provides a simple explanation for a perplexing discrepancy, but it does suffer from the fact that the two calendars would rarely have worked out in such a way that the synoptic date for the supper would have been the same in the Qumran calendar as John's was in the lunisolar arrangement. There is also no evidence that Jesus or any early Christian of the New Testament period used the solar calendar of Qumran — or any other calendar that made them noticeably different from other Jews. Moreover, careful study of John's Gospel soon makes clear that he has a purpose in locating events in the Passion Week as he does. He does not emphasize the communal bread and wine at Jesus' meal; they are not even mentioned. Foot washing and mutual love are highlighted. By dying when he did in John's chronology, Jesus is presented as the Passover lamb of his people.

4. Eschatology

Both the Qumranites and the first Christians can be called eschatological communities in the sense that both were convinced that the end was near and ordered their beliefs and communal practices accordingly. It is useful to distinguish several subjects under this broad heading.

a. Messianism

The people of Qumran and the New Testament Christians looked forward to the arrival of the messiah(s) and shared a number of beliefs about the messianic age. The hopes of the successive generations who lived around Qumran may have changed to some extent, but a whole series of texts reveals that they anticipated two messiahs — one from Israel or David, the other from the line of Aaron, that is, a priest (see chap. 4 B.6). When studying the Qumran evidence for a messianic meal, we noticed that the Rule of the Congregation speaks of a messiah from Israel and his priestly associate. A similar belief emerges, as already noted, from the Rule of the Community: "They shall depart from none of the counsels of the Law to walk in all the stubbornness of their hearts, but shall be ruled by the primitive precepts in which the men of the Community were first instructed until there shall come the Prophet and the Messiahs of Aaron and Israel" (9.9-11; p. 110). In this sentence, the first named is the priestly one — the messiah of Aaron — and the second is the lay one — the messiah of Israel. Several texts mention something of the roles these figures were to play. For example, the Damascus Document says that they will effect atonement (14.19). Other texts relate the messiah from the family of David directly with prophecies of a new Davidide in Isaiah 11. There wisdom, righteous judgment, and killing the wicked are associated with him (11:1-5).

The general lines of the New Testament picture of Jesus are familiar. Both Matthew and Luke trace his descent from the family of David, and throughout the New Testament the title "messiah" (= Christ) is given to him. Many passages also mention how he secures the forgiveness of sins through his atoning work. The New Testament has just one messiah, not two as at Qumran. Also, while the Qumranites expected the two messiahs to be present together and apparently to come at one time in the near future, the New Testament talks of Jesus' two advents — the one described in the Gospels and the other at the end of time.

Although the two literatures differ regarding how many messiahs there would be and who the one from the line of David was, they agree in considering the messianic work to be twofold — kingly and priestly. Jesus' descent from David documents his kingly role. One of the passages where royal language is used for him is Acts 2:29-31 (Peter is speaking at Pentecost): "Fellow Israelites, I may say to you confidently of our ancestor David that he both died and was buried, and his tomb is with us to this day. Since he was a prophet, he knew that God had sworn with an oath to him that he would put one of his descendants on his throne. Foreseeing this, David spoke of the resurrection of the Messiah." His priestly side comes to expression especially in the Letter to the Hebrews. There, as a priest after the order of Melchizedek (and not from Levi's line), he officiates as high priest of the heavenly sanctuary. Aspects of both his kingly and his priestly functions appear in Heb 10:12-14: "But when Christ had offered for all time a single sacrifice for sins, 'he sat down at the right hand of God,' and since then he has been waiting 'until his enemies would be made a footstool for his feet.' For by a single offering he has perfected for all time those who are sanctified." As a result, we may say that the Essenes of Qumran (and other Essenes) awaited two messiahs, one who would carry out royal labors and the other priestly labors, while the New Testament followers of Jesus remembered and also awaited one messiah, who would perform both kingly and cultic functions.

The basic similarities show that the two communities operated with related messianic faiths. Hence, it is not surprising to learn that both, in dependence on the Hebrew scriptures, use some of the same or similar titles for the messiah(s). Of course, both employ the term *messiah*. At Qumran, several texts (Florilegium is one) call the political messiah "the branch of David" (taken from Isa 11:1; Jer 23:5; 33:15). The New Testament does not employ the exact equivalent but does speak of Jesus as "the root of David" (Rev 5:5; 22:16). Another of the titles given to Jesus in the New

Testament is now attested at Qumran for the first time in its Semitic form. In Luke 1:32-33 the angel who appeared to Mary to announce that she would become the mother of a wondrous child predicts to her: "He will be great, and will be called the Son of the Most High, and the Lord God will give to him the throne of his ancestor David. He will reign over the house of Jacob forever, and of his kingdom there will be no end." The child also "will be holy; he will be called Son of God" (v. 35). An impressive parallel to some of these titles comes from 4Q246 (Aramaic Apocalypse), the relevant portion of which reads:

> . . . he will be great on earth . . . will make and all will serve . . . he
> will be called (or: call himself) [gran]d . . . and by his name he will
> be designated (or: designate himself). The Son of God he will be
> proclaimed (or: proclaim himself) and the Son of the Most High
> they will call him. (1.7–2.1; p. 577)

Here one cannot simply dismiss the parallel as one title that happens to surface in two texts; on the contrary, the entire contexts have striking similarities: the individual in question will be great, son of God (a title found in the Hebrew Bible), son of the Most High (a new title), and his kingdom will be eternal (see 4Q246 2.5). It should be added that scholars disagree about the person to whom the titles are applied in 4Q246: are they being attributed to a messianic figure, or are they being claimed by an evil ruler who obviously does not deserve them? The latter seems more likely.

Finally, something should be said about 4Q285, the so-called Pierced Messiah Text (officially known as Rule of War, along with 11Q14), which garnered much attention when it first became available in the early 1990s. At that time, some thought that it confirmed charges that a conspiracy by the original team of editors had kept the text from the public because it was damaging to Christianity (see chap. 7 about the controversies). The fragment in question contains a few words distributed along six lines. The first line mentions "Isaiah the prophet," while the second quotes the first words of Isa 11:1 ("A shoot shall come out from the stump of Jesse"). The sequel continues to use the language of Isaiah 11: it mentions the "branch of David" (line 3), and a verb of judging relates it to Isa 11:3-4. The line that caused the excitement was the fourth. The scholar who brought it to public attention, Robert Eisenman, read it as saying: "And they killed [or: will kill] the prince of the congregation, the bran[ch

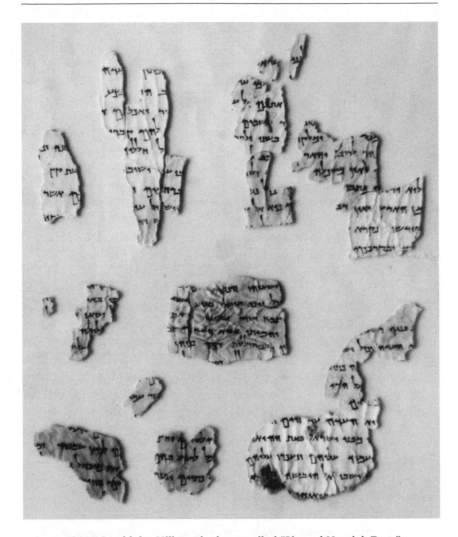

4Q285 Serekh ha-Milhamah, the so-called "Pierced Messiah Text."
Although some suspected it might be a text damaging to Christianity that
had been purposely withheld from the public, further study has shown it fits
well in the familiar scrolls' predictions about the messiahs.
(Courtesy Israel Antiquities Authority)

218

of David]." As already noted, "branch of David" is one of the Qumran names for the nonpriestly messiah. The fifth line has a word that Eisenman took to mean "his wounds" or "his piercings" (hence the once-popular name of the text). Understood in this way, he thought of the Christian use of Isaiah 53 to interpret Jesus' death: "he was wounded for our transgressions" (v 5). The fragment seemed to offer, then, a remarkable prefiguring of the Christian messiah's experience.

The fragment was later subjected to more careful scrutiny, resulting in more cautious conclusions. Here just a few points should be made. First, since the initial line names Isaiah and and the next ones echo the wording of the first verses in Isaiah 11, it is reasonable to expect the next lines also to relate to that chapter. At any rate, that expectation should be tested first before other interpretive moves are made. Second, the fourth line — the controversial one — should be translated: "and the prince of the congregation [another title for the Davidic messiah] . . . will kill [or: killed] him." The three ellipsis points represent the next word, only two letters of which are preserved at the edge of the fragment. Some read them as the first two letters of the Hebrew word for "branch," but the second one remains debatable. It is possible that one should translate: "and the prince of the congregation, the branch of David will kill [or: killed] him." This line reflects the words of Isa 11:4, where the offspring of David "shall kill the wicked." Thus, it is more likely that the prince is doing the killing here; it is quite unlikely, for syntactical and exegetical reasons, that he is being or has been killed. Hence, an eye-catching parallel to the New Testament falls by the wayside.

b. Biblical Interpretation

The two groups also gave voice to their eschatological consciousness through the methods that they applied when interpreting biblical texts. In chapter 2 C.1.a, I noted that the Qumran commentaries reveal a set of assumptions from which the interpreter explicates the meaning of the scriptural text: the biblical authors, who were predicting events of the latter days, were writing about the Qumranites' times and even about their history and leaders. The Teacher of Righteousness was an inspired exegete of the scriptural words. A number of New Testament passages evidence the same eschatological and contemporizing reading of biblical texts.

One of the most helpful examples occurs in the story of Pentecost in Acts 2. Peter, the spokesman for the apostolic band who had experienced the linguistic miracle, quotes scripture to prove that the extraordinary event that had just taken place was part of God's foreordained plan for the end time: "Indeed, these are not drunk, as you suppose, for it is only nine o'clock in the morning. No, this is what was spoken through the prophet Joel: 'In the last days it will be, God declares, that I will pour out my Spirit upon all flesh, and your sons and your daughters shall prophesy, and your young men shall see visions, and your old men shall dream dreams'" (Acts 2:15-17). The Lord had inspired the prophet Joel to write that the divine Spirit would be poured out "in the last days," and that eschatological event, Peter maintains, took place at the first Christian celebration of Pentecost. The words "in the last days," which are crucial to the point being made here, are not present in the Hebrew text of Joel (Joel 2:28: "Then afterward I will pour out my spirit on all flesh . . ."). They represent, apparently, Luke's interpretation of Joel's meaning, and the verses that follow in the prophecy do in fact point to the last days "before the great and terrible day of the Lord comes" (Joel 2:31). The simple fact that Luke inserted these words, however, shows the eschatological nature of the way in which early Christians read the scriptures.

It is especially interesting to compare the ways in which the two literatures explain the same biblical text. We have already seen that the Scrolls community supported its separated life in the wilderness on the authority of Isa 40:3: "And when these become members of the Community in Israel according to all these rules, they shall separate from the habitation of unjust men and shall go into the wilderness to prepare there the way of Him; as it is written, *Prepare in the wilderness the way of . . . , make straight in the desert a path for our God* [Isa 40:3]. This (path) is the study of the Law which He commanded by the hand of Moses" (1QS 8.12-15; p. 109). In the four Gospels, the same passage from Isaiah explains the role of John as the forerunner of Jesus, the one in the wilderness who prepares the way of the Lord (Matt 3:3; Mark 1:3; Luke 3:4-5; John 1:23).

Another example of this sort occurs in 4Q521 (Messianic Apocalypse), a text already referenced several times. It illustrates that a passage in Luke 7 (// in Matthew 11) rests upon a more widely embraced way of associating sections from the book of Isaiah. In Luke, disciples of John ask Jesus on behalf of their teacher: "Are you the one who is to come, or are we to wait for another?" (7:20 // Matt 11:3). Jesus replied: "Go and tell John what you have seen and heard: the blind receive their sight, the lame walk, the lepers are cleansed, the deaf hear, the dead are raised, the poor have good news brought to them" (v. 22 // Matt 11:4-5). In 4Q521 there is a similar list of miraculous actions: "And the Lord will accomplish glorious things which have never been as [He . . .] For He will heal the wounded, and revive the dead and bring good news to the poor (Isa. 61:1)" (2 ii + 4.11-12; p. 392). Both passages draw upon Isa 35:5-6 and Isa 61:1; the unique element added by the two is raising the dead, and both mention it just before bringing good news to the poor. In the Gospels, Jesus is the one who does these miraculous deeds in the present; in 4Q521 the Lord will do them in the future. Further parallels between Luke and 4Q521 arise in connection with their use of Isaiah. Jesus reads and explains Isa 61:1-2 in the Nazareth synagogue: "The Spirit of the Lord is upon me, because he has anointed me to bring good news to the poor. He has sent me to proclaim release to the captives and recovery of sight to the blind, to let the oppressed go free, to proclaim the year of the Lord's favor" (Luke 4:18-19; see also Isa 58:6). 4Q521 2 ii + 4.6-8 reflects some of these elements: "Over the poor His spirit will hover and will renew the faithful with His power. And He will glorify the pious on the throne of the eternal Kingdom. He who liberates the captives, restores sight to the blind, straightens the bent (Ps. 146:7-8)" (p. 392).

Another instance of a text cited in the Qumran literature and in the New Testament is Hab 2:4b. Along with Gen 15:6 it was a proof text to which Paul turned as he proclaimed that faith was the way to become right with God, not performing deeds of the law: "Now it is evident that no one is justified before God by the law; for 'The one who is righteous will live by faith'" (Gal 3:11; cf. Rom 1:17). Paul understood the word *faith* to mean that trustful reliance on the promises God gave to Abraham — a way of life that he contrasts sharply with a legal righteousness. The Qumran Habakkuk commentary takes up the same passage and offers what would appear to be rather different understandings of what *faith* or *faithfulness* (the Hebrew word can have either sense) means in the prophetic text. After citing the verse, the commentator writes: "Interpreted, this concerns all those who observe the Law in the House of Judah, whom God will deliver from the House of Judgement because of their suffering and because of their faith in [or: fidelity to] the Teacher of Righteousness" (8.1-3; p. 482). The first part of the explanation relates the passage to "those who observe the Law in the House of Judah" — an interpretation that seems the opposite of the way Paul read the verse. In addition, the words "House of Judah," whatever the commentator intended by them, limit the application of Habakkuk's words to Judeans (or another limited group such as the one to which the writer belonged, if the phrase is symbolic); Paul found in his doctrine of justification by faith a way to include not only Jews but also other nations within the divine plan. Yet, after explaining the verse in this legal sense, the expositor adds that those who do obey the law in the House of Judah will be delivered for two reasons: because of what they have endured, and due to their *faith* in or *faithfulness* to the Teacher of Righteousness. This second line of interpretation is more in harmony with the way in which Paul read Hab 2:4, although of course he related the faith/faithfulness to Jesus Christ, not to the Teacher of Righteousness.

c. Teachings

One can also see the eschatological nature of these two communities in some of the basic theological tenets that they embraced. Since I sketched the theology of the Qumranites in chapter 4 B, the comparison here need not be exhaustive. It is sufficient to highlight two areas of doctrinal kinship.

First, both groups employed dualistic language to describe the options in the universe: there are just two positions, with no mediating ground between. Since both literatures are fundamentally Jewish, there is no thought of this dualism being ultimate. Instead, the dualism is ethical, and the two opposing camps are characterized as light and darkness. As we have seen, one of the best-known passages in the Scrolls says:

> He [[God]] has created man to govern the world, and has appointed for him two spirits in which to walk until the time of His visitation: the spirits of truth and injustice. Those born of truth spring from a fountain of light, but those born of injustice spring from a source of darkness. All the children of righteousness are ruled by the Prince of Light and walk in the ways of light, but all the children of injustice are ruled by the Angel of Darkness and walk in the ways of darkness. (1QS 3.18-21; p. 101)

The ways of each spirit mentioned in the text — the conduct that they induce in human beings — are then enumerated in a manner reminiscent of Paul's lists of the works of the flesh and the fruit of the Spirit in

Gal 5:19-23. In the Rule of the Community, the two camps are in continual conflict throughout history: "For God has established the spirits in equal measure until the final age, and has set everlasting hatred between their divisions. Truth abhors the works of injustice, and injustice hates all the ways of truth. And their struggle is fierce in all their arguments for they do not walk together" (4.16-18; pp. 102-3). God has, nevertheless, "ordained an end for injustice, and at the time of the visitation He will destroy it for ever" (4.18-19). The War Rule describes at length the final battles between the sons of light and the sons of darkness. Although powerful angels fight on both sides, God will, in his good time, enter the fray decisively and hand victory to the sons of light.

Such language should not sound foreign to students of the New Testament. One can find the same kind of rhetoric in the writings of Paul and John. I have already examined 2 Cor 6:14–7:1 in which a series of Qumran-sounding words and phrases have entered one of Paul's letters. There he asks: "Or what fellowship is there between light and darkness?" (6:14). The Johannine literature in the New Testament has long been considered the most productive source of comparative material in theological matters. Like the Qumran covenanters, John resorts to the light/darkness contrast, not in its literal meaning but in an ethical sense. John 8:12 quotes Jesus as saying: "I am the light of the world. Whoever follows me will never walk in darkness but will have the light of life." For John, the two realms are in long-term conflict: "The light shines in the darkness, and the darkness did not overcome it" (1:5). In 12:35-36a we read Jesus' words: "The light is with you for a little longer. Walk while you have the light, so that the darkness may not overtake you. If you walk in the darkness, you do not know where you are going. While you have the light, believe in the light, so that you may become children of light" (see also 3:19-20; 1 John 1:6; 2:9-10). Thus, followers of Jesus, like the residents of Qumran, styled themselves "the children [literally: sons] of light."

A second doctrinal point concerns the hope entertained by the two communities. Christian beliefs about the end are familiar: Christ will return, there will be a resurrection of the good and evil, and Christ will win the ultimate victory over sin and death (see, for example, 1 Cor 15:20-28, 51-57). Jesus' resurrection is interpreted as a guarantee that those who believe in him will likewise experience a resurrection. As already mentioned, we now have evidence that the Qumran Essenes anticipated a resurrection (4Q521), although the ancient sources regarding this article of their faith may conflict with one another. We have also observed that the residents of Qumran looked to the day when a victorious Davidic messiah would come in the company of a priest. To this extent, then, the eschatological expectations of the Scrolls and the New Testament are similar. Both also believed there would be a judgment, but the expectation of such a judgment was shared more widely in Judaism at the time. When one presses beyond the general points mentioned under this rubric, one does find, however, some differences, among which was that for the Christians the eschatological coming of the one messiah would be a return, not his first appearance.

C. CONCLUSIONS

The survey presented in this chapter comes far short of exhausting what could be said about the similarities and differences between the Qumranites and the first Christians. Whole books have been devoted to the subject. The points selected for discussion here are meant to illustrate the nature of the material. The Qumran literature has shown to a far greater extent than was sensed before 1947 how deeply rooted early Christianity was in the Jewish soil that nourished it. Because of the Scrolls, one can more easily see that a large number of Christianity's beliefs and practices were not unique to it. The major contribution of the Scrolls to New Testament study is to highlight the simple but profound fact that the uniqueness of the early Christian faith lies less in its communal practices and eschatological expectations than in its central confession that the son of a humble woman and a carpenter from Nazareth in Galilee was indeed the messiah and son of God who taught, healed, suffered, died, rose, ascended, and promised to return in glory to judge the living and the dead. By claiming that the historical Jesus was the messiah, the Christians also placed themselves farther along on the eschatological timetable than the Qumran Essenes, who were expecting their messiahs to come in the near future.

BIBLIOGRAPHICAL NOTES

The lines from André Dupont-Sommer appear in his *The Dead Sea Scrolls: A Preliminary Survey* (trans. E. Margaret Rowley; Oxford: Basil Blackwell, 1952) 99.

Edmund Wilson's article "The Scrolls from the Dead Sea" was published in *The New Yorker,* May 1955, 45-131; it later grew into a book, *The Scrolls from the Dead Sea* (London: Collins, 1955). The quotations are from the book, pp. 102 and 114.

For Robert Eisenman's views, see *Maccabees, Zadokites, Christians and Qumran: A New Hypothesis of Qumran Origins* (Studia Post-Biblica 34; Leiden: Brill, 1983); *James the Just in the Habakkuk Pesher* (Leiden: Brill, 1986); and *James the Brother of Jesus: The Key to Unlocking the Secrets of Early Christianity and the Dead Sea Scrolls* (London and New York: Penguin Books, 1997).

Barbara Thiering's hypotheses appear in *Redating the Teacher of Righteousness* (Australian and New Zealand Studies in Theology and Religion; Sidney: Theological Explorations, 1979); in the same series *The Gospels and Qumran: A New Hypothesis* (1981); and *Jesus and the Riddle of the Dead Sea Scrolls* (San Francisco: HarperSanFrancisco, 1992).

The opinions of Millar Burrows are from his *The Dead Sea Scrolls* (New York: Viking Press, 1955) 327-43 (quotation from 343).

Krister Stendahl's comments may be found in "The Scrolls and the New Testament: An Introduction and a Perspective," in *The Scrolls and the New Testament* (ed. Stendahl; New York: Harper & Row, 1957) 16-17. This helpful collection, with a new introduction by James H. Charlesworth, has been reprinted by Crossroad (1992).

Of assistance for this chapter was Joseph Fitzmyer's article "The Qumran Scrolls and the New Testament after Forty Years," *Revue de Qumran* 13 (1988) 609-20. See also his "Paul and the Dead Sea Scrolls," in *The Dead Sea Scrolls after Fifty Years: A Comprehensive Assessment* (ed. P. Flint and J. VanderKam; 2 vols.; Leiden: Brill, 1998, 1999) 2.599-621.

José O'Callaghan's case was made in "Papiros neotestamentarios en la cueva 7 de Qumran?" *Biblica* 53 (1972) 91-100 and more fully in his *Los papiros griegos de la cueva 7 de Qumrân* (Biblioteca de autores cristianos; 353; Madrid: Editorial católica, 1974). His essay was translated into English by William L. Holladay: "New Testament Papyri in Qumran Cave 7?" Supplement to the *Journal of Biblical Literature* 91 (1972) 1-14. For a summary of the evidence and discussion, see James VanderKam and Peter Flint, *The Meaning of the Dead Sea Scrolls: Their Significance for Understanding the Bible, Judaism, Jesus, and Christianity* (San Francisco: HarperSanFrancisco, 2002) chap. 14.

For Lawrence Schiffman's discussion of the meal, see his *The Eschatological Community of the Dead Sea Scrolls* (Society of Biblical Literature

Monograph Series 38; Atlanta: Scholars Press, 1989). The quotation is from p. 67.

On the calendar and the last supper, see the discussion of Joseph Fitzmyer (with his bibliography) in *The Dead Sea Scrolls: Major Publications and Tools for Study* (Sources for Biblical Study 20; rev. ed.; Atlanta: Scholars Press, 1990) 180-86. For Annie Jaubert's views see *The Date of the Last Supper* (trans. Isaac Rafferty; Staten Island: Alba, 1965).

For the Qumran *pesharim* and the Epistles of Paul, see Timothy H. Lim, *Holy Scripture in the Qumran Commentaries and Pauline Letters* (Oxford: Clarendon, 1997).

For a series of essays on a variety of topics including some treated in this chapter, see George J. Brooke, *The Dead Sea Scrolls and the New Testament* (Minneapolis: Fortress, 2005).

CHAPTER 7

Controversies about the Dead Sea Scrolls

Note to the Reader: Parts A and B of this chapter are repeated (with very modest adjustments) from the first edition of *The Dead Sea Scrolls Today*. They therefore reflect the perspective of the early 1990s. The Postscript brings the discussion up to date.

Since 1990 the Dead Sea Scrolls have been transformed from a small, quiet backwater of biblical scholarship into a torrent that has flooded not only the realm of scriptural and Jewish studies but also the media and even popular culture. For a time, especially in late 1991 and early 1992, we came to expect the Scrolls in the headlines, articles about them in the leading news magazines, the *New York Times*, the *Washington Post*, and other important newspapers editorializing on the Scrolls, the "cartel" that held a monopoly on them, and liberation of them by a few brave souls. Often the news coverage included stories of normally peaceful academics trading nasty charges and countercharges. The authors of a best-selling book advanced talk of a Vatican-inspired conspiracy. What had happened? To grasp the current situation, it is necessary to go back briefly to the early days of Scrolls scholarship.

A. EDITING AND PUBLISHING THE SCROLLS

In chapter 1 I told the story about the seven manuscripts removed initially from the first Qumran cave. Those seven texts were made available to the scholarly world with commendable speed. In a sense, one could have expected speedy publication because most of them were in excellent condition and presented relatively few problems of reading and reconstruction. For the biblical scrolls, the editors did not even have to bother translating, since the texts found in them were nearly the same as the Masoretic Text that had been the basis for all translations of the Hebrew Bible/Old Testament.

Preliminary publications of the new texts started to appear in 1948 when the scholars who had obtained them — Eleazar Sukenik and the three experts from the American School in Jerusalem (John Trever, Millar Burrows, and William Brownlee) — began to make their findings known. The first complete edition of any of the scrolls came out in 1950, when, under the editorship of Burrows (with Trever and Brownlee), the American Schools of Oriental Research produced *The Dead Sea Scrolls of St. Mark's Monastery,* volume 1: *The Isaiah Manuscript and the Habakkuk Commentary.* It was followed in 1951 by volume 2, fascicle 2: *Plates and Transcription of the Manual of Discipline.* Fascicle 1 was reserved for the Genesis Apocryphon, which had not been opened at that time; the fascicle has never appeared. Sukenik's three scrolls (the second copy of Isaiah, the War Scroll, and the Hymn Scroll) were published posthumously in 1954 in *The Collection of the Hidden Scrolls in the Possession of the Hebrew University* (in Hebrew). An English edition appeared in 1955: *The Dead Sea Scrolls of the Hebrew University.* The remaining scroll — the Genesis Apocryphon — was edited and published in 1956 by Nahman Avigad and Yigael Yadin (the two scholars who edited Sukenik's work after he died in 1953) under the title *A Genesis Apocryphon.* All of these publications included at least the photographs and transcriptions of the scrolls into printed Hebrew characters. The hundreds of other fragments dug up in the first cave were issued in 1955 as the first volume in Discoveries in the Judaean Desert, the Oxford University Press series devoted to the Dead Sea Scrolls. It was named *Qumran Cave 1* and was edited by Dominique Barthélemy and J. T. Milik, two priests associated with the Ecole Biblique in Jerusalem. By 1956, then, all texts from the first cave were available for study by anyone who wished to examine them.

As the Cave 1 texts were moving promptly into print, other caves were discovered (see chap. 1 B.2). The texts from Caves 2-3, 5-10 and those from Murabba'at were handled expeditiously by a small group of scholars who had been assigned to work on them. The second number of the Discoveries in the Judaean Desert (two volumes, edited by Pierre Benoit, Milik, and Roland de Vaux, and published in 1961) contained the material found in the Murabbaʿat caves, while the third, also in two volumes, appeared in 1962 under the editorship of Maurice Baillet, Milik, and de Vaux. It included all the texts from the so-called minor caves, that is, Caves 2-3 and 5-10. The manuscripts from Cave 11, some of which were in a very good state of preservation, were handled differently. Several were purchased by foreign institutions, and major ones were published in the 1960s and 1970s.

The real problem came with Cave 4, which yielded so many thousands of battered fragments. As the myriad pieces were being purchased by the Jordanian government and brought to the Palestine Archaeological Museum in East Jerusalem, it soon became evident that the task of handling them would be massive and that they would require extra time and special expertise. In 1952 G. Lankester Harding, the director of the Jordanian Department of Antiquities, named de Vaux as chief editor of the Judean desert texts. With more and more fragments pouring into the museum, those in charge determined that an international team of scholars should be appointed to work on the Cave 4 materials. The directors of archeological schools in Jerusalem (they sat on the board of the Palestine Archeological Museum) were asked for assistance in forming such a group; also, leading scholars in England and Germany were asked to name candidates. The experts who eventually constituted the Cave 4 team, their nationalities, and their religious affiliations were, in the order of their appointments: Frank Moore Cross, American, Presbyterian; J. T. Milik, Polish, Catholic; John Allegro, English, agnostic; Jean Starcky, French, Catholic; Patrick Skehan, American, Catholic; John Strugnell, English, Presbyterian, later Catholic; Claus-Hunno Hunzinger, German, Lutheran. These seven, all appointed in 1953 and 1954, joined de Vaux, who had been elected chair of the museum board, as the international team responsible for the Cave 4 fragments. In 1958 Maurice Baillet joined the team, and Hunzinger eventually withdrew, leaving his material to Baillet.

The texts were divided among the members of the elite committee, with Cross and Skehan receiving the biblical material, and the others assigned various sorts of extrabiblical works. It was apparently understood that these scholars had the official right to publish the texts in their respective "lots." Obviously and pointedly missing from the list is the name of any Jewish scholar. The Jordanian government insisted that none be included. During the 1950s the group was able to spend large amounts of time in Jerusalem through the generosity of J. D. Rockefeller, Jr., who donated funds to support the work for six years. Under these favorable circumstances, the tedious labors of cleaning, sorting, reading, and identifying the thousands of fragments proceeded at a good pace. Cross has written a memorable description of the work:

> Unlike the several scrolls of Cave I and XI which are preserved in good condition, with only minor lacunae, the manuscripts of Cave IV are in an advanced state of decay. Many fragments are so brittle or friable that they can scarcely be touched with a camel's-hair brush. Most are warped, crinkled, or shrunken, crusted with soil chemicals, blackened by moisture and age. The problems of cleaning, flattening, identifying, and piecing them together are formidable.
>
> The fragments when they are purchased from tribesmen generally come in boxes; cigarette boxes, film boxes, or shoe boxes, depending on the size of the fragments. The precious leather and papyrus is delicately handled by rough Bedouin hands, for the value of the material is all too keenly appreciated. Often cotton wool or tissue paper has been used by Bedouin to separate and protect the scraps of scrolls; and on occasion they have applied bits of gummed paper to pieces which threatened to crack apart or disintegrate. Not since the clandestine digs of Cave I have owners broken up large sheets or columns to sell them piecemeal.

In 1957 work began on compiling a concordance of all the words that occurred in the hundreds of texts that the team identified. This was done for the convenience of the editors, who would often need to check where a word might occur in other fragments. One should note that fragments continued to arrive at the museum until the late 1950s. By 1960, when the Rockefeller support ended, the team had succeeded in doing a huge amount of the painstaking editorial work and had identified more than five hundred texts in the Cave 4 collection. Their results to that point were recorded in the concordance.

Their labors, however remarkable and admirable, did not entail that the scroll fragments were soon published and on library shelves. All the members of the team did prepare preliminary editions of some of their texts. These appeared regularly in scholarly journals in the 1950s and early 1960s. During the 1960s, Oxford University Press published two more volumes in the Discoveries in the Judaean Desert series: volume 4, *The*

Psalms Scroll of Qumran Cave 11 (11QPs^a) (edited by J. A. Sanders); and volume 5, *Qumran Cave 4, I (4Q158-186)* (edited by John Allegro). The latter volume was the first in the series to offer Cave 4 texts. In 1967 the Six-Day War broke out in the Middle East, resulting in Israeli capture of East Jerusalem and the Palestine Archaeological Museum. It was then that Israel took over the Scrolls from Jordan (which had nationalized the Scrolls in 1961 and had done the same to the museum in 1966) and effectively became their owners, although the question of who the legal owners of the texts might be remains a thorny if theoretical problem. When Israeli authorities assumed control of the museum and its treasures, de Vaux saw to it that the original arrangement with the members of the Cave 4 team was honored, and apparently only one new condition was imposed — that the last two words be removed from the full title of the Oxford University Press series Discoveries in the Judaean Desert of Jordan.

Looking back at what was happening in the late 1960s and beyond, one can clearly see that the project of publishing the Cave 4 texts was losing momentum. The next Discoveries in the Judaean Desert volume did not appear until 1977 (*4Q128-57*, edited by de Vaux [who had died in 1971] and Milik). Another five years passed before volume 7 was published (*4Q482-520*, edited by Baillet). Even granting a delay of several years between the time when the editors submitted their manuscripts to the press and the date of publication, the project was not advancing very rapidly.

Some notable publications continued outside the official series. 1976 saw the appearance in print of Milik's *The Books of Enoch* in which he offered editions, photographs, and extensive commentary on most of the Enoch manuscripts from the fourth cave. Then, in 1977 (English edition in 1983) Yadin's three-volume edition of the Temple Scroll, thought to be from Cave 11, appeared. The extraordinary works by Milik and Yadin illustrate another fact of Qumran life: as time went on, scholars were no longer content to prepare transcriptions and brief treatments of the texts; they preferred to write exhaustive commentaries in addition to doing the basic editing work. The change in the quantity of commentary had disastrous consequences for any publishing timetable that might have existed.

As the years passed, changes began to take place in the official team of scholars. John Allegro's case is strange. He had won the gratitude of many people by getting his texts into print long before any of his colleagues did (Discoveries in the Judaean Desert, vol. V, 1968, preliminary editions in the 1950s), but he seems too often to have sacrificed quality for speed. One result was that Strugnell wrote a 114-page review in which he offered detailed corrections of line after line in Allegro's work. This exchange indicates the tensions that had grown between these former teammates. Allegro's relation with the group had been deteriorating for some time. He had claimed publicly that the Catholic-dominated group was suppressing material because it was known to be harmful to Christianity. His colleagues responded that they had seen all the texts Allegro had and none of them supported his charges. He hardly enhanced his reputation when he went off hunting for the treasures of the Copper Scroll and also published a translation of the scroll, without authorization, before the official edition came out. Later he tarnished his reputation even more by writing *The Sacred Mushroom and the Cross* (1970), a book regretted by friend and foe. Here he sought to trace the origins of Christianity to the effects of the hallucinatory drug psilocybin. Even the publisher apologized for it, and Allegro's mentor Sir Godfrey Driver was one of a number of academics who repudiated its arguments.

As mentioned above, Hunzinger had already resigned his position. De Vaux died on September 10, 1971, and was succeeded as chief editor by Pierre Benoit, who, like de Vaux, was director of the Ecole Biblique in Jerusalem. Before Patrick Skehan died on September 9, 1980, he had transferred his materials to Eugene Ulrich of the University of Notre Dame, who in time also received some of Cross's texts. Benoit made attempts to set a timetable for publication of the texts by the team members, but these efforts seem not to have been taken seriously. Benoit died on April 23, 1987, and John Strugnell, an original member of the team, became chief editor in the same year. Preparations had already been made in 1984 or 1985 to have the succession take place.

To this point, the practice was that when one member was lost to the team, he was replaced by just one other person. The number of people engaged in the work did not grow. One of the trademarks of Strugnell's editorship was an effort to expand the original, small team of scholars and to associate Jewish experts with the work. It seems that having a small team was advantageous during the initial phases of the project because it permitted more efficient interaction as the members consulted and helped one another with the fragments. But the initial editorial work was one thing; preparing the extensive materials for official publication was quite another matter. Here the system was obviously inadequate. Tens of thousands of fragments were more than eight experts, however skilled, could handle, even if the Rockefeller money had continued. When the funds lapsed and were not renewed, the work slowed considerably. Yet no new scholars were brought on board to assist in completing the task. Not until Strugnell became chief editor was the team enlarged to about twenty members. I was one of those added during his stint as chief editor, when in 1989 Milik agreed to give me some of the texts assigned to him.

B. EVENTS SINCE 1989

During Strugnell's tenure as chief editor (1987-90) scholarly annoyance at the continuing delays in publishing the Cave 4 material increased and turned into a public protest. The first year that he held the position marked the fortieth anniversary of the Cave 1 discoveries. By this time the perception was widespread that the team held a monopoly on the Cave 4 texts and that they refused to show them to others before publication, which, of course, kept being delayed. In notable cases team members did share their texts with other scholars (for example, Bible translating teams received them). For a long time one heard a modest amount of grumping in academic circles about what was taking the team so long, but scholars were generally content to wait until the team members produced their editions of the Qumran texts. No one seemed to take seriously the wild charges of people like Allegro. The vast majority of scholars continued waiting quietly year after year.

There were, however, some exceptions. Robert Eisenman of California State University, Long Beach, and Philip Davies of the University of Sheffield in England tried in 1989 to obtain access to some unpublished scrolls. Both men had written several books on Qumran subjects. When they requested permission from Strugnell to examine fragments at the Rockefeller Museum, he refused. Their cause and the general cause of free scholarly access to the many unpublished scrolls soon came to be championed by a new player on the stage, Hershel Shanks, the founder of the Biblical Archaeology Society. Through one of his immensely popular journals, the *Biblical Archaeology Review*, he had begun a campaign (starting in 1985) to raise queries about how the Scrolls were being handled and why they were still not available some forty years after they were found. In this way public awareness of the situation and popular suspicions about it began to grow. The language of monopoly gave way to talk of a Scrolls "cartel" — a term normally used for Colombian drug lords or unpopular oil producers.

With the mounting negative publicity, Israeli authorities began pushing for a specific timetable of publication to which the team members would be held. So, when I was working at the Rockefeller Museum in January 1990, Amir Drori, the director of the Israel Antiquities Authority (IAA), checked carefully into when I planned to have the texts Milik entrusted to me ready for publication. But a whole series of events soon occurred that changed the entire landscape of the Qumran world. The IAA named a three-person Scrolls Advisory Committee in 1989 to help in monitoring the situation. In October 1990 the IAA appointed Emanuel Tov of the Hebrew University to serve as editor alongside Strugnell, with the hope that his presence would speed up the process.

The move did not please Strugnell, but he was soon to be ousted from his position in strange circumstances. He gave an interview to the Israeli journalist Avi Katzman in the fall of 1990. When it was published in the Tel Aviv newspaper *Ha'aretz* on November 9, 1990, it caused an immediate sensation. The interview quoted Strugnell as saying, among other provocative comments, that Judaism was "a horrible religion." He was later to claim that his remarks were taken in an unintended sense. But he was clearly very ill at the time when he said such things. It would not have been surprising if such an interview had caused his dismissal as chief editor of the Jewish texts, but the authorities in Israel had apparently decided on the move even before this interview. Thus in December 1990 the Scrolls Advisory Committee removed Strugnell from his post. The veteran members of the international team chose in his place three general editors — Emanuel Tov, Emile Puech of the Ecole Biblique, and Eugene Ulrich of the University of Notre Dame — to head the project. The IAA appointed Tov to be editor-in-chief. Through their guidance and on the basis of the progress that Strugnell had made, the official team was eventually enlarged to a more realistic size of about fifty members. While this exponential growth was news in itself, several other events soon grabbed the international headlines.

The first happened in the fall of 1991. On September 4, 1991, Ben Zion Wacholder, a senior scholar at the Hebrew Union College in Cincinnati, and Martin Abegg, at the time a graduate student there, issued the first volume in their series *A Preliminary Edition of the Unpublished Dead Sea Scrolls* (published by the Biblical Archaeology Society). The book immediately captured the popular fancy because it resulted from applying computer technology to something so ancient as the Dead Sea Scrolls. The project was born out of frustration at the long delay in publishing the Scrolls. Wacholder and Abegg used a copy of the concordance made from the Cave 4 texts (see above A) and, from the words and phrases in the concordance, reconstructed texts from which the concordance had been made in the first place. Their backwards procedure was successful because in the concordance every word is listed in context; from such information one could reconstruct whole texts. Wacholder and Abegg were hailed for their circumvention of the blockade around the texts that, so it was widely believed, the official team had erected. Some wondered, however, what right Wacholder and Abegg had to publish the work of others (that is, the editors of the texts they published and those responsible for compiling the concordance from their transcriptions). Questions were also raised about the accuracy of their reconstructed texts, since they were based on pre-1960 versions; the scholars on the team had improved many of their earlier readings in the intervening thirty years.

The second event happened in the same month. On September 22, 1991, William A. Moffett, director of the Huntington Library in San Marino, California, announced that the complete set of photographs of the Scrolls which the library owned would be made available to anyone who wished to study them. Not many people knew that the Huntington Library had a set of Scrolls photographs; Moffett himself had learned about them only a short time before. The library had received the photographs from Elizabeth Hay Bechtel, whose generous support of Scrolls research was well known. She had funded the creation of the Ancient Biblical Manuscript Center in Claremont, California, and had obtained permission to house a set of copies of the Scrolls photographs there. After a serious disagreement with the director, she had another copy made and placed in the Huntington Library. There they languished largely unnoticed until Moffett's announcement. The thought of free speech was apparently much on the minds of the staff in September 1991 because a display on the Bill of Rights was then showing at the library. (Some murky questions apparently remain about who controls the library's photographs.) At any rate, the IAA was not pleased by Moffett's decision, and talk of a possible lawsuit floated about for a while. Nevertheless, the praises of Moffett and the library echoed throughout the newspapers of the land. We were told that at last the Scrolls were liberated, despite the best efforts of the editors to keep them locked up.

One of the people who took advantage of the Huntington Library's offer to open its archives to interested parties was Robert Eisenman, the man who had done so much to publicize discontent with the official team. On November 1, 1991, the university where he teaches (California State University, Long Beach) issued a press release in which Eisenman announced that he had found a text that was not only revolutionary but also showed how wrong the official team had been about the Scrolls.

> Robert Eisenman, the first scholar given access to the Huntington Library's collection of Dead Sea Scrolls microfilms, has announced the discovery of a text that refers to the execution of a Messianic leader. "This tiny scroll fragment puts to rest the idea presently being circulated by the Scroll editorial committee that this material has nothing to do with Christian origins in Palestine," said the California State University, Long Beach professor of Middle East religions.
>
> Leading scroll editors have been saying there is nothing interesting in the unpublished scrolls and that they have nothing to do with the rise of Christianity in Palestine.

Eisenman is also quoted as saying that the text (4Q285) "makes concrete reference to 'the putting to death' or 'the execution of the leader of the community,' an individual the text appears to refer to as 'the branch of David.' 'Though this passage can be read in either the past or future tense, the reading is not subject to doubt,' said Eisenman." As noted in chapter 6 B.4.a, Eisenman's reading is very much subject to doubt, since he opted for a less likely interpretation of the key line (it is more likely that the messianic figure does the killing) and failed to draw the proper conclusion from its relation to Isaiah 11. Eisenman's discovery was soon trumpeted abroad in the newspapers. It is only fair to say that the press release is quite misleading. It gives the impression that the official team had a monolithic view about the Scrolls and that they were trying to distantiate them from Christian origins. Anyone who has read the varied opinions of the team members will know that they disagreed on many points and that no one of them tried to separate the Scrolls from the beginnings of Christianity. All of them were quite aware of the significant parallels between the two literatures; they did not, however, draw the thoroughly implausible conclusions (for example, that Jesus' brother James was the Teacher of Righteousness) that Eisenman preferred.

The quick pace of events still did not slow down. On November 19, 1991, the Biblical Archaeology Society published a two-volume work, *A Facsimile Edition of the Dead Sea Scrolls,* edited by Eisenman and James M.

Robinson. In it were 1,785 photographs of the Dead Sea Scrolls. The source of the photographs was not divulged. This, too, was a remarkable breakthrough because it made a huge percentage of the unpublished texts available to those who could afford the volumes ($195 at time of publication) and read the texts on the photographs. The pictures are small and in some instances utterly illegible; many of them are, however, quite usable. The first volume of *A Facsimile Edition* also contained an introductory section (contributed by Hershel Shanks) in which a number of documents (letters, etc.) that had been generated by the recent Scrolls controversies were printed. Among the items was a Hebrew transcription of the 121-line Halakhic Letter (or Some of the Works of the Torah, 4QMMT). For some years, copies of the transcription, made by Strugnell and Elisha Qimron, had been circulating among interested scholars. But here was the text in printed form, and nowhere in the book was Qimron acknowledged as one of the scholars who had produced the transcription.

As these events were unfolding, the IAA was reassessing its position about permitting access to the photographs of the Scrolls. Copies of them were housed in Jerusalem and in four other places: the Ancient Biblical Manuscript Center in Claremont, California; the Huntington Library; the Oxford Centre for Postgraduate Hebrew Studies; and the Hebrew Union College in Cincinnati. The IAA gave permission for these centers to make their photographs available to interested parties, but at first the Israeli authorities wanted to require that those who studied photographs of unpublished texts agree not to produce an edition of them, though they could use the texts in their research. It took about two weeks for the IAA to back down from this position and to relieve the four institutions of the need to obtain such a statement from users of the photographs. Only some moral pressure was to be exerted on users so that team members would not be deprived of the right to first publication of the texts they had been studying for years.

One more publication should be mentioned, even though it has done much to spread misconceptions. Michael Baigent and Richard Leigh authored a book called *The Dead Sea Scroll Deception: Why a Handful of Religious Scholars Conspired to Suppress the Revolutionary Contents of the Dead Sea Scrolls* (New York: Summit Books, 1991). The first part of the book — in which the authors describe the Scrolls, arrangements for publication, the so-called consensus that was developed about them, and all the problems that resulted — makes for interesting and informative reading. It is particularly valuable to read their citations from the letters of

John Allegro and to observe firsthand how his relations with the other team members soured.

But after a rather good start the book quickly degenerates. The authors try to foist on the reader the idea that the delay in Scrolls publication came about because the Catholic-dominated team was under the control of the Vatican, which, fully informed of what was in the unpublished scrolls, was anxious to suppress all the information in the fragments that would undermine Christianity. De Vaux, who according to those who knew him was a pleasant man, turns out to be a monster who masterminded and enforced the Vatican's conspiracy to suppress the Scrolls. After this tortured and remarkable bit of nonsense, they advance a form of Eisenman's theory about the Scrolls — one that somehow gave them satisfactory answers to the questions that the Essene hypothesis just could not handle. It is hard to imagine a book with a more bizarre combination of discipline and credulity. But conspiracy theories tend to get a lot of attention, and Baigent and Leigh's book has become a bestseller. Now that all the Scrolls are available for consultation, no one has been able to find anything damaging to Christianity or anything that the Vatican would be interested in suppressing. One of the beneficial side effects of full access to the Scrolls has been to show that the Baigent-Leigh conspiracy theory is baseless.

The most recent newsmaking publication is the most valuable. E. J. Brill, under the auspices of the IAA, has published a remarkable work entitled *The Dead Sea Scrolls on Microfiche: A Comprehensive Facsimile Edition of the Texts from the Judaean Desert* (Leiden, 1993). On microfiche are photographs (about 6,000) of all the Qumran scrolls and those found in other Judean desert sites. Companion volumes provide a full list of all the manuscripts, the numbers assigned to the different photographs of them, and some history of Scrolls study and photography. Thus, today all the Dead Sea Scrolls are available for use by all who are able to handle them.

Photography has been an essential tool in Scrolls research. The scrolls from Cave 1 were photographed as soon as possible (see chap. 1.1.A), while the thousands of fragments which poured into the Palestine Archaeological Museum in the 1950s were photographed by Najib Albina at various stages in the editorial team's work on them. As anyone who has worked with the fragments themselves knows, the photographs are frequently easier to read than the originals.

In 1993 a consortium of experts from the Ancient Biblical Manuscript Center (Claremont), the Jet Propulsion Laboratory, and West Semitic Research began a new set of infrared tests, using multi-spectral imaging (MSI) techniques. MSI allows the photographer to enhance contrasts between different parts of an image, each of which has a unique spectral signature, through application of computer imaging techniques. In this way the ink and writing surface of a fragment can be presented in far greater contrast with each other than the one visible to the naked eye. The results have been astonishing. A good example is a previously illegible fragment of the Genesis Apocryphon; with MSI technology, the writing on the fragment is now clearly legible, even some letters that were covered by another piece of leather which was stuck to the surface of the first one (see the illustration).

The enlarged official team continues to do its work. In 1990 volume 8 of Discoveries in the Judaean Desert appeared. In it the editor, Emanuel Tov (with Robert Kraft), published *The Greek Minor Prophets Scroll from Nahal Hever* — another Judean desert location, not Qumran. In 1992 Ulrich, Skehan, and Judith Sanderson published Discoveries in the Judaean Desert volume 9, *Qumran Cave 4, IV: Palaeo-Hebrew and Greek Biblical Manuscripts;* volume 10, which contains the long-awaited Halakhic Letter (Some of the Works of the Torah), is at the press and due out in 1994. Several other volumes are in advanced states of preparation.

All the publicity engendered by these events had the unexpected result of making some Scrolls experts into celebrities who were kept busy attending conferences, being interviewed by reporters, and appearing on television or radio. Scholarly conferences have proliferated, as has the number of preliminary editions of texts prepared by official team members and by others. Circumstances have produced some strange results and hard feelings. Publication of the Strugnell-Qimron text of the Halakhic Letter by Shanks in *A Facsimile Edition* led to a lawsuit by Qimron against Shanks, with Qimron winning in an Israeli court, although he did not get all the money for which he was suing (the decision is being appealed). At times scholarly conferences have turned into shouting matches, as the cameras rolled and the media sharpened their pencils. Other results have been hasty, sloppy publications of texts and the use of the work of others without proper acknowledgment. Some scholars who have never been part of the official international team continue to be suspicious of the team and to peddle the notion that the team holds a consensus and suppresses anyone who disagrees. But such perceptions seem to have little basis. A variety of viewpoints is represented on the team, and, as we have seen in the preceding chapters, nearly all areas of Qumran research are today witnessing lively debates, with anyone free to conclude what he or she wishes. There is no consensus on the team and certainly no means for enforcing one even if it did exist.

One other benefit of the controversies has been that learned societies whose members work with and are interested in the Scrolls and other finds from Middle Eastern sites have examined the issue of access to such discoveries and have adopted official positions on them. Both the Society of Biblical Literature (1991) and the American Schools of Oriental Research (1992) have now issued policy statements on the matter. The hope is that, if members follow these policies and urge governmental bodies to do the same, the mistakes and delays that have attended publication (or nonpublication) of the Scrolls could be avoided when the next discoveries are made.

The statements of the two societies are rather different. The policy of the former calls for free and prompt access by all to discoveries and the right of anyone to publish editions of texts. It rejects the idea that any one person or small group of people should have the sole right for any number of years to publish a discovered text. The statement of the latter is more cautious because it comes from a society that is different in character — a society that deals with various governments in several of whose lands it owns property and conducts expensive investigations for which money must be raised. It therefore addresses those concerns and attempts to ensure that the scholars who have found funding and done the work of discovery have rights to first publication for a reasonable amount of time. Both societies are, however, dedicated to the principle that finds must be made accessible to others in an expeditious fashion and not kept out of circulation for as long as they were in the case of the Cave 4 manuscripts. The Qumran experience has made us more aware of what works and what does not. The policies of these two societies are another benefit of the recent controversies and lead us to hope that when the next great discovery of texts is made a better system for publication will be employed.

BIBLIOGRAPHICAL NOTES

Since almost all the references in this chapter are given in the text, they are not repeated here. The only exception is the quotation from Frank Moore Cross, *The Ancient Library of Qumran and Modern Biblical Studies* (rev. ed.; repr. Grand Rapids: Baker Book House, 1980) 35. The experts who are applying multi-spectral imaging techniques to the Scrolls are Gregory Bearman of the Jet Propulsion Laboratory, California Institute of Technology, Bruce Zuckerman of the University of Southern California, Kenneth Zuckerman of West Semitic Research, and Joseph Chiu of California Institute of Technology. Their initial results were presented at the Annual Meeting of the Society of Biblical Literature in November 1993. A report on their presentation, with photographs, appeared in the *New York Times*, Nov. 23, 1993.

Postscript

A fter *The Dead Sea Scrolls Today* appeared in 1994, some of the controversies sketched in chap. 7 continued for a time. The suit filed by Elisha Qimron in an Israeli court against Hershel Shanks, Robert Eisenman, James Robinson, and the Biblical Archaeology Society for printing a transcription of Some of the Works of the Torah (4QMMT) in *A Facsimile Edition* without explicit acknowledgment of Qimron's part in preparing it led to a preliminary injunction prohibiting distribution of the text. Later printings of *A Facsimile Edition* lack the transcription of 4QMMT. On March 3, 1993 the judge, Dalia Dorner, ruled infringement had occurred and imposed the maximum statutory compensation of NIS 20,000. She determined the proper compensation for mental distress and injury to reputation was NIS 80,000, not the 100,000 Qimron sought. She also ordered payment of NIS 50,000 for Qimron's legal fees.

Oxford University Press published the official edition of 4QMMT as volume 10 in the Discoveries in the Judaean Desert series in 1994. Unlike other volumes in the official series of Scrolls publications, this one assigns copyright to an editor — to Qimron, not to John Strugnell who had worked to establish the text for decades, much longer than Qimron had.

Not surprisingly, the defendants appealed the ruling of the Israeli court. On August 20, 2000, Justice Y. Türkel of the Supreme Court of Israel issued a decision upholding the verdict that Qimron owned the copyright to the text and that his copyright had been infringed; he also added payment of attorneys' fees to the defendants' penalty. The court decisions and many other matters relevant to them form the contents of an interesting publication: *On Scrolls, Artefacts and Intellectual Property* (ed. Timothy H. Lim, Hector L. MacQueen, and Calum M. Carmichael; Journal for the Study of the Pseudepigrapha Supplement Series 38; Sheffield: Sheffield Academic Press, 2001).

Florentino García Martínez, a Scrolls scholar now retired from the University of Leuven in Belgium, later examined the photos taken of the fragments of 4QMMT at various times as Strugnell's work on them progressed in the 1950s and the relevant entries in the card concordance for texts as Strugnell read them at the time. He determined that the readings, placement of fragments, and the combination of pieces into a continuous text had been substantially completed in 1961 — 24 years before Qimron began working on the text ("Discoveries in the Judaean Desert: Textes legaux (I)," *Journal for the Study of Judaism* 32 [2001] 71-89). Apparently this evidence was not presented while the courts were adjudicating the case.

On a cheerier note, the world of the Dead Sea Scrolls is very different today than it was in 1994. Making photographs of the unpublished fragments available unleashed a flurry of publications in the 1990s and the first decade of the new millennium. Scholars issued preliminary editions of texts in journal articles and official editions in the Discoveries in the Judaean Desert series. The field has been marked by the participation of a large number of experts from many countries and by a whirlwind of activity, debate, and publication. The following are some of the most helpful works that have appeared.

Discoveries in the Judaean Desert From 1955 to 1982, seven volumes in the series had seen the light of day; since 1990, 32 more have flowed from the press (DJD 8-31, 33-40). Three of the more recent volumes contain material from sites other than Qumran (24 has seals from the Wadi Daliyeh [the first part of 28 has texts from the same site], 27 has texts from Nahal Hever and other places, and 38 offers fragments from various places in the Judean Desert) and one is a work containing indexes and an introduction to the series (39, where the full list of scrolls and scrolls fragments from Qumran and other sites can be found, pp. 27-114). All of the others present editions of Qumran texts. The one volume yet to appear, 32, offers the two Isaiah scrolls from Cave 1. As of this writing (December 2009), it is at the press. Since both of the manuscripts in it have been available for decades, one can say that all of the Dead Sea Scrolls have been published.

Some publications assist the user by combining all of the non-biblical scrolls and scroll fragments from Qumran with English translations.

> Florentino García Martínez and Eibert J.C. Tigchelaar, *The Dead Sea Scrolls Study Edition* (2 vols.; Leiden: Brill, 1997, 1998). The volumes offer the ancient text on the lefthand page, an English translation on the righthand page; brief bibliographies are included. The texts are presented in the order of the caves and then by the number assigned to each text from a cave.
>
> Donald W. Parry and Emanuel Tov, editors, *The Dead Sea Scrolls Reader* (6 vols.; Leiden: Brill, 2004-2005). The volumes include the ancient text on the lefthand page and English translations on the righthand page; both texts and translations are from the DJD editions where possible, with slight updates. The works are arranged by genres.

For the biblical scrolls, one can consult:

> Martin Abegg, Jr., Peter Flint, and Eugene Ulrich, *The Dead Sea Scrolls Bible: The Oldest Known Bible Translated for the First Time into English* (San Francisco: HarperSanFrancisco, 1999). The arrangement is in the order of the books in Hebrew Bibles, with translations offered where the text is available in a Qumran copy or copies.

Eugene Ulrich has published a volume with the texts of the Qumran biblical (that is, the books in the Hebrew Bible) manuscripts:

> *The Biblical Qumran Scrolls: Transcriptions and Textual Variants* (Leiden: Brill, 2010). He presents the scrolls material mostly from the DJD editions and lists variant readings in the Qumran copies and ancient versions.

A valuable tool for those who work with the original texts is:

> Martin G. Abegg, Jr., with James E. Bowley and Edward M. Cook and in Consultation with Emanuel Tov, *The Dead Sea Scrolls Concordance*, Volume One: *The Non-Biblical Texts from Qumran*, Parts One and Two (Leiden: Brill, 2003). The planned second and third volumes will cover the biblical scrolls from Qumran and the texts from other sites in the Judean Desert.

For information on a wide variety of topics the reader can consult:

Lawrence H. Schiffman and James C. VanderKam, editors in chief, *Encyclopedia of the Dead Sea Scrolls* (2 vols.; Oxford/New York: Oxford University Press, 2000).

There are two journals devoted to scholarship on the Scrolls:

Revue de Qumran (1958-)
Dead Sea Discoveries (1994-)

A series in which many technical monographic studies of scrolls and related phenomena have appeared is Brill's

Studies on the Texts of the Desert of Judah

Electronic publications offer vast quantities of information:

The Dead Sea Scrolls Electronic Reference Library, Volume 1, ed. Timothy H. Lim in consultation with Philip S. Alexander (Oxford: Oxford University Press; Leiden: Brill, 1997): three CD-ROMs contain approximately 2700 photographs of scrolls. Each fragment has a card assigned to it, and on the card is a range of searchable information about that fragment (where it is housed, where it was published, publications about it).

The Dead Sea Scrolls Electronic Reference Library, Volume 2, prepared by Noel B. Reynolds, Donald W. Parry, E. Jan Wilson, and Terence L. Szink of the Foundation for Ancient Research and Mormon Studies and the Center for the Preservation of Ancient Religious Texts at Brigham Young University (Leiden: Brill, 1999): a single CD-ROM offers some 800 digitalized photographs of scrolls chosen from the collection at the Ancient Biblical Manuscript Center, transcriptions of the texts, a database of the non-biblical texts, Florentino García Martínez's English translation of them, word lists, the Septuagint, the Vulgate, and the King James Version of the Old Testament. A search feature is also part of the volume.

The Dead Sea Scrolls Electronic Library, by Emanuel Tov and the Neal A. Maxwell Institute for Religious Scholarship, Brigham Young University. Revised Edition 2006, part of the Dead Sea Scrolls Electronic Reference Library of E. J. Brill Publishers (Leiden: Brill, 2006). The work provides the user with the most complete collection of the texts and images of the non-biblical Dead Sea Scrolls, in the original languages and in translation, with morphological analysis and search programs.

THE ACCORDANCE PROGRAM

Included in the immense array of material available in the latest versions of the Accordance Program are:

Qumran Sectarian Manuscripts in Hebrew/Aramaic, with Qumran text and Grammatical Tags, by Martin G. Abegg, Jr.

Qumran Sectarian Manuscripts in English (translation by Michael Wise, Martin Abegg, Jr., and Edward Cook, *The Dead Sea Scrolls: A New English Translation* [San Francisco: HarperSanFrancisco, 1996).

An Index of Qumran Manuscripts, ed. Stephen W. Marler, in consultation with Martin G. Abegg, Jr.

Today there are unprecedented tools available for studying the Scrolls that can now be seen in their full surviving form. All — archeologists and non-archeologists — are hoping that the complete inventory of archeological data will soon become available so that the experts can assess all of the information and use it in formulating more securely based hypotheses about the site.

Index